Research in
Learning Disabilities

Based on a symposium sponsored by the Division of Learning Disabilities of the Council for Exceptional Children, the Utah State Office of Education, the Utah Special Education Consortium, and the Utah Learning Resource Center.

Research in Learning Disabilities
Issues and Future Directions

Sharon Vaughn, Ph.D.

University of Miami
Coral Gables, Florida

Candace S. Bos, Ph.D.

University of Arizona
Tucson, Arizona

A College-Hill Publication
Little, Brown and Company
Boston/Toronto/San Diego

College-Hill Press
A Division of
Little, Brown and Company (Inc.)
34 Bacon Street
Boston, Massachusetts 02108

Library of Congress Cataloging in Publication Data
Main entry under title:

Research in Learning Disabilities: Issues and Future Directions

  "A College-Hill publication."
  Includes index.
  1. Learning disabilities—Research—United States—Congresses.
I. Vaughn, Sharon, 1952-   . II. Bos, Candace, 1950-
LC4705.I87   1987   371.9   87-4233

ISBN 0-316-10305-5

Printed in the United States of America

CONTENTS

Preface   **vii**
Acknowledgments   **x**
Contributors   **xi**
PART I: **Models and Theories**
Chapter 1   A Shared Attribute Model of Learning Disabilities   **3**
              Barbara K. Keogh   **Response** by Susan A. Vogel
Chapter 2   Theoretical Quandaries in Learning Disabilities   **19**
              Kenneth A. Kavale   **Response** by Joseph K. Torgesen
Chapter 3   A Multifaceted Hierarchical Theory of Learning Disabilities   **35**
              Carol Weller   **Response** by Doris J. Johnson

PART II: **Research**
Chapter 4   Thinking about the Future by Distinguishing Between Issues
              That Have Resolutions and Those That Do Not   **55**
              Joseph K. Torgesen   **Response** by James D. McKinney
Chapter 5   Learning Disabilities Research:
              False Starts and Broken Promises   **69**
              G. Reid Lyon   **Response** by Kenneth A. Kavale
Chapter 6   Learning Disabilities as Sociologic Sponge:
              Wiping up Life's Spills   **87**
              Gerald M. Senf   **Response** by Barbara K. Keogh

PART III: **Eligibility**
Chapter 7   Eligibility: Back to Basics   **105**
              Harold J. McGrady   **Response** by Cecil D. Mercer
Chapter 8   Eligibility and Identification Considerations in
              Postsecondary Education: A New but Old Dilemma   **121**
              Susan A. Vogel   **Response** by James C. Chalfant

PART IV: **Assessment**
Chapter 9   Assessment Issues in Learning Disabilities Research   **141**
              Doris J. Johnson   **Response** by Bernice Y.L. Wong

Chapter 10   Beyond Traditional Assessment   **153**
              Cecil D. Mercer   **Response** by Samuel A. Kirk

PART V: **Intervention**
Chapter 11   Intervention Research in Learning Disabilities   **173**
              Samuel A. Kirk   **Response** by Edwin W. Martin
Chapter 12   Conceptual and Methodological Issues in Interventions with
              Learning-Disabled Children and Adolescents   **185**
              Bernice Y.L. Wong   **Response** by G. Reid Lyon

PART VI: **Public Policy**
Chapter 13   Learning Disabilities and Public Policy:
              a Role for Research Workers   **203**
              Edwin W. Martin   **Response** by Gerald M. Senf
Chapter 14   Research on the Identification of Learning-Disabled Children:
              Perspectives on Changes in Educational Policy   **215**
              James D. McKinney   **Response** by Carol Weller
Chapter 15   Providing Services to All Students with
              Learning Problems: Implications for Policy and Programs   **239**
              James C. Chalfant   **Response** by Harold J. McGrady

PART VII: **Conclusions**
Chapter 16   Moving from Consensus to Action: An Agenda for
              Future Research in Learning Disabilities   **257**
              Sharon Vaughn, Candace S. Bos, and Stevan J. Kukic
Author Index   **267**
Subject Index   **273**

PREFACE

There are children and adults whose learning problems consistently challenge the skills of special as well as general educators. They seem to have the ability to achieve, but do not. They require unique instructional designs, geared to their individual needs.

Research in learning disabilities has been dedicated to describing and differentiating subgroups of these individuals, and determining the interventions that promote greatest growth within and across these subgroups. However, research has not yet yielded consistent results in terms of definitions or interventions. The reasons for this are varied: the premises of research studies differ, as do the findings; methodological problems make some "significant" findings insignificant; strong theoretically based research, as well as programmatic research, is often lacking; and research has not been compared either among learning disabilities researchers or with research from different fields of study.

Currently, social and political pressures and the resulting regulations are more powerful determiners of identification and intervention policy than research. If we are to gain respectability and stability as a field, research must provide answers so that identification and intervention can be empirically based.

This book and the research symposium upon which it is based reflect the acceptance of the challenge to give direction to research in the field of learning disabilities. Impetus for this challenge grew from a national task force chaired by James Chalfant, and the direct challenges he made during the Division for Learning Disabilities keynote session at the 1985 International Convention of The Council for Exceptional Children.

In 1984, the task force was named to investigate policies and procedures related to the identification of learning-disabled students. A summary of the report appeared in *Learning Disabilities Focus* in 1985. In this article Chalfant discussed terminology, definition, eligibility and identification, regular education pre-referral activities, identification of high risk students, team decision making, and transition and exit procedures. This report made specific suggestions in the form of issues to be addressed related to the identification of learning-disabled students.

At the 1985 International Convention of The Council for Exceptional Children, the Division for Learning Disabilities (DLD) presented a keynote session in which Chalfant, William Cruickshank, and Barbara Keogh discussed several issues related to the provision of services to learning-disabled students. Chalfant challenged the field to determine:

1. What are the unique characteristics of the learning-disabled population?
2. How many students receiving learning disabilities services are truly learning disabled?
3. What kinds of special teaching techniques do we use with learning-disabled students that good regular education teachers do not use?
4. How effective are we at remediating learning-disabled students.

During the DLD Research Committee's meeting following this session. It was decided that Chalfant's challenges could not be ignored. It was suggested that a long-range plan for research related to these challenges could be generated by bringing together in a think-tank symposium key professionals who might provide guidance and support for future research in learning disabilities. This group of researchers and practitioners would be a select group of individuals whose research is varied, yet who have sought to resolve some of the field's basic problems.

At the same time Stevan Kukic, formerly Coordinator of the Utah Learning Resource Center and currently the Director of Special Education, Utah State Office of Education, and Carol Weller, President of DLD, discussed a similar notion. Thus, the idea of a symposium in Utah to discuss future directions for learning disabilities research was born.

Cyrus Freston, Learning Disabilities Specialist of the Special Education Section of the Utah State Office of Education, secured the funding for the symposium, and the Utah Learning Resource Center was designated as the major planning unit. The Chair of the DLD Research Committee, Sharon Vaughn, gained approval from the executive board of DLD to co-sponsor the symposium.

The DLD Research Committee chose 15 researchers and leaders from around the country to participate in the symposium. The participants were the contributors to this book (except for James Chalfant, who was unable to attend). Stevan Kukic served as facilitator for the symposium. Sharon Vaughn and Candace Bos, Chair of the Publications Committee, served as DLD coordinators.

The symposium consisted of an introduction and six think-tank sessions, in which participants presented position papers reflecting their views on assigned topics, followed by open discussion. The topics were (a) models and theories, (b) research issues and procedures, (c) eligibility, (d) assessment, (e) intervention, and (f) public policy. As the topical discussions proceeded, the symposium facilitator noted what appeared to be agreements. These statements were organized and presented to the participants, who endorsed them as an emerging consensus that could serve as a focus for future efforts at improving the state of learning disabilities research. The consensus was summarized as follows:
Given that

■ Learning disabilites exist based on long-standing broad-based clinical evidence.
■ Learning disabilities are complex and heterogeneous.
■ Research methodologies are at times ill grounded, idiosyncratic,

methodologically imprecise, and/or issue driven.
■ Practice in schools is driven by sociopolitical forces.

Then

■ More than one definition of learning disabilities is needed, some serving the function of delineating eligibility criteria for identifying and serving students in public schools and postsecondary institutions.
■ These eligibility criteria are topics of investigation separate from theory-based issues. These criteria are inappropriate bases for theory-driven research.
■ Theory-driven research should be conducted programmatically within a developmental framework to:
Describe the attributes of individuals who are not successful at achieving the expectations of personal, social, academic and vocational life.
Differentiate reasons for this scientifically observed underachievement.
Develop a classification system that is both sophisticated and usable.
Describe, differentiate, and determine the effect of interventions.
■ This research could have an impact on policy and practice.

The symposium exceeded the expectations of the planners and participants, and the consensus generated at the symposium holds promise for future gatherings and other collaborative efforts.

Using their expertise and the discussions generated at the symposium, each participant has written a chapter focusing on one of the six topical areas. This book is organized around these six areas. The final chapter synthesizes and builds upon the previous chapters to develop an agenda for future research.

Stevan Kukic
Jed Luchow
Cyrus Freston
Candace Bos
Sharon Vaughn

ACKNOWLEDGMENTS

Initial thanks goes to the DLD Research Committee. It was the members of the Research Committee, Jed Luchow, Ken Kavale, and Susan Vogel, who initiated and developed the idea of a research symposium to address Chalfant's challenge.

The symposium never would have been possible if not for the work of Stevan Kukic, at the time Coordinator of the Utah Learning Resource Center and currently the Director of Special Education in Utah, and Cyrus Freston, also from the Special Education Section of the Utah State Office of Education. Stevan played a major role in the logistical planning and served as facilitator during the symposium. Cy gained support for the idea, as well as the all-important funding.

Thanks also is to be extended to the DLD Publications Committee, and Michael Bender and Marie Linvill at College-Hill Press. The members of the Publications Committee, Katherine Garnett, Ken Kavale, and Susan Vogel assisted in obtaining a publishing agreement. Michael Bender and Marie Linvill provided their expertise so as to facilitate the timely publication of this book.

Finally, and most importantly, we would like to express thanks to the authors in this volume. They are leaders and researchers with busy professional schedules, who made the time to participate in the symposium and write chapters for this volume.

Sharon Vaughn
Candace Bos

CONTRIBUTORS

Candace S. Bos, Ph.D.
Associate Professor
Divison of Special Education
and Rehabilitation
University of Arizona
Tucson, Arizona

James C. Chalfant, Ed.D.
Professor and Head
Division of Special Education
and Rehabilitation
University of Arizona
Tucson, Arizona

Cyrus W. Freston, Ph.D.
Specialist for Learning Disabilities
and Staff Development
Utah State Office of Education
Salt Lake City, Utah

Doris J. Johnson, Ph.D.
Professor and Program Chair,
Learning Disabilities
Northwestern University
Evanston, Illinois

Kenneth A. Kavale, Ph.D.
Professor and Chair,
Department of Special Education
College of Education
University of Iowa
Iowa City, Iowa

Barbara K. Keogh, Ph.D.
Professor, Education Department
University of California, Los Angeles
Los Angeles, California

Samuel A. Kirk, Ph.D.
Division of Special Education
and Rehabilitation
University of Arizona
Tucson, Arizona

Stevan J. Kukic, Ph.D.
State Director of Special Education
Utah State Office of Education

Jed P. Luchow, Ed.D.
College of Staten Island
City University of New York
Staten Island, New York

G. Reid Lyon, Ph.D.
Departments of Neurology and
Communication Science and
Disorders
University of Vermont
Department of Special Education
St. Michael's College
Burlington, Vermont

Edwin W. Martin, Ph.D.
President and Chief Executive
Officer
Human Resource Center
Albertson, New York

Harold J. McGrady, Ph.D.
Director of Special Education
Mesa Public Schools
Mesa, Arizona

James D. McKinney, Ph.D.
Professor, Frank Porter Graham
Child Development Center
University of North Carolina
Chapel Hill, North Carolina

Cecil D. Mercer, Ed.D.
Professor, Department of Special
Education
University of Florida
Gainesville, Florida

Gerald M. Senf, Ph.D.
Executive Director
BrainMap Laboratories and
Diagnostic Clinic
Tucson, Arizona

Joeseph K. Torgesen, Ph.D.
Department of Psychology
Florida State University
Tallahassee, Florida

Sharon Vaughn, Ph.D.
Department of Education
University of Miami
Coral Gables, Florida

Susan A. Vogel, Ph.D.
Northeastern Illinois University
Chicago, Illinois

Carol Weller, Ed.D.
Department of Special Education
University of Utah
Salt Lake City, Utah

Bernice Y.L. Wong, Ed.D.
Associate Professor
Faculty of Education
Simon Fraser University
Burnaby, British Columbia

PART I

Models and Theories

CHAPTER 1

A Shared Attribute Model of Learning Disabilities

Barbara K. Keogh

The field of learning disabilities (LD) is often described as fragmented and diverse, as lacking in coherence and focus. These are not positive characteristics from a scientific perspective, yet they have considerable validity. The literature is filled with evidence of diagnostic disagreements, of classification and placement inconsistencies, of treatment and intervention disputes (Shepard, 1983; Shepard & Smith, 1983; Ysseldyke & Algozzine, 1983; Ysseldyke, Algozzine, Richey, & Graden, 1982). These differences of opinion are not trivial, given the magnitude of the field. According to the *Sixth Annual Report to Congress* (prepared in 1984 by the Office of Special Education), in 1982–1983, almost four and one-half million pupils ages 3 to 21 years were identified as handicapped; almost one and three-quarter million of them were classified as LD. The LD figures represent almost 4% of all school children nationally and more than 40% of pupils served in special education programs.

This chapter was supported in part by a NICHD Program grant to the Sociobehavioral Research Group, Mental Retardation Research Center, the University of California, Los Angeles.

While the numbers themselves are of interest and of some concern, two trends in the prevalence of LD are particularly to be noted. First, there has been a dramatic increase in the prevalence of LD—the numbers of identified LD pupils more than doubling over the last 10-year period. Second, there is considerable variation in prevalence according to state or geographic location—LD figures ranging from 64% to 26% of the special education population in different states. These findings underscore the inconsistencies and diversity within the field and raise serious questions about the conceptual underpinnings that drive operational decisions and applications. Clearly, there are a number of perceptions of learning disabilities, yet we refer to the field as though it represents a single, unitary condition.

THE DEFINITION PROBLEM

The heart of the problem lies in our continuing concern with "the definition." Numerous persons and professional groups have wrestled with definition issues, and a number of somewhat different definitions have been proposed (Clements, 1966; Cruickshank, 1981; *Federal Register*, 1977; Hammill, Leigh, McNutt, & Larsen, 1981; National Advisory Committee on Handicapped Children, 1968; see also Hallahan & Kauffman, 1976; and Mercer, Forgnone, & Wolking, 1976). The various definitions have some similarity and a number of points of disagreement, yet each is assumed to be comprehensive and inclusionary and to provide the basis for decisions about individual children. Clearly, this is not so, as evidenced in the disparities in numbers of LD pupils identified in various places and at various times, and in the heterogeneity within and across research samples. Both research and services within the LD field have been diluted and confounded by continuing arguments about what LD *really* is. A good deal of the argument appears to be based on the assumption that there is a single definition that identifies a single condition. Such an assumption is not defensible either conceptually or empirically.

A Range of Definitions

Examination of the current literature (Keogh, 1987) suggests that definitions of LD can be placed on a hypothetical continuum ranging from specific syndromes at one end to broadly defined learning problems at the other. A variety of syndromes (e.g., Developmental Dyslexia, Strauss Syndrome, Minimal Brain Dysfunction) impute an underlying neurologic cause and specify symptoms or signs that presumably identify the condition. At the other end of the continuum is a general category in which the defining criterion is a discrepancy between presumed aptitude and actual achievement. In the latter definition, etiology is important only as the basis for exclusion. Under the broad term *learning disabilities*, or in any group of pupils classified as learning disabled, we may find representatives of both ends of the continuum. Thus, it should not surprise us that there may be more differences than similarities in any LD group. The way in which we handle this diversity reflects, in part, our approach to definition.

An analogy from a related field may be relevant. In medicine, diagnostic and nosologic efforts differ according to whether the organizer is a "lumper" or a "splitter" (Beauchamp, 1985). In the latter case, disease states or conditions, although having some features in common, are viewed as separate, specific syndromes. In the former case, the same conditions are viewed as a single syndrome with many manifestations. Applied to LD, we may define a broad condition (or single syndrome), which includes many attributes and has many expressions, or we may define a series of separate and relatively independent conditions or syndromes, recognizing that they may have features in common. The term *learning disabilities* means different things, depending upon which approach is taken. The implications of definitional differences for identification, diagnosis, and treatment are real. The implications for the conduct of research on LD are equally powerful. Who and how many persons are identified as learning disabled will differ depending upon which approach to definition is taken. Our problem to date is that we are not sure which definition is being referred to when the term *learning disabilities* is used. Both our understanding of and our efforts to treat LD are influenced by these confusions.

A Shared Attribute Model

A major consequence of different definitional approaches and criteria is diversity of characteristics of persons identified as LD. This is to be expected, given that different professionals hold such different views about definition. In a recent analytic discussion of research in LD, Senf (1986) suggested that issues of subject variability have led to a number of questionable inferences about the nature of LD and have also provided a rationalization for less than powerful design and analytic strategies. His interpretation has considerable merit and allows the further inference that much of the problem in studying and understanding LD relates more to how we deal with heterogeneity than to the heterogeneity itself.

Acceptance of the reality of the diversity in the field suggests that we must change the way we think about LD. The search for a single definition is no longer defensible or necessary. It is time to put "the definitional problem" behind us. Rather, the argument presented here is that we must adopt a multidefinitional approach to LD; we must tie definitions to purposes; and, we must understand LD within a sociopolitical context. Such an approach requires acceptance of the diverse attributes that characterize LD conditions. Some LD definitions may include neurologic signs, but neurologic signs will not be criterial in all definitions. Such an approach also implies that research on LD must be conceptualized and directed by the reason for the research. Study of instructional effects may, thus, require a different definition of LD than will research on specific cognitive or perceptual processes. Part of our task is to determine patterns of shared attributes, taking into account number, severity, and chronicity of attributes or signs, and to demonstrate the relevance of these findings to the purpose(s) of identification. This is a call for a reasonable classification system or taxonomy of LD.

Need for a Taxonomy of Learning Disabilities

The need to describe, order, and organize the content of a field of study is basic in any scientific effort. All scientific fields are confronted with questions of classification. Taxonomies and typologies provide a working framework for study of a phenomenon or condition. Taxonomies organize content, bring order to diverse attributes, and determine membership in classes or categories. Some classification is monothetic—membership in a class is based on the presence or absence of single criterial attributes, for example, the presence of mammary glands ensures membership in the class mammalia. Other classification systems are polythetic—membership is not guaranteed by any single attribute but by the presence of a number of shared attributes. The latter classification approach is common in the social sciences and in medicine.

It is unlikely that monothetic classification will be useful in LD. Even the infamous and much argued ability–achievement discrepancy does not guarantee classification as learning disabled. As noted by Reynolds (1984–1985) and Reynolds and associates (1984–1985), Reynolds, Berk, Boodoo, Cox, Gutkin, Mann, Page, & Willson, 1984–85), discrepancy formulae merely establish an eligibility "pool" for further diagnosis. The pool contains persons with a wide range of characteristics. For example, many but not all children with ability–achievement discrepancies have symptoms of hyperactivity, impulsivity, and clumsiness or have visual processing problems, perceptual confusions, and reversals. Although few children have *all* the symptoms associated with LD, many share *some* attributes in common. Thus, a polythetic classification scheme may help us organize the diverse array of attributes associated with LD. The shared attribute conceptualization of LD is a polythetic approach to classification, which takes explicit account of the lack of a single criterial attribute that might define the condition(s). It allows us to consider the range of LD characteristics and the probability of their association. Adoption of this approach renders the definitional task, in part, an empirical one, and takes us out of the continuing debate about the definition.

Empirical Approaches to Definition

A number of empirical efforts toward resolving definitional problems are underway (Fletcher & Morris, 1986; Keogh, 1987; McKinney, 1986; Siegel & Heaven, 1986; Senf, 1986; Wong, 1986). Promising approaches involve research on LD subtypes (Lyon, 1983; McKinney, 1984, 1986); on rationally defined subgroups (Torgesen, 1982; and, on the routine use of marker variables (Keogh, Major-Kingsley, Omori-Gordon, & Reid, 1982). The subtype work is well described in the literature; therefore, it will not be discussed in detail here. It is important to emphasize, however, that although subtype research is being carried out from a number of different perspectives, these efforts are beginning to yield subgroups that are coherent and interpretable and that have some consistency across studies and investigative groups (Doehring, Hoshko, & Bryans, 1979; Lyon, 1983, 1985; McKinney, 1984, 1986; Satz & Morris, 1981; Speece, McKinney, & Appelbaum, 1985). There are some differences in findings that likely relate to specifics of sampling criteria, procedures, measures, and statistical methods. Yet, the subtype work as a whole supports the viability of a "multiple syndrome paradigm" (Doehring, 1978).

Of particular importance to the future of LD is the possibility that there may be functional links between subtype membership and instructional needs. Extensive literature (Lloyd, 1987) documents the failure to identify LD–instructional interactions when LD is imprecisely defined. Pupils with diverse characteristics may be diagnosed or identified as LD, yet all pupils may be assigned to the same instructional program. Availability of program, not pupil characteristics, is often the determiner of mode of instruction. The subtype work, by delineating replicable and reliable subtypes within the broad LD rubric, may provide impetus to refinement of intervention and treatment decisions.

Another empirical approach to the problem of heterogeneity within LD programs and LD research is the UCLA Marker Variable

System (Keogh, et al., 1982). Markers are defined as common reference points, as descriptive benchmarks that allow determination of similarities and differences of subjects across research samples and/or educational programs. The specific markers identified in the UCLA research were derived from a comprehensive search of the empirical literature in LD and were tested in a series of field studies. The final system is composed of four groups of markers: Descriptive, Substantive, Topical, and Background (Table 1).

As noted by Senf (1986), the use of detailed markers would increase awareness of sample distinctiveness but would not address issues of sample selection bias, a point to be elaborated in a subsequent section of this chapter. However, routine reporting of characteristics of learning–disabled pupils and research subjects using a common format of agreed upon markers could greatly reduce problems in interpreting findings from research and evaluation studies. It would also provide information about learning–disabled pupils that could increase our ability to "map" the many expressions of LD and to identify patterns of shared attributes.

Whatever the particular approach, the empiric work to date underscores the generalization that LD is a plural concept. Our task is to identify conceptually and empirically valid subgroups and describe the functional organization of these groups. A much needed product would be a workable taxonomy of learning disabilities.

TABLE 1-1. *UCLA Marker Variables*

Descriptive Markers	Topical Markers
Sample size	Activity level
Chronologic age	Attention
Grade level(s)	Auditory perception
Locale	Fine motor coordination
Race/ethnicity	Gross motor coordination
Sample source	Memory
Socioeconomic status (SES)	Oral language
Language	Visual perception
Educational history	
Educational placement	
Physical and health status	
Substantive Markers	**Background Markers**
General intellectual ability	Year of study
Reading achievement	Georgraphical location (state or county)
Arithmetic achievement	Exclusionary criteria
Behavioral and emotional adjustment	

MULTIPLE PURPOSES OF CLASSIFICATION

Closely related to the notion of LD as a plural concept is recognition that classification has many purposes (Keogh, 1986, 1987; Senf, 1986; Wong, 1986). As proposed elsewhere (Keogh, 1983), at the minimum, classification in LD may be for purposes of advocacy, for the provision of services, or for study of a condition. These purposes involve different selection criteria and practices and may lead to the identification of different numbers and different types of learning-disabled persons. For purposes of advocacy, we wish to bring attention and support to the needs of many pupils with a range of learning disabilities. For provision of services, classifications are required that group together learning-disabled pupils with similar instructional or treatment needs. Yet, neither of these classifications may include learning-disabled pupils who meet the criteria for study of particular LD conditions, for example, visual perceptual or auditory processing problems. Research on particular aspects of LD requires selection criteria that relate to the purpose of the research (e.g., the studies on short-term memory in LD by Torgesen & Houck, 1980).

Problems in understanding LD have come in part because we have assumed that persons identified as learning disabled for one purpose are representative of another group of LD. Most studies of the characteristics of learning-disabled persons are based on subjects selected for other purposes, such as special programs in schools, clinic rosters, or remedial referrals. These "system-identified" subjects (Keogh & MacMillan, 1983; MacMillan, Meyers, & Morrison, 1980) reflect the criteria and procedures that lead to referral and placement in schools and clinics. Different service facilities have somewhat different operational criteria for defining LD and, thus, may select different persons.

Using qualitative procedures and working within ongoing programs, Mehan, Meihls, Hertweck, & Crowdes (1981) described the identification and placement process within school districts. They found that many extra-pupil influences were important in identification and selection decisions. School psychologists' work load, space in the resource room, numbers and kinds of other services in the school, and level of funding were among the many factors that determined who and how many pupils were processed for special education services. Senf (1986) also argues that classification and placement decisions are influenced by political and economic conditions, noting that the number of learning-disabled pupils identified in a given school district relates to the level of available financial support. In addition, Senf (1978, 1986) emphasizes that identification of pupils as learning disabled is in part a function of the power and position of the advocates who represent children, that is, middle-class and upper middle-class, well-educated, articulate, and assertive parents are persuasive representatives for the children. Less well-educated and less "school-wise" parents from nonmajority language, social, and/or cultural groups may be less effective in dealing with school professionals.

Economic and social factors may explain, in part, why LD is often viewed as an Anglo, middle-class problem. These characteristics describe the majority of pupils identified as LD in schools. Such pupils may accurately reflect the operational criteria applied in particular school settings. However, they cannot be assumed to represent LD defined for other purposes or the learning–disabled population. One wonders at the prevalence and nature of LD in groups with other handicapping conditions or from different linguistic and cultural backgrounds. Senf's (1986) admonition about the need to specify population, not just sample, characteristics, deserves emphasis: "To examine a subgroup from an unknown population is to learn only about that specific subgroup—an undertaking of dubious value." (Senf, 1986, p. 39).

Unfortunately, the bulk of the research and program evaluation in LD consists of specific subgroups selected from unspecified populations. Most studies of LD were conducted without consideration of, or reference to, the population from which the sample was drawn. It should not surprise us that research findings frequently differ or that generalizations about LD are limited. In most studies of LD, the sampling base is system-identified subjects. These subjects are part of a population defined by socioeconomic and sociopolitical conditions as well as by personal or individual attributes. Samples may accurately reflect specific population parameters but may not represent a broader LD population.

The point to be emphasized is that the term *learning disabilities* may vary in meaning for the purpose of classification. Classifications for educational services differs from classification for the study of the condition. This is not an issue of rightness or wrongness of classification, but rather underscores the fact that definition is tied to purpose. Thus, inferences across classification systems must be drawn with caution.

CLASSIFICATION AND IDENTIFICATION

The focus of this chapter has been on definitional and classification issues. Yet understanding the state of the art in LD requires acknowledgment of the distinction between classification and identification. As noted by Bailey (1973), classification is conceptual and is measurement free. Decisions about organization or taxonomic structure can be made on the basis of logic alone. Identification is measurement bound, however, because it involves decisions about who or what fits into given classes or groups. As part of the process of determining who goes into what class or category, we necessarily move from conceptual to operational levels, and, thus, we are faced with serious measurement questions.

To illustrate, a number of governmental agencies and many researchers consider the ability–achievement discrepancy criterial in defining LD. On a conceptual level, this may be a defensible criterion that specifies a given class of problems. Problems characterized by an ability–achievement discrepancy are different from problems in which there is no discrepancy. This is a straightforward and logical distinction when establishing an organization or classification of problem conditions. The difficulty comes when we attempt to decide which persons will or will not be placed in the category of discrepancy problems. Identification is measurement bound, because we must operationalize the constructs if we are to determine which persons do or do not fit the class or category. In the case of the ability–achievement discrepancy, the literature is replete with detailed criticism of tests used to measure both ability and achievement and contains much criticism of the methods and criteria used to define discrepancy (Cone & Wilson, 1981; Page, 1980; Reynolds, 1984–85; Reynolds, et al., 1984–85; Shepard & Smith, 1983). Unreliability of measures and differences in the formulae for determining discrepancy result in the identification of varying numbers of learning–disabled persons (Epps, Ysseldyke, & Algozzine, 1983; Forness, Sinclair, & Guthrie, 1983).

One issue is to be faced in LD is whether our problems of subject heterogeneity relate to the defining criteria for classification or to our methods of identification. It seems likely that much of the present confusion in the LD field relates directly to problems at the identification level, because these operational decisions are directly embedded in a host of social, political, and economic influences. The problems are also exacerbated by the lack of a clear and consensual classification system or taxonomy. Thus, the development of such a classification system appears to be a necessary conceptual step. A paralleling step relates to questions of how to operationalize these definitional criteria.

CONCLUSIONS AND FUTURE DIRECTIONS

A multidimensional and multidefinitional approach to defining LD may clarify, but at the same time may complicate, the conduct of research on the topic. It underscores the need to take into account both individual and situational or contextual variables; it argues for clearer conceptualization of research questions and increased methodologic sophistication; and it suggests the need for research on a number of levels. If we take seriously the notion of a shared attribute definition of LD, it is possible to propose a comprehensive research agenda for LD. At the very least, such a program of research would include several major efforts.

First, there is clearly a need for a classification system or taxonomy of LD that takes into account and orders the diversity of conditions subsumed under this rubric. This will require both conceptual and empiric approaches and will necessarily cut across disciplinary and professional perspectives. Second, understanding LD requires understanding other expressions of problem development. Our shared attributes may be shared, in part, by other diagnostic or classification groups. Thus, it is imperative tht the similarities and differences between LD and other categories of mildly handicapped pesons be addressed. Research on LD will likely yield more powerful insights when conducted within cross-categoric designs. Third, the course of LD over time requires description and analysis, and the many influences on LD require specification. Patterns of growth and change may vary widely among subgroups of learning-disabled children. Understanding how the many personal and social contributions to development and to the expressions of LD interact and transact over time requires commitment to longitudinal, developmental research designs. Fourth, the interactive links between LD conditions and intervention and treatment approaches must be identified and tested. We have often intervened on faith, and sometimes this has been enough. Too often, however, our successes, as well as our failures, have occurred for unknown reasons. Better understanding of both LD and interventions should improve the level of services for many children.

Finally, the time seems right for this field of study to become part of a larger scientific tradition. This would involve improved and more rigorous research methods, as well as improved and more rigorous thinking. We have evolved from an applied need and a pragmatic perspective. We face many serious and pressing "real world" problems. Yet, we are not likely to understand the many expressions of LD unless we make the topic a legitimate focus of scientific study. This means, in part, that we support and encourage research that does not necessarily have an immediate practical payoff. Earlier in this chapter, I suggested that classification must be tied to purpose. Similarly, the conduct of research must be tied to purpose, and one purpose is to understand the condition(s) of LD. Understanding learning disabilities will require a continued tolerance of ambiguity, along with a commitment to theoretical as well as to applied research.

Susan A. Vogel

No one in the field of LD has had as significant an impact on research as Barbara Keogh. Her seminal, common sense, yet profound thinking has riveted our attention on the essential research and practice problems in the field: (1) the rapid increase in the prevalence of LD and the variations in prevalence across states and geographic areas of the country, (2) definitional problems leading not only to placement inconsistencies but also to heterogeneity within and across research samples, (3) our lack of sound principles to guide identification–intervention decisions and establish treatment–condition links, (4) the underlying confusion regarding the nature of LD or, in her terminology, the diversity of attributes that characterize LD conditions, and (5) the lack of ". . .a reasonable classification system or taxonomy of LD."

Keogh's special contribution in identifying and clarifying these problem areas is that she provides us with a theoretic framework that, like other such theoretical constructs, explains a host of previously inexplicable phenomena, or, in the field of LD, of previously discrete and somewhat contradictory observations, findings, and practices. For example, can and, if so, how does Keogh's discussion of monothetic and polythetic classification systems relate to definitional problems and eligibility of learning–disabled adults in postsecondary settings? How can a diagnosed learning–disabled college student be ineligible to receive service in a college with a well-developed program specializing in the treatment of dyslexia and, after being dismissed for academic failure, apply to a college in a neighboring state where she/he is accepted and deemed eligible to receive assistance from the staff that provides support services to learning–disabled students on campus? This question is even more perplexing since the development of eligibility criteria in postsecondary settings is in its infancy (see discussion in Vogel's chapter), and, in only one state, California (and then only in the community college system) has there been an attempt at implementing a uniform set of eligibility criteria (Best, Howard, Kanter, Mellard, Pearson, 1986). One could easily attribute these circumstances to incompetence of college personnel, the complexity of identifying and assessing learning disabilities in adults (Vogel, 1985), or declining enrollment in higher education. But assuming that none of these circumstances is the case, does Keogh's discussion of shared attributes explain these phenomena, and, if so, how?

According to Keogh, one of our tasks is to determine the number of attributes necessary for membership in a class. In the monothetic classification system, membership is based on the presence or absence of a single attribute, for example, in this first college setting, reading ability, and, even more specifically, word attack skills was that attribute. Only students with existing decoding skills weaknesses were eligible for service; in other words, the documentation of present deficits in knowledge of grapheme–phoneme correspondences determined membership in the class of dyslexia.

In the second type of classification system, polythetic, membership is determined by the presence of a cluster of attributes. This model was used in the second setting, in which history of a learning disability, an aptitude–achievement discrepancy, intraindividual discrepancies, and processing deficits had to be present. Determination of the presence or absence of all of these attributes is fraught with difficulties, including instrumentation, measurement, methodologic, and discrepancy formulae problems. But what we do not know is how severe a deficit must be to interfere with success in a postsecondary setting. Keogh recommends that we take into account each type of deficit and individual settings in our research (be situational specific and context specific).

Many other factors, however, must also be taken into consideration according to Keogh. Because educational background; home environment; emotional stability; physical health; life experiences; type and degree of LD; and type, duration, and effectiveness of intervention will all vary considerably in the learning–disabled adult population, there is an even greater need to explore the long-term effects of learning disabilities in a wide range of aptitudes (low average to gifted range) throughout the range of variability in aptitude–achievement discrepancies (from mild to severe) and in those with a variety of subtypes of learning disabilities. Questions to be addressed include:

1. How does the nature of learning disabilities change over time (chronicity)?
2. Are certain aspects of functioning ameliorated while others are more resistant to intervention or to the effect of maturation?
3. As a corollary to this question, do learning–disabled males differ from learning–disabled females in the pattern of their shared attributes at each developmental stage throughout the life span, indicative of a different pattern of shared attributes, different subtypes, differing rate of learning, and a different prognosis? If so, how?
4. How should the definition of LD in adults differ not only by

number of attributes, patterns of shared attributes, severity, and chronicity, but also by purposes of identification?

Returning again to the first vignette, the purpose of identification in the first college setting was to identify those learning–disabled students who needed intensive training in decoding skills. The monethetic approach, that is, selecting one attribute to determine eligibility, is, in fact, appropriate. If, however, the purpose of identification is provision of a broad spectrum of basic skills instruction, of teaching bypass strategies and self-advocacy skills, rather than instruction in a specific remedial program, the polythetic model is more appropriate. Therefore, by applying Keogh's analysis to specific subtypes, settings, and different purposes, the utility and power of her discussion become evident.

Lastly, I wish to suggest that there has never been a more critical period to implement Keogh's (1986) recommendation regarding a comprehensive research agenda. Such a program is needed to counteract the imminent danger of federal budget cutbacks for special education combined with the regular education/special education initiative, which considers the learning disabled under the broad umbrella of persons with "learning difficulties" rather than as those with an identifiable, handicapping condition.

Moreover, a research program to describe and analyze the long-term effects of LD is likewise needed, because just as we witnessed the dramatic increase in the number of learning–disabled children and adolescents in the last decade, there has been a tenfold increase in the number of self-identified learning–disabled college freshmen, constituting 14.3% of all handicapped freshmen (as reported by HEATH, May 1986). This percentage is, I believe, a minimal estimate of the prevalence of LD among college students, since students were excluded from this study if they were part-time or transfer students (thus excluding many learning–disabled persons).

The definitional problems, classification issues and intervention/treatment dilemmas follow these adults into postsecondary settings just as the residual effects of their learning disability do. With the help of Keogh's comprehensive, scholarly analysis and recommendations combined with the synergistic energy generated by the group of researchers who came together in this symposium, we can design and implement such a research agenda.

REFERENCES

Bailey, K.D. (1973). Monothetic and polythetic typologies and their relation to conceptualization, measurement and scaling. *American Sociological Review, 38*(1), 18–33.

Beauchamp, G. R. (1985). Personal communication.

Best, L., Howard R., Kanter, M., Mellard, D., Pearson, M. (April 1, 1986). Program standards and eligibility criteria for learning disabled adults in California community colleges. Presentation at the 64th Annual Convention of the Council for Exceptional Children, New Orleans.

Clements, S. D. (1986). *Minimal brain dysfunction in children: Terminology and identification* (NINDS Monograph No. 3, U. S. Public Health Service Publication No. 1415). Washington DC: U. S. Department of Health, Education, and Welfare.

Cone, T.E., & Wilson, L.R. (1981). Quantifying a severe discrepancy: A critical analysis. *Learning Disability Quarterly, 4*(4), 359–371.

Cruickshank, W.M. (1981). Learning disabilities: A definitional statement. In W.M. Cruickshank (Ed.), *Selected writings* (Vol. 2). Syracuse, NY: Syracuse University Press.

Doehring, D.G. (1978). The tangled web of behavioral research on developmental dyslexia. In A.L. Benton & D. Pearl (Eds.), *Dyslexia: An appraisal of current knowledge.* New York: Oxford University Press.

Doehring, D.G., Hoshko, I.M. & Bryans, B.N. (1979). Statistical classification of children with reading problems. *Journal of Clinical Neuropsychology, 1*(1), 5–16.

Epps, S. Ysseldyke, J.E., & Algozzine, B. (1983). Impact of different definitions of learning disabilities on the number of students identified. *Journal of Psychoeducational Assessment, 1*(4), 341–352.

Federal Register (1977). 42,65082–65085.

Fletcher, J.M., & Morris, R. (1986). Classification of disabled learners: Beyond exclusionary definitions. In S.J. Ceci (Ed.), *Handbook of cognitive, social, and neuropsychological aspects of learning disabilities* (Vol. 1). Hillsdale, NJ: Lawrence Erlbaum Associates.

Forness, S.R. Sinclair, E., & Guthrie, D. (1983). Learning disability discrepancy formulas: Their use in actual practice. *Learning Disability Quarterly, 6*(2), 107–114.

Hallahan, D.P., & Kauffman, J.M. (1976). *Introduction to learning disabilities: A psycho-behavioral approach.* Englewood Cliffs, NJ: Prentice-Hall.

Hammill, D.D., Leigh, J.E. McNutt, G., & Larsen, S.C. (1981). A new definition of learning disabilities. *Learning Disability Quarterly, 4*(4), 336–342.

Information from HEATH, Vol. 5, No. 2 (May, 1986) Washington, D.C.

Keogh, B.K. (1983). A lesson from Gestalt psychology. *Exceptional Education Quarterly, 4*(1), 115–127.

Keogh, B.K. (1987). Learning disabilities: Diversity in search of order. In M. Wang, M. Reynolds, & H. Walberg (Eds.), *The handbook of special education: Research and practice.* Oxford, England: Pergamon Press.

Keogh, B.K. (1986). Future of the LD field: Research and practice. *Journal of Learning Disabilities, 19,* 455–460.

Keogh, B.K., MacMillan, D.L. (1983). The logic of sample selection: Who represents what? *Exceptional Education Quarterly, 4*(3), 84–96.

Keogh, B.K., Major-Kingsley, S., Omori-Gordon, H., & Reid, H. P. (1982). *A system of marker variables for the field of learning disabilities.* Syracruse, NY: Syracruse University Press.

Lloyd, J.W. (1986). Learning disability interventions. In M. Wang, M. Reynolds, & H. Walberg (Eds.), *The handbook of special education: Research and practice.* Oxford, England: Pergamon Press.

Lyon, G.R. (1983). Learning disabled readers: Identification of subgroups. In H.R. Myklebust (Ed.), *Progress in learning disabilities: Vol. V.* New York: Grune & Stratton.

Lyon, G.R. (1985). Educational validation studies of learning disability subtypes. In B. Rourke (Ed.), *Learning disabilities in children: Advances in subtypes analyses.* New York: Guilford Press.

Macmillan, D.L., Meyers, C.E., & Morrison, G.M. (1980). System-identification of mildly mentally retarded children: Implications for interpreting and conducting research. *American Journal of Mental Deficiency, 85*(2), 106–115.

McKinney, J.D. (1984). The search for subtypes of specific learning disability. *Annual Review of Learning Disabilities, 2,* 19–26.

McKinney, J.D. (1986). Research in conceptually and empirically derived subtypes of specific learning disabilities. In M. Wang, M. Reynolds, & H. Walberg, (Eds.), *The handbook of special education: Research and practice.* Oxford, England: Pergamon Press.

Mehan, H., Meihls, J.L., Hertweck, A., & Crowdes, M.S. (1981). Identifying handicapped students. In S.B. Bacharach (Ed.), *Organizational behavior in schools and school districts.* New York: Praeger.

Mercer, L.D. Forgnone, C., & Wolking, W.D. (1976). Definitions of learning disabilities used in the United States. *Journal of Learning Disabilities, 9*(6), 376–386.

National Advisory Committee on Handicapped Children (1986). *Special education for handicapped children: First annual report.* Washington, DC: Department of Health, Education, and Welfare.

Page, E.B. (1980). Tests and decisions for the handicapped: A guide to evaluation under the new laws. *The Journal of Special Education, 14*(4), 423–483.

Reynolds, C.R. (1984–1985). Critical measurement issues in learning disabilities. *The Journal of Special Education, 18*(4), 451–476.

Reynolds, C.R., Berk, R.A., Boodoo, G.M., Cox, J., Gutkin, T.B., Mann, L., Page, E.B., & Wilson, V.C. (1984–1985). *Critical measurement issues in learning disabilities.* Report of the Work Group on Measurement Issues in the Assessment of Learning Disabilities.

Satz, P., & Morris, R. (1981). Learning disability subtypes: A review. In F.J. Pirozzola & M.C. Wittrock (Eds.), *Neuropsychological and cognitive processes in reading.* New York: Academic Press.

Senf, G.M. (1978). Implications of the final procedures for evaluating specific learning disabilities. *Journal of Learning Disabilities, 11*(3), 124–126.

Senf, G.M. (1986). LD research in sociological and scientific perspective. In J.K. Torgesen & B.Y.L. Wong (Eds.), *Psychological and educational perspectives on learning disabilities.* Orlando, FL: Academic Press.

Shepard, L.A. (1983). The role of measurement in educational policy: Lessons from the identification of learning disabilities. *Educational Measurement: Issues and Practice, 2*(3), 4–8.

Shepard, L.A., & Smith, M.L. (1983). An evaluation of the identification of learning disabled students in Colorado. *Learning Disability Quarterly, 6*(2), 115–127.

Siegel, L.S., & Heaven, R.K. (1986). Categorization of learning disabilities. In S.J. Ceci (Ed.), *Handbook of cognitive, social, and neuropsychological aspects of learning disabilities* (Vol. 1). Hillsdale, NJ: Lawrence Erlbaum Associates.

Sixth Annual Report to Congress on the Implementation of Public Law 94-142: *The Education for All Handicapped Children Act* (1984). Office of Special Education, U.S. Department of Education.

Speece, D.L., McKinney, J.D., & Appelbaum, M.I. (1985). Classification and validation of behavioral subtypes of learning–disabled children. *Journal of Educational Psychology, 77*(1), 67–77.

Torgesen, J.K. (1982). The use of rationally defined subgroups in research on learning disabilities. In J.P. Das, R.F. Mulcahy, & A.E. Wall (Eds.), *Theory and research in learning disabilities.* New York: Plenum Press.

Torgesen, J.K., & Houck, D.G. (1980). Processing deficiencies in learning disabled children who perform poorly on the Digit Span test. *Journal of Educational Psychology, 72*(2), 141–160.

Vogel, S.A. (1985). Learning disabled college students: Identification, assessment, and outcomes. In D. Duane and C.K. Leong (Eds.), *Understanding learning disabilities: International and multidisciplinary views.* New York: Plenum Press.

Wong, B.Y.L. (1986). Problems and issues in the definition of learning disabilities. In G.K. Torgeson & B.Y.L. Wong (Eds.), *Psychological and educational perspectives on learning disabilities.* New York: Academic Press.

Ysseldyke, J.E., & Algozzine, B. (1983). LD or not LD: That's not the question! *Journal of Learning Disabilities, 16*(1), 29–31.

Ysseldyke, J.E., Algozzine, B., Richey, L., & Graden, J. (1982). Declaring students eligible for learning disability services: Why bother with the data? *Learning Disability Quarterly, 5*(1), 37–44.

CHAPTER 2

Theoretical Quandaries in Learning Disabilities

Kenneth A. Kavale

Theoria is the highest form of activity.

-Aristotle
Nicomachean Ethics

T he field of learning disabilities (LD) is in a perpetual state of crisis. Several fundamental complications are the cause of this crisis, which results in confusion, ambiguity, and legitimate disagreement about the optimal study of LD. When these complications and the individual characteristics of LD researchers become entwined, a variety of quandaries are created that can only be gradually understood and overcome.

Although most LD researchers would agree that this is a scientific field, almost no one believes entirely that it is a science (Kavale & Forness, 1985b). In fact, it is possible to take such a jaundiced view of LD that it may be considered a form of sorcery compounded by magic and fantasy (Andreski, 1972). It would be wrong to take this view, but equally wrong is the hope that if we proclaim unsubstantiated ideas and concepts loud and long enough they might be believed. The LD field must pull together in order to halt the continuing fragmentation of the discipline. This chapter addresses the almost perennial question in LD: Why aren't we doing better and how can we improve?

THE PROBLEMS

The tough, intellectual challenges in LD appear to be the result of two forces: (1) the fundamental complications facing the field, and (2) the diverse intellectual backgrounds and interests of LD researchers. To understand the current difficulties we must examine the interplay between the following factors:

1. The LD phenomenon is probably even far more complex than is currently realized (Kavale & Nye, 1986). Explanations must be both multivariate and probablistic. Yet, we often study only single variables in isolation that are not linked to any larger system.

2. Measurement problems in LD are formidable. The physical sciences are accustomed to indirect measurement (e.g., mass, heat), where the assumptions required to link operational measures to physical properties are much more precise and justifiable than in LD (Blalock, 1982). For example, to infer perceptual abilities on the basis of test scores requires a complex auxiliary measurement theory that is far more difficult to justify.

3. There exists a tremendous variety of behaviors in LD that we wish to explain. Are there any systematic ways by which we can reduce the complexity by identifying a smaller number of more inclusive variables? The answer is probably yes, but problems of comparability loom large. How, for instance, can one compare word attack skills, attention deficits, or peer status across a variety of contexts? Must procedures change as we move from more structured to less structured situations? If so, how do we distinguish artifactual from substantive differences across settings?

4. The confines of LD are often fuzzy or imprecise. Even when we desire precision, it is often necessary to make arbitrary decisions, each of which may then yield somewhat different conclusions. For example, the boundaries of average achievement or social acceptance are relatively indeterminate. There is consequently a kind of analog to Heisenberg's Uncertainty Principle, placing limits on the degree of precision in our measuring instruments.

5. There is no obvious way to divide the labor involved in understanding LD (Boalt, 1969). Certainly, there are some rather arbitrary disciple-based boundaries that have been arrived at mostly through historical accident. The problem is that important variables

spill across many current disciplines, and any large fraction of these variables cannot be omitted arbitrarily without doing injustice to the reality of LD.

In addition to these complicating factors, there are a number of inherent characteristics of LD researchers that tend to compound the already difficult intellectual challenges (Mitroff, 1974). We have been attracted to LD for a variety of reasons, but it is highly probable that most LD researchers represent a cross between scientist and humanist. Those who take a ''hard science'' orientation were probably initially drawn to LD because they were fascinated by problems of underachievement and wanted to see them corrected. Others probably have a much more hostile orientation toward the sciences and believe we should seek an understanding of LD with a more phenomenologic bent. Still others probably believe that their role is one of critic, whose principal task is to improve LD—to point out its assets and liabilities, with a view toward modifying them in a positive direction. Thus, LD researchers themselves are far from homogeneous in their intellectual orientations. We are probably a very heterogeneous group of scholars, so much so that greater differences may exist within the LD discipline than between LD and some other fields.

THE PROPER STUDY OF LEARNING DISABILITIES

The LD field, lodged as it is somewhere between a natural science and a human science (i.e., helping profession), is fertile ground for debate over the suitability of natural science models to the study of human behavior (Winch, 1958). A common argument against a natural science-oriented approach is based on the thesis that human behavior is a different kind of phenomenon, one that is not best studied by scientific means that attempt to break a totality into parts to be analyzed separately. But such a position suggests that there exists some sort of deeper understanding that can never be communicated (Rescher, 1970).

The LD field will never be considered a scientific field until it achieves success with scientific methods, and this will not occur until there is a fundamental restructuring of the LD field (Kavale & Forness, 1985a). The LD field is indeed complex and suggests that our scientific aspiration level, for the present, must be realistically lower. It must be understood that the status of a ''science'' comes slowly. A ''science'' (e.g., geology, meteorology) may exist even though natural forces are highly complex, making precise prediction practically impossible. If the level of aspiration was realistically lowered, there would be less of a tendency to slavishly imitate the physical sciences in the hopes of gaining prestige (Northrop, 1947). In an effort to appear scientific, the problems studied are theoretically or practically trivial. Important questions are avoided in favor of less important questions, the rationale being that important questions are scientifically tractable only when less important ones are resolved. Methods dictate the problems studied rather than vice versa. Success, however, will never be achieved unless there is a break from such misguided efforts.

Science, in its simplist and most fundamental sense, means knowledge. Given this definition, much of contemporary LD research is respectably scientific. But science has come to be more than just knowledge; it implies knowledge of a particular sort obtained in particular ways. In this refined sense, science has come to mean physics, chemistry, and possibly biology, with their highly systematized theories describing lawful relationships based on the logic of mathematics.

These theories are similar in conception to Cronbach and Meehl's (1955) notion of nomologic network used to designate the system of laws assumed to exist between theoretical entities and between theoretical entities and their observable indicators. No theory in LD approaches an optimal realization of a nomologic network (Kavale & Forness, 1985b). In a field such as LD, the nomologic network is coordinated directly with observable events in only a few instances. The connections with observation are more likely only through other regions of the network using weak statistics (e.g., means, correlations, tendencies, and probabilities). The nomologic network in LD is not composed of strict lawlike relationships that permit explicit assumptions. Instead, this network possesses many implicit assumptions which suggest that their practical implications are often arrived at through metaphoric argument rather than by rigorous logical derivation. This is easily verified by noting the large number of intervening variables incorporated into LD theory. The presence of intervening variables prevents a formally complete and parsimonious theory in LD that specifies all the linkages between independent and dependent variables (MacCorquodale & Meehl, 1948).

DATA AND THEORY IN LEARNING DISABILITIES

The LD field is literally inundated with data, so it ostensibly looks scientific (Summers, 1986). There exists a veritable catalog of empirical evidence in LD that probably provides some insight into the nature of the phenomenon but does little to justify theories in LD. The reason for this is that data are not facts in the ordinary sense. Facts must also include some theory, that is, information that arises independent of the collections of data. In short, facts depend upon the interpretation of data (Goodman, 1955).

The notion that theories may be demolished by facts is, by and large, historically incorrect. The framework of a science is provided by the integrated set of propositions that make up a theory (Nagel, 1961). A theory cannot be displaced by facts; it can be displaced only by another theory, a theory that gives rise to more comprehensive facts, more useful facts, or simply more recent facts (Lakatos & Musgrave, 1970). Science is then, above all, distinguished by the presence of facts that represent the conjunction of data and theory. Theory in the absence of data is not science, but equally clear is the fact that data alone do not make a science. The intellectual value of any particular fact comes from the plausibility of the theory behind it, not necessarily from the particulars of observation (Nagel, 1961). Thus, when we way that something is fact within the framework of a theory, we mean that the factual status of that observation depends entirely upon the adequacy of the theory. The adequacy of the theory, in turn, depends upon a complicated structure of theory and observation (i.e., nomologic network) (Hempel, 1974).

The lack of theory is thus a primary reason why we seldom, if ever, experience any dramatic breakthroughs in LD. Although we accumulate much data, the absence of theory prevents us from discovering new facts. At times, however, we exaggerate findings to make it appear as though we have done so. This is accomplished by magnifying the importance of small differences and placing the emphasis on statistical signficance and probability levels, rather than on magnitudes of relationships and explained variance. In the reporting such results, the emphasis is on "significant" differences without regard to the fact that within-group differences may also be large when compared to between-group differences (Weener, 1981).

THE STATUS AND FUNCTION OF LEARNING DISABILITIES THEORY

In the LD field, there are some theories, but these might best be included under the heading of LD classics. They represent the sociology of knowledge in LD in the sense of who said what, who influenced LD at specific times, and who provided intuitive insights (Merton, 1973). The primary difficulties with previously proposed LD "theories" (probably better understood as conceptual schemes) are twofold: (1) they have typically been unidimensional conceptualizations, and (2) they have incorporated only a narrow and isolated context (Wong, 1979). Such single-paradigm notions have encompassed many areas (e.g., minimal brain dysfunction, psychoneurologic disturbance, linguistic processing, as well as deficits in attention, memory, perception, psycholinguistic functioning, sensory integration and the like). These notions, however, were confined to these specific deficits and thus presented a circumscribed focus that could not explicate the entire LD phenomenon (Kavale & Forness, 1985b).

The basic aims of theory are to explain and to predict (Toulmin, 1961). The available theories in LD do not explain a sufficient number of cases to be useful and predict even fewer cases. For LD to overcome its present chaotic state, it is necessary for theoretic formulations to explain and to predict LD in general rather than LD in particular. Such macro-level theories are the only means by which a superstructure in LD can be achieved (Blalock, 1979). A comprehensive and unified theory would serve as the primary vehicle for scientific knowledge about LD, because facts can then be placed in perspective (Ziman, 1978). In terms of levels of explanation, theories permit enhanced explanation by allowing for a greater degree of generality than that which is to be explained. Facts are explained by lawlike generalizations. Laws, in turn, are explained by theories and suggest that explanation consists in subsuming whatever is to be explained under higher order (more inclusive and comprehensive) principles. The logical outcome, then, is that to explain theory, one must have a more inclusive theory (Feigl, 1973).

This analysis suggests that it is necessary to distinguish between two types of theory. In the standard sense, theory denotes a very specific set of related doctrines (e.g., hypotheses, axioms, principles), which can be used for making specific experimental predictions and for giving detailed explanations of a phenomenon (e.g., Maxwell's theory of electromagnetism, the Freudian theory of the Oedipel complex) (Feigl, 1970). By contrast, the term *theory* is also used to refer to much more general sets of assumptions. For instance, it is possible to speak about "the kinetic theory of gases" or "the theory of evolution." In these cases, the reference is not to a single theory, but to a whole spectrum of individual theories. Although "the theory of evolution" does not refer to any single theory, the variety of instantiations, historically and conceptually related, all work from the assumption that organic species have common lines of descent (Laudan, 1977).

The two types of theories are quite different, but both are integral components of science. Fidelity to scientific practice suggests that the LD field take these larger theoretical units seriously. These larger units contain the epistemic features that are characteristic of science and may be overlooked by focusing on theories in the narrower sense (Rescher, 1970). It has been argued persuasively that more general theories are the primary tool for understanding and appraising scientific progress (Lakatos & Musgrave, 1970). These general theories have been formalized as "research programmes" (Lakatos, 1978) presenting a set a general assumptions about the entities and processes in a domain and about the appropriate methods to be used for investigating the problems and constructing the theories in that domain. In short, a research programme is a set of ontologic and methodologic "dos" and "don'ts" for an entire phenomenon (Lakatos, 1978).

The LD field has no research programmes; rather, it is a patchwork alliance of very different intellectual enterprises. Ostensibly, the identifiable enterprises study the same phenomenon, but do so with such tremendous variation in attitudes, techniques (scientific and otherwise), and standards for judging outcomes that it is difficult to observe the commonality (Mitroff, 1974). Consider, for example, the divergence between those with a developmental view of LD and those with a behavioral framework. Research on the social variables of LD is as narrow as that focusing on the medical aspects of LD. What is the proper role of neuropsychologic research in LD compared and contrasted with information processing research? How is research focused on schooling made compatible with efforts examining extra-school influences? Where does the strong psychometric tradition in LD fit?

The LD field is marked by a pluralism that is both healthy and unhealthy (Ravetz, 1971). It is healthy since most facets of LD possess a respectable research base and little is not studied about the LD phenomenon. It is unhealthy because these facets have remained isolated and discrete. Because the efforts in LD are so varied, it is possible to question whether there is a single discipline of LD. There appears to be a need for more structural studies in LD that have the goal of describing relationships among the components of the larger system (i.e., LD in general) (Turner, 1971). The phenomenon of LD is not a series of discrete entities, yet, through historical tradition and conceptual parsimony, it has been easier to handle LD in this manner. But the whole is probably even more than the sum of its parts. Without the development of research programmes, in the sense discussed, the LD field will not resolve its almost perpetual state of crisis (Lakatos & Musgrave, 1970).

WHY LEARNING DISABILITIES THEORY?

The primary aim of this chapter has been to lobby for increased effort in the LD field directed toward theory development, especially the general type of theory that can provide a comprehensive and unified perspective about LD. It may be argued that increased attention in theory development is unwise for an applied field whose efforts are directed at practical matters such as assessing and teaching children who are experiencing learning problems. Practice appears concrete, whereas theory seems esoteric. It was John Dewey (who certainly did not neglect practice) who said, "There is nothing so practical as a good theory" and sought to demonstrate that theory construction has pragmatic value. Unfortunately, the LD field has been affected by a general mistrust of theory and probably views it as a lofty, fanciful, and seemingly worthless activity. But theory can serve useful purposes in an applied field. Polansky (1986) suggested the following:

1. Theory mobilizes a field's energies.
2. Theory selects attention toward critical matters.
3. Theory infuses a field with dynamism.
4. Theory allows the field to transcend known facts.
5. Theory articulates prior knowledge.
6. Theory protects against unconscious forces and motivations.
7. Theory simplifies by providing a parsimonious perspective.
8. Theory allows for the extension and elaboration of knowledge.

Although these are important uses of theory, perhaps the most important function of theory is to provide a mechanism for correcting the deficits in our intellectual sphere (Churchman, 1971). Although achievements in LD are many, we, as insulated scholars, often become so accustomed to whatever practices we see around us that we fail to see that many of them are dysfunctional to the development of scholarship, as well as to the image of LD that we portray to others.

Because of the rewards for contributing to knowledge (or appearing to do so), it would be strange indeed if LD researchers did not develop vested interests in seeming to be in possession of great stores of knowledge. As Merton (1968) pointed out, whenever ends become highly important, whereas means come to be evaluated primarily in terms of their technical efficiency, one may expect strains toward deviance from whichever legitimate norms are less efficient than illegitimate ones. There also will be strains to modify the rules and to redefine the norms of legitimacy so as to favor whatever means are most efficient.

The pressures toward deviance are considerable, particularly when LD researchers are attempting to follow the model of physical science and where we find ourselves being compared to fields that have a long head start in building the status of science. The public tends to look at science in terms of *results* rather than as a *process* of learning (Ravetz, 1971). People want to see applications with immediate payoffs. We, in LD, must thus modify our own scholarly norms to permit ourselves to engage in a broad range of research activities with little guilt or feelings of intellectual insecurity. We must convince ourselves that our field is legitimate from a scholarly viewpoint, and, perhaps, practical applications may have to be secondary until such time that we convincingly understand what we are talking about (Kavale & Forness, 1985a).

HOW CAN WE IMPROVE THE INTELLECTUAL CLIMATE OF LEARNING DISABILITIES?

There are several means for accomplishing the necessary modifications:

1. *Eliminate the use of jargon and ideological language.* Since it is difficult to distinguish between technical terms useful in scientific context and words that are bandied about but have no clear meaning, the use of "big words" can often substitute for knowledge. Consider, for example, the differences between technical terms in statistics such as covariance or multicollinearity, both of which have well-understood meanings, and LD concepts such as "psycholinguistic" or "metacognition," which do not possess the same precision.

2. *Eliminate the proliferation of data.* The LD field seems enamored with data. Research reports are replete with so much statistical information that it appears that a surfeit of data is made to compensate for a paucity of ideas.

3. *Stop ignoring simplifying assumptions.* This suggestion surrounds the question of how much LD researchers differ in terms of the degree to which their assumptions are presented "out front." When compared to scientific theorizing, where almost all assumptions are explicit, LD "theories" are almost always based on loose-knit verbal associations possessing numerous implicit assumptions, which makes it almost impossible to test for robustness (Popper, 1959).

4. *Stop making ex post facto interpretations.* Given the complex nature of LD and the LD researchers' inclination to interpret findings so as to be consistent with known information, it is relatively easy for LD researchers to look good. Why is this child LD? Answers can always be found, not only by LD researchers but also by charlatans and demagogues.

5. *Eliminate nonproductive "theoretical" disputes.* It is important to recognize that LD researchers are human actors with individualistic goals that are not necessarily compatible with long-term scientific development. Rather than seeing issues as challenges that should be attacked cooperatively, we often perceive the situation as a zero sum

game, in which it is ourselves or our opponents who will discover the truth (Boalt, 1969). We must recognize that many disputes in LD stem only from ideologic differences, for instance, between skill (behavioral) and ability (process) schools. Although dispute is healthy, it also leaves scars in the form of fruitless debates and professional animosities—the latter have even infiltrated the major professional organizations in LD.

Ideologic debate also leads to another source of difficulty. When rhetoric is added to an already complex subject matter, it becomes difficult to distinguish between conflicts that will eventually be resolved amicably and those that will produce endless bickering. The consequences are a tendency to oversimplify opponents arguments and to set up "straw men." To avoid such disputes, a self-selective mechanism may develop, through which persons wishing to avoid conflict merely retreat from one area and enter another (Platt, 1976). Many researchers began by studying LD, probably now view themselves as primarily in the domain of dyslexia, attention deficits, or language-learning disabilities. The outcome here is a proliferation of subfields that are highly concrete but probably prevent the development of a single intellectual core for LD.

CONCLUSIONS AND FUTURE DIRECTIONS

The most fortunate part of our current quandary is that much of the situation is under our control. Whether or not we will choose to do something about it undoubtedly depends upon the extent to which we are frustrated and disturbed by the present chaotic state of affairs. The choices necessarily will entail costs before any gain. That which appears least satisfactory, however, is a laissez-faire attitude that accepts the status quo as inevitable or as a natural consequence of the search for understanding.

Dissatisfaction with the current state of affairs appears essential for collective action and productive debate (Kuhn, 1977). The LD field, first and foremost, needs to focus upon the development of a comprehensive and unified intellectual core (Ziman, 1978). This might be conceived of as similar to Kuhn's (1970) notion of paradigm, with the essential question being: To what degree do LD researchers orient their empirical and theoretical work to a research programme that denotes clearly the relevance of each particular work to a larger body of knowledge? Two ingredients are essential. First, there might be a theoretical formulation that can be modified into an even more general formulation as new information is secured (Feigl, 1973). The second ingredient consists of systematic efforts to check the general theory with empirical information in such a way that modifications are brought about in a cumulative manner. These ingredients are ordered, but it makes sense to put the theoretical horse before the empirical cart only if the two can be hitched in a secure and flexible manner. Too often in LD, lengthy theoretical discussions and debates take place without any reference to the quality of the empirical evidence or even to the kinds of data needed to test the theoretical propositions at issue (Popper, 1978). Given the many existing biases in the LD field, the development of an intellectual core would be a difficult endeavor (Merton, 1973). Two primary suggestions are offered:

1. The major orienting principles in LD should be organized around concepts that are sufficiently general in nature, so that they may be described and analyzed in terms of propositions that are not bound to particular points in space and time.

2. A greater emphasis should be placed on scholarly norms that encourage cooperative efforts in the LD field and that would allow researchers to work back and forth between the general and the specific as the situation demands.

Ideally, how should we proceed to build an intellectual core? One model (expensive) is the "think tank" (e.g., Center for Advanced Studies in Learning Disabilities), where a critical mass of scholars can spend their sabbatical leaves with other scholars to pursue common interests. Another model, less ambitious but appropriate as a "bootstrap" type of operation, is a brief working session that takes place over several days. The DLD/Utah Symposium represents such an effort and, with the publication of the proceedings, may also serve as a catalyst for additional activities.

What if we do not engage in any effort at all? Will we be satisfied to drift or to allow forces over which we have little control to determine the future of LD? And, can we predict what that future might be? We all probably have our own ideas and visions. Mine are not sufficiently optimistic to justify the status quo and a laissez-faire attitude. I have, therefore, tried to argue that we need to give increased attention to theory, especially the development of general, comprehensive, and unified theory. This should not be viewed as an esoteric venture, but rather a practical step in deciding where we are heading, where the impediments to progress are, and what steps might be taken in whatever direction we choose to take.

Joseph K. Torgesen

I heartily agree with Kenneth Kavale that we have no reason to be satisfied with the status quo in our field. Although children with LD have had effective political representation and services for them have proliferated in both the public and private sphere, there are still many serious gaps in our understanding of their basic learning difficulties. I am also in agreement with Dr. Kavale on at least three major problems that have limited scientific progress in this area.

First, there can be no doubt that the term *learning disabilities* has been used to designate an extremely complex range of phenomena. Scientific work in this area is attempting to understand not only the reasons why some children fail to learn reading, writing, spelling, or math skills as expected, but also how to help them overcome these learning problems. Certainly, an understanding of the reasons children with normal intelligence fail to learn basic reading skills requires a well-developed understanding of the reading process itself. Although research within the information processing paradigm over the last 20 years has added greatly to our knowledge of how humans read, there are still many interesting controversies to be resolved. Although we still lack scientific understanding of most basic academic tasks with which learning-disabled children have difficulty, we have set for ourselves a much more ambitious goal than simply understanding the processes by which these tasks are accomplished in normal children. We are concerned with trying to understand the diverse ways that acquisition of a broad range of academic skills is curtailed by interactions between child characteristics, task demands, and aspects of the instructional setting.

Second, the methods we have used to study the complex problems in our field have often been far from adequate. Some of these methodologic problems are caused by the complex nature of the phenomema under study; adequate methods have simply not been available. Other problems result from improperly trained and insufficiently careful researchers. In these cases, we could do better simply by drawing upon the best methodologies currently available from supporting sciences such as psychology, biology, or mathematics.

The historical weakness of our scientific methodology is a major factor underlying much of the current weakness in our knowledge of learning disabilities.

A third area of concern is the lack of good theory to help us organize the data that we do possess. Although I agree with Kavale that this is an important area of concern, my point of view about our current progress in this area, and ways of approaching the problem, is somewhat different than his.

First of all, I disagree with the proposition that "the LD field possesses no research programmes." In my view, almost all current research in learning disabilities is conducted within one of three scientific paradigms; information processing, neuropsychology, and applied behavior analysis (Torgesen, 1986). Although there is clearly wide variation in the sophistication of research within each of these areas, the best work in each paradigm shares similar ideas about basic assumptions, important questions to be addressed, preferred explanatory concepts, and methodologies that are most appropriate. For these and other reasons, each of these areas of inquiry qualifies as a scientific paradigm within which useful theories about learning disabilities may be developed. Since both theories and paradigms are accepted or rejected on the basis of their usefulness in generating research and explaining data, we currently have no defensible way of selecting one or another of these paradigms as the framework for a single theory about learning disabilities. Althougth paradigmatic pluralism does create a sense of confusion at times, it seems compatible with the complexity of the phenomena we are studying and with the maturity of our field. In my view, we are now far advanced from the situation faced by the pioneers in our field when there were simply no scientific paradigms available to support the kinds of questions they were asking about learning disabilities.

Kavale also suggests that a primary goal of theory development in our field should be to develop a comprehensive *general* theory of learning disabilities. In my view, efforts in this direction, if conceived as a serious attempt to develop a viable general theory, would be a fruitless and empty intellectual exercise. My own preference is to develop reasonably tight conceptualizations (or theories) of individual differences in performance within very restricted domains. If we can produce enough facts (defined as data embedded in theory) at this level, we may have some hope of eventually recognizing general principles that apply across domains. Without a better basis for our general theorizing, however, I am afraid that we may be led unnecessarily toward controversies that can only dissipate our energies and produce more confusion and division in our field.

REFERENCES

Andreski, S. (1972) *Social sciences as sorcery*. London: Andre Deutsch.

Blalock, H.M. (1979). Dilemmas and strategies of theory construction. In W. Snizek, E. Fuhrman, & M. Miller (Eds.), *Contemporary issues in theory and research*. Westport, CT: Greenwood Press.

Blalock, H.M. (1982). *Conceptualization and measurement in the social sciences*. Beverly Hills, CA: Sage.

Blalock, H.M. (1984). *Basics dilemmas in the social sciences*. Beverly Hills, CA: Sage.

Boalt, G. (1969). *The sociology of research*. Carbondale, IL: Southern Illinois University Press.

Churchman, C.W. (1971). *The design of inquiring systems*. New York: Basic Books.

Cronbach, L.J., & Meehl, P.E. (1955). Construct validity in psychological tests. *Psychological Bulletin, 52*, 281–301.

Feigl, H. (1970). The 'orthodox' view of theories: Remarks in defense as well as critique. In M. Radner & S. Winokur (Eds.), *Minnesota studies in the philosophy of science: Vol IV. Analysis of theories and methods of physics and psychology*. Minneapolis: University of Minnesota Press.

Feigl, H. (1973). Research programmes and induction. In R. Buck & R. Cohen (Eds.), *Boston studies in the philosophy of science* (Vol. 8). Dordrecht, Holland: Reidel.

Goodman, N. (1955). *Fact, fiction, and forecast*. Cambridge, MA: Harvard University Press.

Hempel, C.G. (1974). Formulation and formalization of scientific theories. In F. Suppe (Ed.), *The structure of scientific theories*. Urbana, IL: University of Illinois Press.

Kavale, K.A., & Forness, S.R. (1985a). Learning disability and the history of science: Paradigm or paradox? *Remedial and Special Education, 6*(4), 12–24.

Kavale, K.A., & Forness, S.R. (1985b). *The science of learning disabilities*. San Diego: College-Hill Press.

Kavale, K.A., & Nye, C. (1986). Parameters of learning disabilities in achievement, linguistic, neuropsychological, and social/behavioral domains. *Journal of Special Education, 19*(4), 443–458.

Kuhn, T.S. (1970). *The structure of scientific revolutions* (2nd ed.). Chicago: University of Chicago Press.

Kuhn, T.S. (1977). *The essential tension: Selected studies in scientific tradition and change*. Chicago: University of Chicago Press.

Lakatos, I. (1978). *The methodology of scientific research programmes*. Cambridge: Cambridge University Press.

Lakatos, I., & Musgrave, A. (Eds.). (1970). *Criticism and the growth of knowledge*. Cambridge: Cambridge University Press.

Laudan, L. (1977). *Progress and its problems*. Berkeley: University of California Press.

MacCorquodale, K., & Meehl, P.E. (1948). On a distinction between hypothetical constructs and intervening variables. *Psychological Review,* 55, 95–107.

Merton, R.K. (1968). *Social theory and social structure.* New York: Free Press.

Merton, R.K. (1973). *The sociology of science.* Chicago: University of Chicago Press.

Mitroff, I. (1974). *The subjective side of science.* Amsterdam: Elsevier.

Nagel, E. (1961). *The structure of science.* New York: Harcourt Brace & World.

Northrop, F.S.C. (1947). *The logic of the sciences and the humanities.* New York: Macmillan.

Platt, J. (1976). *Realities of social research.* New York: John Wiley & Sons.

Polansky, N.A. (1986). "There is nothing so practical as a good theory." *Child Welfare,* 65(1), 3–15.

Popper, K.R. (1959). *The logic of scientific discovery.* New York: Basic Books. (Originally published 1934.)

Popper, K.R. (1978). *Conjectures and refutations.* London: Routhledge & Kegan Paul. (Originally published 1962.)

Ravetz, J.R. (1971). *Scientific knowledge and its social problems.* Oxford: Oxford University Press.

Rescher, N. (1970). *Scientific explanation.* New York: Free Press.

Summers, E.G. (1986). The information flood in learning disabilities: A bibliometric analysis of the journal literature. *Remedial and Special Education,* 7(1), 49–60.

Toulmin, S. (1961). *Foresight and understanding.* New York: Harper & Row.

Turner, M.B. (1971). *Realism and the explanation of behavior.* New York: Appleton-Century-Crofts.

Weener, P. (1981). On comparing learning disabled and regular classroom children. *Journal of Learning Disabilities,* 14(5), 227–232.

Winch, P. (1958). *The idea of a social science.* London: Routledge & Kegan Paul.

Wong, B.Y.L. (1979). The role of theory in learning disabilities research: Part I. An analysis of problems. *Journal of Learning Disabilities,* 12, 585–595.

Ziman, J. (1978). *Reliable knowledge.* Cambridge: Cambridge University Press.

CHAPTER 3

A Multifaceted Hierarchical Theory of Learning Disabilities

Carol Weller

When the issues addressed in the DLD/Utah Symposium on Research in Learning Disabilities are considered in retrospect, one is struck by a persistent theme: the need for an empirically validated theoretical perspective that accounts for the diversity, variability, and heterogeneity of the learning-disabled population. The theory should be sufficiently multifaceted to include all learning-disabled persons regardless of age, strength and weakness pattern, severity, or intellectual ability. The theory should extend beyond the boundaries of the school years, should not be confined to persons classified as learning disabled for administrative purposes, should allow for inclusion of persons with learning disabilities (LD) regardless of categorical classification, and should not represent conditions observable only in the classroom (Torgesen, 1986). The theory should be conceived in such a way that validation is possible and that research plans are delineated.

Because of the lack of a multifaceted theory, systematic investigation of the learning-disabled population has not been feasible. As a result, issues of definition, description, classification, policy, service delivery, assessment, and intervention have become quagmired in examination of details. Therefore, it is the purpose of this chapter to propose a theory and a plan for validation of the theory that will describe, assess, and confirm or reject the multiple configurations of traits evidenced by learning-disabled persons.

DESCRIPTION OF A THEORY

Snow (1973) defined *theory* as "a symbolic construction designed to bring generalizable facts into systematic connection" (p. 78). Consisting of a set of units, such as concepts, facts, and variables, and a systematic relationship among the units, theories may be derived from subsets of data, existing models, metaphors, or explicitly stated postulates without direct supportive evidence (Turner, 1967). The importance of a theory lies, not in its derivation, but in its ability to "implicitly define the legitimate problems and methods of a research field for succeeding generations of practitioners" (Kuhn, 1962, p.10).

Two levels of theories can be developed: higher level and lower level (Boring, 1963; Snow, 1973). Higher level theories include axiomatic, broken axiomatic, and conceptual theories. These theories are derived from pre-existing massed data and result in mathematical formulations elemental to scientific laws. Lower level theories include descriptive, elementism, and formative hypotheses theories and are characterized by postulated summarization of relationships provocative for research and practice. Through the development of generalized distinctions, categories, and principles, lower level theories lead to the acquisition of facts about the structures they address. Lower level theories may develop into higher level theories as masses of validation data confirm, reject, or modify their constructs.

RATIONALE FOR THE PROPOSED THEORY

The lack of cohesive massed data in LD precludes the development of a higher level theory. Instead, the accumulated propositions, hypotheses, and concepts of the field can be used to generate a lower level theory that is of a descriptive nature. To develop a descriptive theory, two criteria must be met. First, the theory must conceptually account for diversity and, second, the theory must be capable of moving from theory to operation (Underwood, 1957). According to Campbell and Fisk (1959), these criteria can be met by the development of a multifaceted theory that can be statistically validated by a multitrait-multimethod matrix.

To generate a multifaceted theory, two or more discrete variables (traits) held by a given population are selected. These traits are described as discernible entities and are assumed to be independent of one another. Following theory generation, each trait is confirmed by testing with two or more distinctly definable variables (methods). The simultaneous interaction of traits and methods, as designated by a matrix, operationalize the validity of the traits (Campbell and Fisk, 1959).

Theories that have been developed specifically for validation with the multitrait-multimethod matrix have tended to be relatively simplistic. These theories have assumed strict independence of variables and have not allowed for situations in which the interrelationship of some variables may define another variable (Cronbach, 1970). To minimize the magnitude of this problem and to allow for complexity in theory development, the statistical concept of confirmatory factor analysis can be added to the multitrait-multimethod matrix (Long, 1983). In this procedure, the simultaneous investigation of the multitraits and multimethods of the matrix is not circumvented, and the procedure is expanded to allow for hierarchical prediction of relationships of layers of multiple traits with layers of multiple methods. Therefore, theories developed to be confirmed by these combined procedures can address more diversity within populations and interactions of specific methods with specific combinations of traits and subtraits.

DESCRIPTION OF THE PROPOSED THEORY

The proposed theory has been designed to be validated by the statistical procedures of the multitrait-multimethod matrix and confirmatory factory analysis. Two layers of multiple traits and two layers of multiple methods have been selected from the research and propositional literature in LD. All traits and methods have been selected on the basis of the conceptual assumptions that (1) learning-disabled persons constitute a heterogeneous group; (2) the traits and methods selected are measurable by appropriate instrumentation that has been or can be developed; (3) identification of learning-disabled persons on the basis of these traits and methods will contribute to the knowledge base of the field; and (4) analysis of the interaction of the traits and methods will positively impact research and practice.

DESCRIPTION OF TRAITS

The traits that have been selected for the proposed theory are considered generally representative of the LD population. These traits can be observed under more than one experimental condition and can be meaningfully differentiated from one another. The traits constitute two layers of the multifaceted hierarchy and are definable by the methods that will be used to confirm them.

Layer I Traits

Layer I of the trait hierarchy consists of two traits, subgroup and severity. Since heterogeneity within the learning disabilities population is a widely accepted notion and since heterogeneity can be described by the traits of severity and subgroup, these traits appear to be logical variables for the first layer of a multifaceted theory. Traits of subgroup are described by at least five discrete taxonomic categories. These categories are assumed to be independent of one another, distinguishable by their salient characteristics, present across the life cycle, measurable regardless of classification or program placement, and equal in impact on persons' lives. Traits of severity are described by a linear progression within subgroups. This progression is assumed to range from mild to severe with designatable breaking points being arbitrarily determinable.

Subgroups

Torgesen (1982) has hypothesized that subgroups of learning disabilities exist within the LD population and that investigation of the characteristics of these groups can lead to more adequate descriptions of diagnostic categories. Senf (1986) and Wong (1986) have purported that delineation of subgroups can lead to increased pragmatic knowledge about group correlates and features that group members have in common.

Weller and Strawser (1987) have consolidated current subgroup literature by numerous authors to designate five discrete subgroups: non-learning-disabled, production deficits, verbal organization disorders, nonverbal organization disorders, and global organization disorders. These subgroups were derived from research with students receiving service in LD programs, clinically defined learning-disabled populations, and self-referred learning-disabled adults. Although a random sample of the learning-disabled population may not have been described in the studies, representation of the condition outside the LD classroom has been included.

The first of the aforementioned subgroups, non-learning-disabled, has been identified from studies that used samples of school-identified learning-disabled subjects. Persons of this subgroup lack the amount of discrepancy between potential and performance required for LD classification but show achievement below expectation for their grade and age (Strawser & Weller, 1985). They demonstrate mild behavior problems, cultural differences, mental retardation, slowed learning, or sensory deficits (Speece, McKinney, & Applebaum, 1984). Because of these characteristics, this subgroup could be excluded from the proposed theory of LD. However, since the subgroup comprises approximately 25% to 38% of persons identified in subtype studies, exhibits degrees of severity, and may be useful to differentiate LD from other handicapping conditions, a decision has been made to retain it.

The second subgroup, production deficits, has been identified in studies using school-classified and self-referred learning-disabled adults as subjects. The subgroup comprises approximately 23% to 30% of the samples and is delineated by deficts in production and task analysis. Persons of this subgroup exhibit poor work habits, lack of efficient learning, and inadequate study skills. They have been described as messy and annoying (Denckla, 1972), lacking in attentiveness (McConaughty & Ritter, 1985), impulsive and lacking practical planning skills (Wiener, 1980), and immature during transition from school to community (Buchanan & Wolf, 1986). Their performance tends to suffer in situations that demand sustained attention and task-oriented behavior.

The next three subgroups—global organization disorders, verbal organization disorders, and nonverbal organization disorders—have been identified in studies using samples of school-classified, clinically diagnosed, and self-referred adult subjects. The first of these subgroups comprises approximately 8% to 10% of the samples; the second, 14% to 17%; and the third, 11% to 15%. In subtype studies, these subgroups are differentiated by their presenting configuration of strengths and deficits in verbal, nonverbal, behavioral, and educational areas.

The global organization disorder subgroup is distinguished from other subgroups by uneven configurations within several areas, rather than within one area. Limited research has indicated that some persons in this subgroup exhibit both deficits and strengths in combinations of academic and behavioral skills (Speece & McKinney, 1984); others exhibit deficits in both verbal and nonverbal skills (Boder, 1973). Some persons of this subgroup have been found to show scatter among WISC-R subtests (McKinney, 1984) and subtests on Part One of the Woodcock-Johnson Psycho-Educational Battery (Buchanan & Wolf, 1986). Because this subgroup comprises such a small percentage of the samples in existing subtype studies, further verification of these findings is necessary.

Difficulties within the verbal area discriminates persons of the verbal organization disorder subgroup from those in other subgroups. Because of problems in organizing thoughts into verbalizations, persons of this subgroup tend to communicate and solve problems physically (Wiener, 1980) and exhibit poor verbal logic and reasoning (Ozols & Rourke, 1985). Difficulty with analysis and synthesis of verbal information affect performance in situations requiring language competence. When nonverbal skills can be used without linguistic requirements, problems are not encountered (Strawser & Weller, 1985).

The nonverbal organization disorder subgroup is discriminated from others by deficits in visual, spatial, motor, and other nonverbal performances. Persons of this subgroup tend to become lost and disoriented (Strang & Rourke, 1985), have difficulty relating in and with large groups (Lahey, Stempniak, Robinson, & Tyroler, 1978), and exhibit rigidity in interpersonal relationships and affect (Ozols & Rourke, 1985). Performance is limited by inflexibility in comprehensive conceptual thinking, which obscures the ability to express available verbal knowledge (Strang & Rourke, 1985).

Severity

Studies that address the severity of learning-disabled persons are less numerous than those that address subgroup. However, if one accepts the proposition that some learning-disabled persons possess the disability to a greater extent than others, the inclusion of severity as a Layer I trait can be justified.

Senf (1981, 1986) hypothesized that a continuum of severity ranging from normal human variation to extremes of deviance was present in the learning-disabled population. According to Keogh (1986), this continuum could be identified by characteristics related to chronicity, salience, and intensity of individual differences and the effect that these differences have on the person throughout his or her life span.

Historically, hypotheses of severity within the learning-disabled population have been based on presence of academic performance deficits, clinical judgment (Horvath, Kass, & Ferrell, 1980), scatter on intelligence test profiles (Vance, Walbrown, & Blaha, 1978), and uneven performance on tests of processing (Kirk & Kirk, 1974). Since none of these hypotheses has individually withstood empirical scrutiny, it has been suggested that single identifiers of severity may be inappropriate (Ryckman, 1981).

Weller (1980) proposed a consolidated model to describe a continuum of severity for learning-disabled persons. She hypothesized that the intercorrespondence of social skills and academic performance, the alteration of life span needs, the amenability of the problem to remediation or compensation, and the strength and weakness pattern evidenced by an individual could account for the severity of a given learning-disabled person. This model was investigated by

DeLoach, Earl, Brown, Poplin, and Warner (1981), who found that teachers could readily identify degrees of severity among students. Strawser and Weller (1985) confirmed these findings through the analysis of scores from a battery of intelligence, linguistic, achievement, process, and adaptive behavior measures.

Layer II Traits

Layer II of the trait hierarchy extends the Layer I traits to encompass 25 traits that combine subgroup and severity. These traits are conceptualized as five parallel strands (one strand for each subgroup) with the expectation that, despite differences in characteristics among subgroups, a range of severity will be present within subgroups, levels of severity will be equal across subgroups, and the subgroups themselves do not constitute a continuum of severity. When cutoff points in the severity continuum are arbitrarily set, each severity level of each subgroup and its proportional representation of the learning-disabled population can be discretely identified, described, and validated (Fig. 3-1).

Several conceptual propositions are relevant to Layer II traits. It can be hypothesized that the traits described in this layer represent

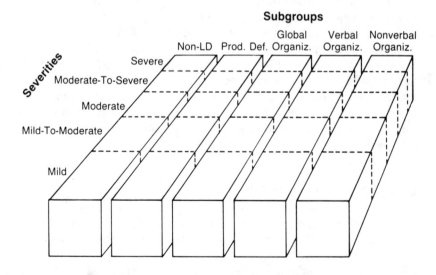

Figure 3-1. Multitrait hierarchy.

diversity and proportional representation in subgroups ranging from normal deviation to extremes of deviance. Depending upon the subgroup, persons at the mild and severe ends of the continuum may, at present, be classified as a category other than LD (i.e., mild—nonhandicapped with normal variation; severe—mental retardation, autism, aphasia, or emotional disturbance with extreme deviation). In this respect, the proposed theory may address more than the current conceptualization of LD.

The continuum of severity within each subgroup may correspond with the levels of severity hypothesized in the consolidated perspective (Weller, 1980). This perspective characterizes the variability attributable to a mild severity level as isolated learning difficulties that do not interfere with other learning and performance behaviors. These difficulties are amenable to remediation using standard teaching methods and allow persons to use the difficulty area throughout the school years and adulthood to an efficient, though not proficient, degree. At a moderate level, the consolidated perspective characterizes problems as less isolated. Problems affect other learning areas, require remediation by means of alternative, but standard, teaching methods, and lead to avoidance of problem areas in tasks that do not specifically require their use. Problems transitioning to and coping with adult environments are evident, and guidance and intervention during the school years is necessary for social difficulties associated with the problems. At a severe level, problems are purported to have a profound impact on most areas of performance throughout the life cycle. One or more performance areas are depressed totally, radical teaching methods and prosthetic alternatives are required for compensatory teaching, and active solicitation of alternative avenues of learning are necessary throughout life. Upon leaving school, ongoing special accommodations are needed for procuring and maintaining productive employment. Continuing guidance is needed to create appropriate interpersonal and peer relationships. Severity levels of mild-to-moderate and moderate-to-severe were not addressed in the consolidated perspective.

DESCRIPTION OF METHODS

To confirm Layer I and II traits, one or more layers of methods are required for a multitrait-multimethod matrix. If two layers of methods are used, Layer I methods are general constructs that conceptually catagorize the systematically defined behavioral variables of Layer II (Campbell, 1953, 1956). Through the statistics of the multitrait-multimethod matrix and confirmatory factor analysis, Layer I and II methods are differentially discriminated from one another, differentially discriminated from the traits they are being used to validate, and used to discretely define the traits under investigation. Methods may be measurement instruments or constructs for which measurement instruments have been or can be developed. Both layers of methods are simultaneously examined with layers of traits to test and confirm the validity of the theory.

Layer I Methods

For purposes of the proposed theory, three methods, assumed to be broad-based constructs that define learning-disabled persons, have been selected for Layer I. These methods, including cognitive competence, adaptability, and experiential competence, are derived from Sternberg's (1982) Triarchic Theory of Intelligence and relate to the problem-solving abilities, social and practical competence, and level of experience that a persons brings to a task. These methods were selected because they are conceptually different from traits, interaction of their components may define subgroups, and their configurations may reflect severity within subgroups. Although it is assumed that the constructs from which these methods are derived are independent and mutually exclusive, the probability exists that they are not. As these methods are investigated simultaneously with Layer I and II traits and Layer II methods through the multitrait-multimethod matrix, the validity of this assumption will be examined.

Cognitive Competence

Although the term *cognitive* tends to be connotatively interchanged with the term *intelligence*, its denotation is much broader. By definition, cognition is the process of knowing or perceiving as applied to the range of knowledge possible through observation. Cognitive competence refers to the expertise with which a given person uses these powers of observation to gain knowledge. Sternberg (1980) described cognitive competence in terms of the executive processes used in planning, monitoring, and evaluating behavior, the metacognitive processes used in performing tasks, and the skills used in the acquisition of knowledge. Ryan, Weed, and Short (1986) expanded this definition to include the awareness of task and strategy variables and the use of this awareness to regulate performance.

Experiential Competence

Experiential competence denotes the demographic, physical, sociologic, environmental, personal, educational, and instructional factors that impact a person's task approach behaviors. Based on the assumption that every facet of a person's background affects the manner in which that person performs throughout his or her life cycle, experiential competence can be considered dynamic, accumulative, and developmental (Feuerstein, 1980; Kirk & Gallagher, 1986). According to these authors, the experiences that persons encounter set the stage on which learning and learning difficulties must be judged.

Adaptability

The concept of adaptability is not new. In 1967, Guilford hypothesized the construct of adaptability in his behavioral content domain. Adaptability, also called adaptive behavior, social competence, social intelligence, and social comprehension, is a construct that refers to a person's typically demonstrated competencies in adjusting to the culture as expected for chronological age (Meyers, Nihira, & Zetlin, 1979). According to Sternberg (1980), the construct of adaptability incorporates the domains of tacit knowledge (practical know-how) and selection (creating a desired environment from an existing one). Although many recent operational definitions of adaptability have tended to emphasize practical environmentally based behaviors and generally ignored the domains of interpersonal and behavioral effectiveness (Greenspan, 1981), the global construct of adaptive behavior of learning-disabled persons hypothesized and assessed by Weller and Strawser (1981) has incorporated both tacit knowledge and selection.

Layer II Methods

Layer II of the methods hierarchy specifies discrete, observable behaviors that describe each method of Layer I. The selection of these methods is based on the assumption that specific behaviors that have been identified in research or proposition as functions of "LDness" should be the methods included, tested, and subjected to statistical scrutiny in the validation of traits. All methods are not expected to appear in definition of every trait, but it is expected that differential patterns of methods will be identified. It is assumed that through the multitrait-multimethod matrix and confirmatory factor analysis, unique configurations of Layer II methods will emerge to define different Layer II traits.

Because the potential number of Layer II methods is immense, selected examples are presented in this chapter. These methods have been distributed within the three categories of Layer I methods by a conceptual assumption of best-fit. Studies using the multitrait-multimethod matrix and confirmatory factor analysis will determine the actual fit of these methods and others used in the validation process. For adequate validation, as many Layer II methods as possible should be used.

Examples of Layer II methods have been selected from studies of LD behavior conducted by numerous researchers. Methods of cognitive competence have been drawn from the work of Torgesen (Torgesen & Licht, 1983) and Deshler (Schumaker, Deshler, & Ellis, 1986). These authors have isolated insufficient skills in task-specific learning strategies, memory strategies, visual-image formation, active learning, phonologic processing, strategy generation, and strategy generalization as behavioral manifestations of inadequate cognitive competence. Also included are situational behaviors that use these skills in academic, career, and nonschool settings and behaviors of knowledge acquisition such as selective encoding, selective comparison, inference, reflection, logic, induction, deduction, and time allocation.

Methods of experiential competence have been identified in several categories. Marker variables described by Keogh, Major-Kingsley, Omori-Gordon, and Reid (1982) have been selected and include descriptive markers (e.g., age, grade, ethnicity, socioeconomic status, and physical and educational history); substantive markers (achievement level and intellectual attainment); topical markers (experiences in attention, memory, perception, and language); and background markers (years of study, placement criteria, and geographic location). Sociologic variables of family contribution, legal mandates, and social policy that impact the experiences contributing to a person's learning career (Senf, 1981, 1986) and interactive instructional variables described in Jenkins' (1979) tetrahedral model of memory research have also been selected. These latter variables include the learning activities in which the subject has engaged and is engaged, the nature of the stimuli that have been and are being used in tasks, the organization of the task-related stimuli, the manner in which stimuli have been presented, and the criteria that have been used for ascertaining task acquisition.

Methods of adaptability have also been selected from several categories. The adaptive behaviors from the categories of social coping, relationships, pragmatic language, and production described by Weller and Strawser (1981) and the social behaviors described by Pearl, Donahue, and Bryan (1986) have been included. These variables encompass difficulty understanding the nonverbal communications of others, difficulty reading emotions, inaccuracy in understanding social interactions, lack of compassion for others, inadequate adherence to social norms, evidence of off-task behavior, lack of attention to content-related information, and negative self-images about academic but not nonacademic competence. Adaptations of language to social situations such as negative attitudes held toward a person's language by others and inadequate reflectivity, persistence, considerateness, and temperament have been selected from studies of other researchers (Wiig & Harris, 1974; Wiig & Semel, 1980).

CONCLUSIONS

Conclusions about the proposed multifaceted hierarchical theory should not be a restatement of content, a list of potential implications, or a defense of assumptions, but an invitation for the field to challenge. According to Estes (1957), the steepest obstacle to theory. . .

is not the complexity of behavior. It is the mountain of stereotypes deposited by centuries of prescientific attempts to comprehend behavior and capped by academicians who have always known, apparently by divine inspiration, exactly what kind of theory is possible and proper. . . This barrier must be undermined by uncertainty before it can be toppled by experiment (p. 617).

Since the field of LD encompasses a disorganized miscellany of unmassed data based on tidbits, constructs, unsubstantiated theories, models, and hypotheses that have not addressed the diversity or heterogeneity of the population, the multifaceted hierarchical theory is provided as an uncertain proposition that can be empirically explored. Snow (1973) admonished theoreticians to invest solid research efforts in their ideas, and consumers, critics, and adherents of the theories to do the same. Emotional confirmation, rejection, and modification were considered unworthy of a scientist. The multifaceted hierarchical theory is proposed in Snow's spirit of inquiry. It has been generated to be confirmed, rejected, or modified, but, it is hoped, not ignored.

Doris J. Johnson

Most participants in the DLD Symposium concluded that more theory-based research is needed in LD. Weller emphasizes the need for a more comprehensive, multifaceted theory that encompasses many variables. I agree that it is important to incorporate both intraindividual factors and external variables in future research to explain possible reasons for learning success and failure. However, rather than arguing for a single theory, I believe that it is healthy to have diverse theories to provide various perspectives.

Weller emphasizes the distinctions between severity and subtypes in her proposed approach, and, again, I agree. The current trend toward looking only at severe LD in certain school systems may prevent children with mild to moderate disorders from receiving help. As with all handicapping conditions, one expects mild, moderate, and severe conditions.

In her discussion of subgroups, Weller notes that one group does not have specific LD. These include problems typically considered in the exclusion clause of the definition. If she is correct, that such persons constitute 25% to 38% of persons in subtype studies, it would appear that those studies are designed to investigate subtypes of underachievers rather than subtypes of LD. Furthermore, they do not constitute one, but several subgroups.

Within the field of LD, there are many approaches to subtype research, each of which varies with the theoretical orientation of the investigator. Much of the early work began with dyslexia and language disorders when clinicians and neuropsychologists observed different symptoms among poor readers. Some early studies also subtyped according to sensory modality, that is, according to the person's ability to process information by way of one or more channels. More recently, investigations have been carried out using theories from neuropsychology and brain-behavior relationships. Still others have examined subtypes of behavior disorders, attention problems, and so on. In certain instances, the studies were designed to explore learning problems that tended to co-occur, whereas in others, the subtypes emerged from an analysis of error patterns in spelling or reading.

In the area of mathematics, subtype studies were done using factor analytic techniques as well as some constructs from neuropsychology.

Weller's approach is somewhat more global in that she looks more broadly at organization, verbal, and nonverbal problems. This approach may be beneficial, but she will need to provide more specific attributes of the people within each subtype in order to foster replicable research. For example, it is not clear how various problems in reading, written language, or mathematics might be manifested in her subtypes. Nevertheless, she recognizes nonverbal and organizational disorders that are often overlooked in other subtype studies and emphasizes the persistent problems in adulthood. However, she does not provide the theoretical base used for determining these subgroups.

The latter half of Weller's paper includes several features of learning and behavior that are important to consider in studying people with LD. However, some of the factors derive from so many different theories that it is difficult to determine how they can be combined into a single model. Nevertheless, she highlights the complexity of the problem and lists many variables that have been studied in previous research.

REFERENCES

Boder, E. (1973). Developmental dyslexia: A diagnostic approach based on three atypical reading-spelling patterns. *Developmental Medicine and Child Neurology, 15,* 663–687.

Boring, E.G. (1963). The role of theory in experimental psychology. In R.I. Watson & D.T. Campbell (Eds.), *History, psychology, and science: Selected papers by E.G. Boring* (pp. 5–25). New York: John Wiley & Sons.

Buchanan, M., & Wolf, J.S. (1986). A comprehensive study of learning disabled adults. *Journal of Learning Disabilities, 19,* 34–38.

Campbell, D.T. (1953). *A study of leadership among submarine officers.* Columbus: Ohio State University Research Foundation.

Campbell, D.T. (1956). *Leadership and its effects upon the group.* Monograph No. 83. Columbus: Ohio State University Bureau of Business Research.

Campbell, D.T., & Fiske, D.W. (1959). Convergent and discriminant validation by the multitrait-multimethod matrix. *Psychological Bulletin, 56*(2), 81–104.

Conbach, L.F. (1970). *Essentials of psychological testing.* New York: Harper & Row.

DeLoach, T.F., Earl, J.M., Brown, B.S., Poplin, M.S., & Warner, M.M. (1981). LD teachers' perceptions of severely learning disabled students. *Learning Disability Quarterly, 4,* 343–358.

Denckla, M. B., (1972). Clinical syndromes in learning disabilities: The case for "splitting" vs. "lumping." *Journal of Learning Disabilities, 5,* 401–406.

Estes, W.K. (1957). Of models and men. *American Psychologist, 12,* 609–617.

Feuerstein, R. (1980). *Instrumental enrichment: An intervention program for cognitive modifiability.* Baltimore: University Park Press.

Greenspan, S. (1981). Social competence and handicapped individuals: Practical implications of a proposed model. In B.K. Keogh (Ed.), *Advances in special education* (Vol. 3, pp. 41–81). Greenwich: JAI Press.

Guilford, J.P. (1967). *The nature of human intelligence*. New York: McGraw Hill.

Horvath, M.J., Kass, C.E., & Ferrell, W.R. (1980). An example of the use of fuzzy set concepts in modeling learning disability. *American Educational Research Journal, 17*, 309–324.

Jenkins, J.J. (1979). Four points to remember: A tetrahedral model and memory experiments. In L.S. Cermak & F.I.M. Craik (Eds.), *Levels and processing in human memory* (pp. 429–446). Hillsdale, NJ: Erlbaum.

Keogh, B. (1986). Abstract: Learning disabilities symposium. Paper presented at the DLD/Utah Symposium, January 30–31.

Keogh, B., Major-Kingsley, S., Omori-Gordon, H., & Reid, H.P. (1982). *A system of marker variables for the field of learning disabilities*. Syracuse, NY: Syracuse University Press.

Kirk, S.A., & Gallagher, J.J. (1986). *Educating exceptional children* (5th ed.). Boston: Houghton Mifflin Co.

Kirk, S.A., & Kirk, W.D. (1974). *Psycholinguistic learning disabilities: Diagnosis and remediation*. Urbana, IL: University of Illinois Press.

Kuhn, T.S. (1962). *The structure of scientific revolutions*. Chicago: University of Chicago Press.

Lahey, B.B., Stempniak, M., Robinson, E. J., & Tyroler, M.J. (1978). Hyperactivity and learning disabilities as independent dimensions of child behavior problems. *Journal of Abnormal Psychology, 87*, 333–340.

Long, J.S. (1983). *Confirmatory factor analysis: A preface to LISREL*. Sage University Paper Series on Quantitative Applications in the Social Sciences 07-034. Beverly Hills and London: Sage.

McConaughty, S.H., & Ritter, D.R. (1985). Social competence and behavioral problems of learning disabled boys aged 6–11. *Journal of Learning Disabilities, 18*, 547–553.

McKinney, J. D. (1984). The search for subtypes of specific learning disability. *Journal of Learning Disabilities, 17*, 43–50.

Meyers, C.E., Nihira, K., & Zetlin, A. (1979). The measurement of adaptive behavior. In N.R. Ellis (Ed.), *Handbook of mental deficiency: Psychological theory and research* (2nd ed, pp. 431–481). Hillsdale, NJ: Erlbaum.

Ozols, E.J., & Rourke, B.P. (1985). Dimensions of social sensitivity in two types of learning disabled children. In B.P. Rourke (Ed.), *Neuropsychology of learning disabilities: Essentials of subtype analysis* (pp. 281–301). New York: Guilford Press.

Pearl, R., Donahue, M., & Bryan, T. (1986). Social relationships of learning-disabled children. In J.K. Torgesen and B.Y.L. Wong (Eds.), *Psychological and Educational Perspectives on Learning Disabilities* (pp. 193–224). Orlando: Academic Press.

Ryan, E.B., Weed, K.A., & Short, E.J. (1986). Cognitive behavior modification: Promoting active, self-regulatory learning styles. In J.K. Torgesen and B.Y.L. Wong (Eds.), *Psychological and Educational Perspectives on Learning Disabilities* (pp. 367–397). Orlando: Academic Press.

Ryckman, D.B. (1981). Searching for a WISC-R profile for learning disabled children: An inappropriate task? *Journal of Learning Disabilities, 14,* 508–510.

Schumaker, J.B., Deshler, D.D., & Ellis, E.S. (1986). Intervention issues related to the education of LD adolescents. In J.K. Torgesen and B.Y.L. Wong (Eds.), *Psychological and Educational Perspectives on Learning Disabilities* (pp. 329–365). Orlando: Academic Press.

Senf, G.M. (1981). Issues surrounding the diagnosis of learning disabilities: Child handicap versus failure of the child-school interaction. In T.R. Kratochwill (Ed.), *Advances in school psychology* (Vol. 1, pp. 83–131). Hillsdale, NJ: Erlbaum.

Senf, G.M. (1986). LD research in sociological and scientific perspective. In J.K. Torgesen and B.Y.L. Wong (Eds.), *Psychological and Educational Perspectives on Learning Disabilities* (pp. 27–53). Orlando: Academic Press.

Snow, R.E. (1973). Theory construction for research on teaching. In R.M.W. Travers (Ed.), *Second handbook of research on teaching* (pp. 77–112). American Educational Research Association.

Speece, D.L., & McKinney, J.D. (1984, March). The academic and social consequences of maladaptive behavior in subtypes of learning disabled children. Paper presented at the Gatlinburg Conference, Gatlinburg, TN.

Speece, D.L., McKinney, J.D., & Appelbaum, M.I. (1984). Classification and validation of behavioral subtypes of learning disabled children. *Journal of Educational Psychology, 77,* 67–77.

Sternberg, R. (1980). Sketch of a componential subtheory of human intelligence. *Behavioral and Brain Sciences, 3,* 573–584.

Sternberg, R. (1982). A componential approach to intellectual development. In R. Sternberg (Ed.), *Advances in the psychology of human intelligence* (Vol. 1, pp. 413–463). Hillsdale, NJ: Erlbaum.

Strang, J.D., & Rourke, B.P. (1985). Adaptive behavior of children who exhibit specific arithmetic disabilities and associated neuropsychological abilities and deficits. In B.P. Rourke (Ed.), *Neuropsychology of learning disabilities: Essentials of subtype analysis* (pp. 302–328). New York: Guilford Press.

Strawser, S., & Weller, C. (1985). Use of adaptive behavior and discrepancy criteria to determine learning disability severity subtypes. *Journal of Learning Disabilities, 18*(4), 201–204.

Torgesen, J.K. (1982). The use of rationally defined subgroups in research on learning disabilities. In J.P. Das, R.J. Mulcahy, & T.E. Wall (Eds.), *Theory and research in learning disabilities* (pp. 111–131). New York: Plenum Press.

Torgesen, J.K. (1986). Learning disabilities theory: Its current state and future prospects. *Journal of Learning Disabilities, 19*(7), 399–407.

Torgesen, J.K., & Licht, B. (1983). The learning-disabled child as an inactive learner: Retrospect and prospects. In J.D. McKinney, & L. Feagans (Eds.), *Topics in learning disabilities* (Vol. 1, pp. 3–32). Rockville, MD: Aspen Press.

Turner, M.B. (1967). *Philosophy and the science of behavior.* New York: Appleton-Century-Crofts.

Underwood, B.J. (1957). *Psychological research.* New York: Appleton-Century-Crofts.

Vance, H., Walbrown, F.H., & Blaha, J. (1978). Determining WISC-R profiles for reading disabled children. *Journal of Learning Disabilities, 11,* 657–661.

Weller, C. (1980). Discrepancy and severity in the learning disabled: A consolidated perspective. *Learning Disability Quarterly, 3,* 84–90.

Weller, C., & Strawser, S. (1981). *Weller-Strawser Scales of Adaptive Behavior for the Learning Disabled.* Novato, CA: Academic Therapy.

Weller, C., & Strawser, S. (1987). Adaptive behavior of subtypes of learning disabled individuals. *Journal of Special Education, 21*(1).

Wiener, J. R. (1980). A theoretical model of the acquisition of peer relationships of learning disabled children. *Journal of Learning Disabilities, 13,* 506–511.

Wiig, E.H., & Harris, S.P. (1974). Perception and interpretation of nonverbally expressed emotions by adolescents with learning disabilities. *Perceptual and Motor Skills, 38,* 239–245.

Wiig, E.H., & Semel, E.M. (1980). *Language assessment and intervention for the learning disabled.* Columbus, OH: Charles E. Merrill.

Wong, B.Y.L. (1986). Problems and issues in the definition of learning disabilities. In J.K. Torgesen and B.Y.L. Wong (Eds.), *Psychological and Educational Perspectives on Learning Disabilities* (pp. 3–26). Orlando: Academic Press.

PART II

Research

CHAPTER 4

Thinking About the Future by Distinguishing Between Issues That Have Resolutions and Those That Do Not

Joseph K. Torgesen

O ne way of approaching any complex problem is to make a distinction between elements of the problem that are immediately solvable and those for which there is no currently available solution. Such a distinction helps to focus energy on the elements that can be dealt with successfully while limiting debate and misguided efforts to immediately resolve issues that are outside one's control.

Improving the quality of research in learning disabilities (LD) certainly qualifies as a complex problem. Weaknesses in our research base are the result of many different kinds of problems acting together and in isolation to limit the utility of our knowledge. The goal of this book is to clarify issues and discuss directions and solutions that may be helpful in improving the quality and utility of future research in learning disabilities. One means of doing this is to distinguish between inadequacies and problems in present and past research that are solvable from present knowledge and those for which solutions are not immediately apparent. This chapter is organized around this distinction. Problems that we are currently capable of solving will be discussed first, and those whose solutions must await further research will be treated last.

SOLVABLE PROBLEMS

The problems and issues discussed in this section are those that have right and wrong, or at least better and worse, answers. Although these issues can be dealt with in a more correct manner by thoughtful, careful, and well-trained researchers, they are frequently ignored or dealt with inappropriately in LD research. Because this type of problem is still widespread in research in our field, we can improve the quality of our work substantially by paying careful attention to these issues. In the following list of problem areas, I have tried to overcome the temptation to compile a general list of good and poor experimental methods. Problems that are general to many areas of psychological and educational research are less likely to be included than those that are particular problems in LD research.

Weak Control Procedures

Control procedures are used in experiments to help isolate the factors responsible for a given pattern of results. The most common problems in LD research involve failure to use proper control procedures in treatment studies and to select proper control groups in assessment studies. Control for the effects of general intelligence is a special problem in LD research that is dealt with in another section.

Selecting proper control groups and procedures is mainly a matter of understanding experimental logic and identifying the extraneous variables that are likely to affect the dependent measures or processes under study. For example, if one's goal is to isolate a particular disability that may *cause* academic difficulties, it is almost always inappropriate to use a control group of normal children who are the same age as the LD children in the study. This is not good practice because LD and non-LD groups are different in so many areas (failure history, academic achievement, test anxiety, self-confidence, motivation, general knowledge base) that can affect performance on most dependent measures. Differences between same-age groups of LD and non-LD children are essentially correlational and say nothing about causation. Use of same age control groups are appropriate if one is simply interested in describing differences that exist between LD and non-LD children of a given age. This, of course, does not add to our theoretical understanding of the causes of learning disabilities, but may be useful information for planning intervention programs.

Three methods that are preferable to simple contrasts between same age groups of LD and non-LD children include (1) use of control groups that vary in age but are matched for a critical ability such as reading (Bradley & Bryant, 1978); (2) using an additional control group of children with similar failure experiences but who do not have the particular cognitive disability being investigated (Torgesen & Houck, 1980); or, (3) using longitudinal designs coupled with training studies (Bradley & Bryant, 1985). The recent monograph by Bradley and Bryant provides an excellent example of careful control procedures in an intervention study.

Failure to Report Characteristics of Samples Studied

The essence of scientific research is to make systematic observations that can be repeated precisely by someone else. In the case of LD research, a very common problem is failure to specify important characteristics of the samples of children observed. This, of course, makes it difficult to compare one study with another so that observations can either be confirmed or disconfirmed. The definitive study of this problem (Keogh, Major-Kingsley, Omori-Gordon, & Reid, 1982) found that large numbers of investigators failed to report such essential characteristics of their samples as age range, sex, general intelligence, socioeconomic status, and academic skill levels. Other surveys (Torgesen & Dice, 1980) have noted that even when characteristics are reported, they are frequently given in a manner that does not allow precise comparison between samples.

The solution to this problem lies in the careful specification of as many characteristics of our samples as possible. Although there may be some disagreement about which characteristics should be reported, most researchers would agree that more should be reported than is currently the case. The Marker Variable Guide at the end of the report by Keogh et al. (1982) provides useful suggestions as to which characteristics should be reported.

Failure to Embed Research in a Theoretical Framework

Theory is useful to research because it makes possible the formulation of systematic questions about a given phenomenon. Without a theory to guide research, the investigator is left to ask essentially random questions of nature. Although useful practical information may occasionally result from such research, it will not lead to the creation of an integrated knowledge base.

There are at least two important reasons why research in learning disabilities has been criticized as being atheoretical. One reason is that the most important theoretical paradigms that support research on LD have matured only recently (Torgesen, 1986). Until the last decade, researchers in LD were faced with a task (understanding the psychological or neuropsychological factors responsible for specific learning disabilities) for which there was not an adequate theoretical paradigm in basic science. Now, however, information processing, neuropsychological, and applied behavioral research are all supported by scientific paradigms that supply a range of methods and theoretical constucts sufficient to sustain useful research programs.

Another reason for the atheoretical nature of much of LD research is related to the training of many investigators in the field. Trained in special education, these investigators often know a great deal about the practical and educational aspects of learning disabilities, but less about the basic sciences. More complete knowledge of the basic sciences would allow them to formulate theoretically coherent research programs. This was a serious problem 10 years ago (Torgesen, 1975), when much of the research in the field lagged substantially behind the basic sciences in the theoretical concepts that were being used. We have made important strides in this area, and there are a number of theoretically coherent bodies of knowledge about learning disabilities that are beginning to emerge (Licht, 1983; Mann, 1986; Schumaker, Deshler, & Ellis, 1986; Stanovich, 1984; Vellutino, 1979). The solution of this problem is for investigators to become thoroughly familiar with research on normal development (empirical and theoretical literature) in a given area before they attempt to study individual differences on the topic.

Use of Samples Biased in Unknown Ways

Many researchers select their samples by simply drawing from classes of learning-disabled children identified by school district procedures. However, these samples are biased in unknown ways because most selection procedures are influenced not only by objective test results but also by political and social factors operating within the school district (Senf, 1986; Ysseldyke, 1983). Thus, these children are not appropriate as samples if our goal is to study groups selected by scientifically defensible (objective, replicable) procedures.

What are our alternatives to using school-identified samples? One solution is simply to divide randomly selected or intact groups of children from regular classrooms into skilled and less-skilled learners on the basis of a group-administered, standardized test of academic skills. General intellectual level could be controlled by using a group-administered screening test. Although these procedures are technically defensible on grounds of replicability, they often do not identify groups containing a very high proportion of children with serious learning disabilities. Thus, studies using these procedures are often criticized as not necessarily contributing to an understanding of clinically identified, seriously impaired, learning-disabled children.

Another alternative would involve following essentially the same outline just discussed, but extending it to identify more seriously impaired children. If one were interested in studying children with reading disabilities, for example, one might scan a large number of standardized test results for a pool of poor readers and then conduct individual assessments to be certain of selecting children with the kind and severity of reading problems about which one is interested. Following this assessment, the children would need to be screened for general intellectual level. The group of children who showed a discrepancy between reading and intellectual ability of sufficient size could then be individually tested to ensure an accurate measure of intelligence. This latter method is relatively difficult and involves selection of groups of children by a simple discrepancy between IQ and achievement—a method that some researchers regard as inaccurate and sterile (Senf, 1986).

A final alternative would be to administer a theoretically coherent battery of tests to a large sample of children and then select subgroups for further study based on the patterning of their scores on the battery. If the original sample were large enough, one would probably form one or more subgroups of children who would meet traditional criteria for classification as learning disabled. These subgroups would have been identified by replicable procedures, and their relationship to the population from which they were selected would be clearly understood. The major difficulty with this method at present involves the identification of tests for the selection battery. Batteries of standardized psychometric tests usually suffer from a lack of theoretical cohesion, and more theoretically interesting batteries of experimental tasks often have unknown psychometric qualities.

In this consideration of alternative subject selection procedures, we have moved in the direction of increasing defensibility, but also in the direction of increasing difficulty. Because of the expense of giving a comprehensive battery of tests to large numbers of children, even if a satisfactory battery was available, the latter discussed alternative is not within the means of many researchers who would like to study learning disabilities.

As a final alternative, we might consider starting with a school-identified group, but selecting from that group only those children who meet a particular, and extensive, set of specific criteria (Pavlidis,

1985). This procedure does not eliminate possible biases in the original selection procedure, but it does ensure that our subjects have in common *at least* a well-defined set of characteristics that are reliably measured. If the characteristics we measure are chosen carefully, it may be possible to eliminate much of the bias inherent in using school-identified samples.

Lack of Appreciation for Heterogeneity of Groups

This is a problem that will be discussed in both this section and in the next section. Although an ultimate solution to the problem is still beyond our grasp, there are some steps that can be taken immediatly to improve our present methods for dealing with the heterogeneity of most samples of LD children.

The most common mistake in this area is to base generalizations about "learning-disabled children" on findings of an average deficiency on some measure. In a study that carefully examined both the within sample variability of scores and the overlap in scores between samples of LD and non-LD children, Shepherd, Gelzheiser, and Solar (1985) have shown how misleading simple average differences can be. Researchers who conduct two group comparison studies should indicate, in some detail, the distributions of scores in their groups and should note the issues of overlap between groups. Also of interest is information about numbers of children in both LD and non-LD groups who produce extreme scores on the measures used in the study. Reporting this kind of data is a post hoc, or "Band-aid" (Senf, 1986), solution to the problem. However, it is clearly better than not attending to the range of variation within samples. More fundamental solutions in this area are discussed in the following section.

Controlling for Influence of General Intelligence

The goal of most research on LD is to understand the factors responsible for poor academic achievement when adequate general intelligence and normal learning opportunities exist. The typical research strategy has been to compare groups of children with and without learning problems who are otherwise similar on these background "control" variables. Relatively poor performance by the LD group on a given dependent measure is taken as evidence that the LD children have a special disability in this area and that this special disability may have a unique causal relationship to their academic problem. Crucial to this design, of course, is adequate control of general intelligence differences between the LD group and the normal contrast group. These controls are necessary for two kinds of conclusions. First, they are necessary to conclude that the *academic* differences between the contrast groups are not primarily the result of differences in general learning aptitude. Second, they are necessary before one can conclude that differences in the *dependent variable* are not the result of mild but pervasive intellectual differences between groups.

Stanovich (1986) argued persuasively that many of the differences between LD and normal children identified in previous research may actually reflect differences in general intellectual ability rather than specific cognitive limitations. His argument is based on the twin facts that (1) most studies have used an IQ matching procedure that is subject to regression artifacts (Crowder, 1984); and (2), most studies do not, in fact, precisely match IQ levels between contrast groups (Torgesen & Dice, 1980; Wolford & Fowler, 1984). Since most of the cognitive abilities studied in research on LD are correlated with IQ, many studies have probably identified "ability deficits" in LD children that are expressions of general intellectual limitations in their LD sample.

Although, as we shall see in a later section, there may be little agreement about *which* aspects of intelligence should be controlled when selecting LD children for study, it is obvious that better *procedures* should be used than is often the case. A good discussion and explication of some of these procedures can be found in an article by Crowder (1984).

PROBLEMS WITH NO IMMEDIATE SOLUTION

Other problems that frequently cause people outside our field to criticize work in LD and contribute to a sense of confusion in the knowledge base about learning disabilities are those that have no immediate solutions. Such problems reflect the complexity of the phenomenon under study and will only gradually be resolved as one or another approach proves more productive or is more convincingly argued by its advocates. For these issues that have no immediate answers, it is most helpful to have a clear understanding of the consequences that result from taking one or another approach to the problem.

How Should Samples Be Operationally Defined?

One aspect of this problem reflects the fact that the dominant approach to defining LD samples involves selecting children as LD whose poor academic achievement is not predicted by their score on a test of general cognitive ability (IQ). Because IQ itself is not a theoretically defined entity, but rather is derived from a sampling of abilities designed to predict achievement, there are no easily defensible conventions about which aspects of "intelligence" to control when selecting samples of LD children. Of course, differences in the way that "IQ" is controlled is one likely cause of different findings about the "unique" intellectual characteristics of LD children.

For example, some investigators include in their research samples children with reading problems who have *either* a performance or verbal IQ in the average range (Vellutino, 1979). As a result of the strong correlation between reading ability and verbal IQ, their samples usually score considerably lower than their non-LD contrast groups on the tests of broad verbal ability included on IQ tests. The fact that they allow verbal ability to vary over a broader range than other investigators (who might require *both* verbal and performance IQ to be in the normal range) makes it more likely that they will discover a variety of verbal deficits in "LD" children when they contrast them with normal learners.

The problem we are discussing here is simply a small part of the overall problem of definition of learning disabilities (Wong, 1986). Similar insurmountable problems in operationalizing the criteria for sample selection occur with regard to other elements of the LD concept. How does one define "adequate educational opportunities," "absence of emotional disturbance," or "adequate cultural support for learning?" One way to deal with this problem is to avoid it. The problem disappears if we no longer use the general term *learning disabilities* as a cover title for all the children we study. Rather, we should be more willing to recognize that generalization is limited to groups selected by similar criteria. For example, it might be better to eschew the use of broad IQ controls altogether and simply describe different subgroups of poor learners in terms of their performance on a clearly defined sample of theoretically meaningful cognitive, neuropsychological, or behavioral measures. Rather than defining a subgroup because their poor academic performance is not predicted by an IQ test (which depends to a large degree on the measure of IQ that is used), one would simply describe the particular kind of variability in intellectual performance shown by each subgroup of poor learners. Presumably, these patterns of performance would eventually be explicable in terms of a coherent theory of human abilities that specifies the variables important to academic achievement.

Selecting a Theoretical Paradigm

The three dominant scientific paradigms currently used in studies of learning-disabled children are information processing, neuropsychology, and applied behavior analysis (Torgesen, 1986). Each of these paradigms uses different methods to study children with LD and uses different concepts to explain them. They each have particular strengths and weaknesses. None of them are, at present, demonstrably the "best" way to approach the study of LD. Only more, and better, research accomplished within each paradigm will lead to consensus about the relative utility of each paradigm in explaining and treating LD.

Solutions to Sample Heterogeneity

This last problem is partially the result of lack of consensus about the preceding two issues. Arguably, the best approach to the problem of heterogeneity in the LD population is to start with a sound general theory of the factors that contribute to good and poor school performance, develop valid measures of these factors, give this battery of tests to a large, randomly selected sample of children who represent the full range of naturally occurring variation in the factors being measured, and then identify clusters of children who show similar patterns of performance on these measures. Once clusters are identified, follow-up research would be conducted on the subgroups of children who show poor academic performance to determine what other characteristics they might have in common and which treatment approaches work best with them.

Unfortunately, we do not have any generally agreed upon theories that can be used to guide the selection of measures to use in empirical subtyping studies. Thus, researchers are free to use neurological, psychoneurological, information processing, or behavioral measures (or any combination of them), and it is likely that the clusters identified by using different measures will not easily be compared with one another. The issue of which measures to use in forming empirically defined subtypes will only be resolved as one or another system is able to provide the most useful subcategorization of children with learning problems.

Another approach to the problem of sample heterogeneity has sometimes been called the *clinical/intuitive* (McKinney, 1984), or *rational* (Torgesen, 1982) *approach* to subgrouping. These approaches rely on clinical experience or theory to suggest a priori the character-istics of a subgroup of LD children that might be homogeneous in their learning characteristics. Although it would be impossible to construct a systematic subtyping system using this approach (all possible subtypes are never considered simultaneously, so it is impossible to place the target subgroup in relation to other types of LD children), carefully constructed studies following a clinical/intuitive or rational approach might be helpful in suggesting the kinds of measures that should be used in larger studies of empirically derived subgroups.

CONCLUSION

We have seen that there are essentially two kinds of research problems that limit the strength of our present knowledge base about learning disabilities. The first type of problem relates mostly to technical issues in research methodology. We can begin immediately to eliminate many of these problems by applying knowledge that is already available. Concerted efforts by journal and book editors, research training programs, funding agencies, and researchers themselves could help to reduce the impact of this type of problem on our knowledge base within the immediately forseeable future.

The second type of problem is less amenable to immediate solution. Our capacity to deal with these intransigent theoretical and methodological problems is limited not only by our lack of reliable knowledge about learning disabilities, but also by gaps in theory and method in the basic sciences that support the study of individual differences in school achievement (Torgesen, 1986).

Our best approach at present is to (1) attend carefully to the problems we know how to solve, (2) keep current with the most recent developments in the basic sciences that support inquiry in our field, and, (3) continue to experiment with a variety of approaches to the issues on which there is no consensus at present.

RESPONSE*

James D. McKinney

There has been considerable discussion in recent years about how to improve the knowledge base in the field of LD. In this chapter, Torgesen draws a useful distinction between problems in LD research that are due to a lack of scientific rigor and those that can be attributed to inadequate theory and operational criteria. He is more optimistic about solving the former set of problems than the latter, and, in general, I agree with this assessment.

*This paper was prepared while the author was the Frank Talbot Visiting Professor at the Curry School of Education, University of Virginia.

The failure to describe research samples adequately and to use appropriate controls in research design has weakened the credibility of existing knowledge. Although it is the case that LD research often fails to meet the highest scientific standards, these problems can be addressed readily through the traditional means of research training at the graduate level and tighter quality control at the professional level. I agree with Torgesen that we must devote greater attention to these matters. Also, I concur that we have much to learn from advances in the basic sciences, particularly with respect to developmental theory.

On the other hand, I do not believe that better research per se and attending to more recent developments in the basic sciences are sufficient to produce major new directions in LD research that would necessarily have a profound and lasting impact on the field. Although these factors are essential to the conduct of better science in the field, I would also argue that we must critically evaluate the basic paradigms that have guided LD research and seek to improve the fundamental nature and style of the research to better address the complexity of the research questions that have been identified by Torgesen (1986) and others (Keogh, 1983, 1986; McKinney, 1983).

As Torgesen points out, much of the research on LD has been confined to the search for differences between the learning-disabled population and normals in what is basically a correlative paradigm. Since this approach is essentially descriptive, it provides little understanding about how different kinds of LD develop or how they result in educational handicaps. The field suffers from a lack of knowledge that explains the phenomenon of LD and predicts its consequences. Such knowledge is essential to practice because it provides the conceptual foundations for classification, treatment, and primary prevention. While it was important to demonstrate that differences exist in the early stages of the field, I do not believe that conducting better research in the same vein will expand our knowledge base significantly.

Also, I am concerned that much of research on LD is issue driven and not programmatic in focus. There are, of course, notable exceptions to this conclusion (e.g., see Keogh, 1983 and McKinney, 1983 for discussion), and Torgesen's work on memory stands as one outstanding exception. Nevertheless, I believe that this criticism is a fair characterization of the bulk of LD research. Unless we invest more resources in long-term programmatic research that reflects a systematic logical progression of studies on a given question, I fear that LD research will remain primarily descriptive and not explanatory in focus.

In this regard, certain types of programmatic research might be particularly timely and profitable in the near future. Many of these suggestions for new directions in research have been discussed previously (Keogh, 1986; McKinney, 1983, 1987; Torgesen, 1986); however, I believe that they are worth repeating in the context of the present volume. Briefly, they are as follows:

1. *Developmental research* to determine how specific LD emerge and change and how they affect learning and adjustment.

2. *Intervention research* carried out in an experimental-manipulative fashion to determine the factors that explain group differences and to develop a functional knowledge base to guide practice.

3. *Cross-categorical research* to elucidate the common and dissimilar characteristics of LD, mentally retarded (MR), and emotionally disturbed (ED) students and slow learners.

4. *Experimental research* to test the utility of current developmental theories and theories of risk for understanding the nature of LD as it influences student performance.

5. *Classification research* aimed at the development of a useful taxonomy to guide sample selection in future research and clarify the problem of definition.

REFERENCES

Bradley, L., & Bryant, P.E. (1978). Difficulties in auditory organization as a possible cause of reading backwardness. *Nature, 221,* 746–747.

Bradley, L., & Bryant, P. (1985). *Rhyme and reason in reading and spelling.* Ann Arbor: University of Michigan Press.

Crowder, R.G. (1984). Is it just reading? *Developmental Review, 4,* 48–61.

Keogh, B.K. (1983). A lesson from Gestalt psychology. *Exceptional Education Quarterly, 4*(1), 115–128.

Keogh, B.K. (1986). The future of the LD field: Research and practice. *Journal of Learning Disabilities, 19*(8), 455–460.

Keogh, B.K., Major-Kingsley, S., Omori-Gordon, H., & Reid, H.P. (1982). *A system of marker variables for the field of learning disabilities.* Alexander R. Luria Research Monograph Series, Syracuse University Press.

Licht, B.G. (1983). Cognitive-motivational factors that contribute to the achievement of learning disabled children. *Journal of Learning Disabilities, 16,* 483–483.

Mann, V.A. (1986). Why some children encounter reading problems: The contribution of difficulties with language processing and phonological sophistication to early reading disability. In J.K. Torgesen & B.Y.L. Wong (Eds.), *Psychological and educational perspectives on learning disabilities.* New York: Academic Press.

McKinney, J.D. (1983). Contributions of the institutes for research on learning disabilities. *Exceptional Education Quarterly, 4*(1), 129–144.

McKinney, J.D. (1984). The search for subtypes of learning disability. *Journal of Learning Disabilities, 17,* 43–50.

McKinney J.D. (1987). Research on conceptually and empirically defined subtypes of learning disabilities. In M. Wang, H. Walberg, & M. Reynolds (Eds.), The handbook of special education: Research and practice. Oxford, England: Pergamon Press.

Schumaker, J.B., Deshler, D.D., & Ellis, E.S. (1986). Intervention issues related to the education of LD adolescents. In J.K. Torgesen & B.Y.L. Wong (Eds.), Psychological and educational perspectives on learning disabilities. New York: Academic Press.

Senf, G.M. (1986). LD research in sociological and scientific perspective. In J.K. Torgesen & B.Y.L. Wong (Eds.), Psychological and educational perspectives on learning disabilities. New York: Academic Press.

Shepherd, M.J., Gelzheiser, L.M., & Solar, R.A. (1985). How good is the evidence for a production deficiency among learning disabled students? Journal of Educational Psychology, 77, 553–561.

Stanovich, K. (1984). The interactive-compensatory model of reading: A confluence of developmental, experimental, and educational psychology. Remedial and Special Education, 5, 11–19.

Stanovich, K.E. (1986). Cognitive processes and the reading problems of learning-disabled children: Evaluating the assumption of specificity. In J.K. Torgesen & B.Y.L. Wong (Eds.), Psychological and educational perspectives on learning disabilities. New York: Academic Press.

Torgesen, J.K. (1975). Problems and prospects in the study of learning disabilities. In M. Hetherington and J. Hagen (Eds.), Review of research in child development (Vol. 5). Chicago: University of Chicago Press.

Torgesen, J.K. (1982). The use of rationally defined subgroups in research on learning disabilities. In J.P. Das, R.F. Mulcahy, & A.E. Wall (Eds.), Theory and research in learning disabilities. New York: Plenum Press.

Torgesen, J.K. (1986). Learning disabilities theory: Its current state and future prospects. Journal of Learning Disabilities, 19, 399–407.

Torgesen, J.K., & Dice, C. (1980). Characteristics of research on learning disabilities. Journal of Learning Disabilities, 13, 531–535.

Torgesen, J.K., & Houck, G. (1980). Processing deficiencies in learning disabled children who perform poorly on the digit span task. Journal of Educational Psychology, 72, 141–160.

Vellutino, F. (1979). Dyslexia: Theory and research. Cambridge: The MIT Press.

Wong, B.Y.L. (1986). Problems and issues in the definition of learning disabilities. In J.K. Torgesen & B.Y.L. Wong (Eds.), Psychological and educational perspectives on learning disabilities. New York: Academic Press.

Wolford, G. & Fowler, C.A. (1984). Differential use of partial information by good and poor readers. Developmental Review, 4, 16–35.

Ysseldyke, J.E. (1983). Current practices in making psycho-educational decisions about learning disabled students. Journal of Learning Disabilities, 16, 209–219.

CHAPTER 5

Learning Disabilities Research: False Starts and Broken Promises

G. Reid Lyon

ENDURING FOIBLES AND FUTURE DIRECTIONS

Despite the dedication and hard work of countless teachers, diagnosticians, clinicians, and researchers, the greatest concensus of thought relative to learning disabilities (LD) continues to be that the field lacks both scientific validity and clinical utility. This conclusion is apparent from reviews of the extant literature (Kavale & Forness, 1985a) as well as from open and honest discussions with colleagues in classrooms and research programs. The field's limited stature and lack of credibility as a clinical science is, according to many observers, inevitable and expected for several reasons.

First, the field's limitations as a clinical science may be related to its young chronologic age (McKinney, 1987; Mercer, 1979). Learning disabilities (LD) has been in existence, as a federally designated handicpping condition, for only 17 years (U.S.O.E., 1968). According to this line of reasoning, there simply has not been time to collect and consolidate all the necessary information that will lead to a better understanding of the nature of LD and determine how best to educate the learning disabled. This explanation makes sense given the incredibly complex nature of human cognitive development and the demands of school learning.

Second, the vagaries associated with definition, assessment, and teaching practices in LD may reflect the multidisciplinary nature of the field (Lerner, 1985; Senf, 1981). Because many disciplines contribute to both research and clinical practice in the field, consolidating information derived from different specialties into a common corpus of facts is difficult (Satz & Fletcher, 1980). Furthermore, competition by various disciplines for learning-disabled students and monies tied to the LD category impede cooperation among the vying fields, further limiting the possibility of codifying important information into unifying concepts (Senf, 1986a).

Third, the number of different professional vocabularies spoken and written by researchers working with learning-disabled students does not bode favorably for mutually comprehensible discourse about definition and the salient attributes of learning-disabled persons. Thus, replicability and generalizability of research outcomes, necessities for scientific inference, are not exemplars of research in the field (Kavale & Forness, 1985a; Torgeson & Dice, 1980).

What is clear from this discussion is that a series of influences hinder, in a synergistic manner, the development of what Kuhn (1970) calls a *disciplinary matrix*, or *paradigm*. As such, professionals do not share a common set of fundamental beliefs, exemplars, and symbolic generalizations about LD. Therefore, disagreements regarding what should be done to advance the field of LD and what constitutes good research are prevalent.

Although the enigmatic issues facing the LD research and clinical communities are to be expected, the important question becomes what to do about them. Given time, will the researchers in the LD field, using those procedures utilized over the past decade or so, eventually share and endorse a set of fundamental beliefs, exemplars, symbolic generalizations, and, very importantly, "best" assessment and teaching practices? Probably not. The field has been, and continues to be, beset with deep and pervasive disagreements about definition (Kirk & Kirk, 1983; McLeod, 1983), assessment practices (Ysseldyke & Algozzine, 1983), eligibility criteria and adherence to them (Tucker, Stevens, & Ysseldyke, 1983), and the efficacy of specific and pertinent teaching interventions for learning-disabled children (Belmont & Belmont, 1980; Lyon, 1983, 1985b). Given the recalcitrant nature of these disputes and the insidious social and political influences that help to propagate and maintain them (Senf, 1986a), it is unlikely that a genuine increase in our understanding of LD will emerge simply with the passage of time.

Unfortunately, it may be that greater resistance to productive change will characterize the field of LD in the future unless thoughtful modifications in research practices and applications are made to tighten definition. As Senf (1981, 1986a) has pointed out elsewhere, the perennial disputes concerning definition, assessment, and eligibility criteria serve to forge and reinforce ambiguous interpretations of "LDness" because they actually benefit many with vested interests in the LD enterprise, and thus slow the forces of productive change. For example, ambiguous interpretations allow some children to be diagnosed as learning disabled when they are not and allow others who are learning disabled to be overlooked. This generally results as a matter of convenience to administrators, teachers, and parents (Ysseldyke, Algozzine, & Epps, 1982). In addition, vagueness of definition and federal eligibility regulations provide a context that can be manipulated inadvertently or willfully, sometimes to help subsidize clinics, privte practitioners, and teacher-training institutions whose need to produce more professionals is linked directly to the number of children to be served in specific categorical areas. Although it may be uncomfortable to mention these factors, they exist and restrict the forces of productive change.

It seems clear that if the field of LD is to survive as a valid clinical science, it must evaluate where it has been, where it is going, and where it wants to end up. Within this process of self-inspection, there is a need to actively identify shortcomings and address them honestly and aggressively. No where is this need for scrutiny and change more apparent than in the research practices and procedures traditionally carried out in the study of LD. As Torgeson and Dice (1980) reported several years ago, pervasive problems endemic to LD research limit its contribution to knowledge and its implications for educational practice with children. Unfortunately, these problems remain, even though LD research is increasingly being called upon to address the critical issues of definition, assessment, and instruction, as well as questions concerning public policy and legal concepts—tasks for which the research community is totally unprepared. Making the need for change in research practices even more compelling, is the increasing number of false and unrealistic expectations concerning the field of LD that are held by parents, teachers, psychologists, school administrators, policymakers, and lawyers. Clearly, these persons need to have accurate information in order to make appropriate decisions about the welfare of learning-disabled children.

A number of suggestions for future research directions in the field of LD could be presented, given the limited state of the art and knowledge base. Two very important areas pertain to the technical quality of our research practices and the manner in which we define samples for study. Recently, thoughtful suggestions for improvement in these areas were made at the DLD/Utah Symposium by Torgeson (1986) and Senf (1986b). What remains to be addressed are issues related to the more global concerns of what and how to study, such that our contributions to both theory and practice in LD are maximized.

Within this context, the remainder of this chapter is organized to address specific research needs and future directions, including (1) the need for developmental longitudinal research programs, (2) the need to develop a theoretically based taxonomy of LD that has clinical significance, and, (3) the need to critically examine some assumptions upon which current conceptualizations of LD are based.

THE NEED FOR DEVELOPMENTAL
LONGITUDINAL RESEARCH PROGRAMS

With some exceptions (Fletcher & Morris, 1986; McKinney & Feagans, 1984; Satz et al., 1978), the majority of research efforts carried out in the study of LD have consisted primarily of single investigations (as contrasted with studies conducted within the context of a program of research) that compared learning-disabled persons with normally achieving persons on one or more dependent variables of interest. Most studies have investigated a particular question at a single point in time using either broad or truncated developmental age spans. These efforts have produced a massive amount of information over the years that ostensibly suggests that learning-disabled students differ from their normally achieving counterparts on measures of attention, perception, linguistic skills, memory, conceptual thinking skills, social skills, and academic achievement variables. It would be advantageous if the data derived from the extensive number of studies could be compared for instances of replicability and then integrated to produce reliable observations about different expressions of LD. Unfortunately, this has not occurred for several reasons, some of which are presented below.

First, learning-disabled students who compose the samples selected for study frequently vary widely among themselves in terms of relevant classification criteria (e.g., IQ, age, SES) (Kavale & Forness, 1985a; Senf, 1986a). These differences could confound results if not accounted for or controlled.

Second, samples of learning-disabled children may differ radically from one another across identification and programmatic variables, depending upon the setting or state from which the sample is selected (Keogh et al., 1982). As Senf (1981) and others (Ysseldyke & Algozzine, 1983) have indicated, these shortcomings are directly related to the lack of specificity in the definition of LD. Definitional ambiguity, in turn, allows professionals in different settings and regions (and even within settings and regions) to identify learning-disabled persons according to a wide variety of eligibility criteria. Obviously, such variability in sample characteristics prohibit replicability and generalizability of findings.

Third, as mentioned earlier in this section, many studies have ignored developmental factors since the majority of investigations have been conducted at one point in time and may not have accounted for developmental differences within a sample, even when they existed. Because of the developmental nature of the learning process, it would be expected that disabilities in learning could be expressed in different ways at different age levels. As such, differential assessment, classification, intervention, or remediation might be required, depending upon the type of disability and the developmental level of the person. This type of information is clearly necessary to establish diagnostic criteria and efficacious educational programs.

This lack of programmatic research suggests a need to examine the manner in which subjects are selected for study and hypotheses are tested. Some significant strides have been made along these lines by Keogh and colleagues (1982) by introducing the concept of marker variables to ensure adequate measurement and description of those persons under study.

However, it is doubtful that even strict use of marker variables in subject selection, assessment, and reporting of results will significantly improve the field's ability to generalize findings from individual studies to the learning-disabled population as a whole. This may be due to both population-specific factors and sociopolitical reasons. In terms of the former, even within well-defined samples of learning-disabled students, heterogeneity of characteristics is the rule rather than the exception (Lyon, 1983, 1985a, 1985b). As such, research methodologies that detect relationships among entities in multivariate space are necessary to identify patterns of attributes that reliably characterize different subtypes of learning-disabled persons (Rourke, 1985). Clearly, LD research underutilizes these types of designs.

The major impediments to generalizability of research findings, even when selecting and describing samples using marker variables, are social and political in nature. These sociopolitical influences impede the development of a clear definition and set of eligibility criteria. As pointed out in the first section of this chapter, ambiguities within the definition of LD are maintained, in part, because they satisfy a number of social, political, and emotional needs. For example, there is no reason to expect that parents, professionals, school administrators, and politicians will embrace a more precise definition of LD if such a change redirects services for children, funds for programs, research subjects, or votes. As such, the many states and school communities that identify learning-disabled persons using different criteria will most likely continue to do so. Because most studies have been, and continue to be, carried out with "school" or "clinic" identified LD samples, there is little reason to believe that the results of an investigation conducted in one setting or state will corroborate other studies carried out in other locations or generalize to learning-disabled children studied at a different site.

In a sense, then, the traditional research practices that have been used in the study of LD will continue to have minimal impact on its understanding LD primarily because of nonscientific factors that are not under the researcher's control. It seems appropriate to consider using research strategies that circumvent the insurmountable definitional problems that the field faces as well as strategies that account for the various expressions of LD that may emerge at different points during the life span.

Within this context, developmental longitudinal research studies, where the same subjects are repeatedly observed and studied, appear to be one of the most powerful means to not only trace the development of learning and LD, but also obtain data for the construction of a focused and succinct definition (Achenbach, 1974, 1978; Achenbach & Weisz, 1975a, 1975b). One major advantage in studying LD from a longitudinal perspective is that there need not be any a priori assumptions about what LD is, particularly if children are studied initially during the preschool years and then followed with consistent probes for several years. Subjects selected randomly from the population as a whole (regardless of IQ level, achievement level, SES, race, and so on) could be observed over time across a wide range of multiple assessment and teaching contexts. In doing so, descriptions of the attributes of persons who are underachieving academically and socially could be obtained, thus identifying critical characteristics that may be manifested in different ways at different age periods. These characteristics could then serve as the relevant elements of a more precise and parsimonious definition of LD. Moreover, by conducting longitudinal studies that are initiated during the preschool years, there exists a possibility that reliable predictors of achievement and under-achievement could be developed for different developmental levels. The identification of such predictors could serve to increase our understanding of etiologic factors as well as to differentiate students for different forms of education and remediation.

Longitudinal developmental research programs will require financial, logistic, and professional commitments far beyond those necessary for the type of "single-shot" or cross-sectional investigations historically carried out with learning-disabled subjects. However, the expense and commitment appear justified given the persistent impotence of our traditional research practices. Unless research strategies are developed and applied in ways that examine the complex interactions among child, teacher, and cultural and social variables at different age levels, the LD field could be in for a continuous litany of false starts and broken promises.

THE NEED TO DEVELOP A THEORETICALLY BASED TAXONOMY OF LEARNING DISABILITIES

Classification plays a pivotal role in producing operationally meaningful accounts of what may constitute human learning and behavior. In a general sense, classification is inextricably linked to human thinking, since, by nature, man has survived through the ability to recognize, measure, and describe similarities and differences between objects and events in his universe. Humans have an apparent need to name, number, sort, and search for order among that which appears to be amorphous. Therefore, it is not surprising that a number of attempts have been made to classify children with LD into homogeneous subtypes (Lyon, 1983, 1985a; McKinney, 1984, 1987; Satz & Morris, 1981). The identification of distinct subtypes represents an important scientific step because the derived typologies can provide a less amorphous data set for intensive study and description. Subtypes can also serve as a starting point for the establishment of general theories that explain and predict particular events. Moreover, empirical multivariate classification procedures could have a powerful and helpful influence on research practices in LD, since it seems relatively clear, at a clinical level, that not all children who underachieve in school learn inefficiently for the same reasons or respond equally well to the same teaching interventions or tactics. Given these clinical insights, it could be hypothesized that the learning-disabled population is composed of a number of distinct homogeneous subtypes, each characterized by particular patterns of strengths and weaknesses across measured attributes. The application of objective classification methodologies could serve to support or refute these clinical impressions in an empirical manner.

The opportunity for misuse of classification procedures, on the other hand, is great. Subtypes can be identified using any data set and on the basis of children's performance on any measures, regardless of their reliability, validity, or conceptual and theoretical significance. As Fletcher (1985) has pointed out, the fact that different LD subtypes emerge through either clinical inspection of diagnostic data or the application of multivarate statistical algorithms to test scores does not ensure the meaningfulness or validity of the resultant typology.

It is reasonable to suggest, however, that one direction for future research lies in more precise descriptions of, and differentiation among, learning-disabled children. Without precision in identification and diagnosis, research findings will be obscured by contaminating factors associated with heterogeneity. Thus, to pursue this research direction in a manner that is both conceptually and methodologically sound, several components, or benchmarks, underlying an integrated paradigm for classification research must be addressed and adhered to in LD subtyping research. These components, derived from Skinner's (1981) seminal work in psychiatric classification, include (1) theory formulation, (2) internal validation, and (3) external validation. A fourth related component concerns the need to carry out subtyping research within a developmental framework.

Theory Formulation

When conducting LD subtyping classification research, it is imperative that several theoretical and empirical considerations be addressed. First, the variables to be used for classification should be selected on the basis of:

1. Their relationships to known paths of development or theoretical developmental frameworks (Adams, 1985).
2. The relationship of the variables to more general experimental psychology concepts of the construct being measured.
3. Evidence for the validity of the variables.
4. Evidence for the reliability of the variables.
5. Their relationship to predecessor theories (Magee, 1973).

Second, the theoretical model underlying the choice of classification procedures must be specified (Skinner, 1981; Wilson & Risucci, 1986). Third, the theory or theories underlying the selection of variables and classification procedures must lead to explicit hypotheses that can be tested. This particular consideration is extremely important. For a theory to serve as a guide in systematizing knowledge, it must be open to falsification. As Popper (1972) has pointed out, it is necessary that theories be formulated so as to expose them most unambiguously to refutation. This will be impossible to do if the theoretical constructs are faulty, the variables for measurement are technically weak, or a particular experiment fails to provide an adequate test of the hypothesis.

Internal Validation

Internal validity refers to the stability and replicability of the typology. As Everitt (1980) and others (Fletcher, 1985; Lyon, 1983; Satz & Morris, 1981; Wilson & Risucci, 1986) have pointed out, an ideal typology would yield reliable, homogeneous subtypes that can be replicated across samples using different techniques. In addition, when assessing the internal validity of a subtype solution, the researcher must ensure that the typology permits classification of a majority of the subjects in the population (coverage) and produces decision rules for identifying new members of subtypes.

External Validation

For a typology to have empirical and clinical utility, predictive, descriptive, and clinical validities must be established (Skinner, 1981). Predictive validity is exemplified by studies that have tested the efficacy of various intervention procedures as a function of subtype membership (Lyon, 1983; 1985b). Descriptive validity is represented in studies that have attempted to show convergent and discriminant validity for the subtypes using parallel measures (Lyon & Watson, 1981; Lyon et al., 1981; Lyon, Stewart, & Freedman, 1982; Satz & Morris, 1981; Wilson & Risucci, 1986). Clinical validity is exemplified in studies that incorporated input from clinicians as a guiding force in interpretation and validation of subtypes (Wilson & Risucci, 1986).

Developmental Classification of Learning Disabilities Subtypes

As pointed out earlier in this chapter, there exists a significant need to study LD from a developmental longitudinal framework that does not require adherence to the a priori assumptions reflected in current definitions. It was argued that a definition could best be provided by investigations that study representative groups of children over time, beginning during the preschool years and observing how differences among subjects emerge, change, and influence school learning. Within this context, the development of typologies for LD should also be conducted within a developmental framework. Using empirical classification approaches, atypical learners could be differentiated from normally achieving learners at all age levels represented in the longitudinal design and then subtyped to identify the existence of distinct homogeneous subgroups and their stability over time. One expectation would be that at certain ages, some subtypes of learning-disabled children would not differ in some abilities from normal learners or from other subtypes but may differ in these abilities at other ages or in eventual outcome.

Thus, the formation of a robust developmentally based typology of LD has both theoretical and clinical significance. At a theoretical level, the constructs used in subtype classification research may provide heuristics for the development of theories of LD. Moreover, delineation of specific subtype patterns of attentional, cognitive, linguistic, perceptual, memory, and academic skills at different age levels can enhance extant theory and knowledge of meaningful continuities in development. At a clinical level, identification of children with putative LD provides a research framework for the design of studies to investigate two major questions: One, do different patterns of attentional, cognitive, and linguistic skills, for example, influence the acquisition of reading, written language, and mathematics skills in different ways? Two, do specific and predictable relationships exist between subtype membership and response to particular teaching approaches or interventions?

THE NEED TO EXAMINE SOME ASSUMPTIONS

It might be surprising to many researchers that a number of basic assumptions underlying current definition of LD, as well as prevalent identification and educational practices in the field, have little basis in fact, at least as yet. Even more concerning is that some assumptions, for example, that learning-disabled children can be reliably differentiated from "normally achieving" and "slow-learning" students, have been found to be erroneous (Ysseldyke & Algozzine, 1983) and yet are still believed by a significant number of professionals and parents (Tucker et. al., 1983). Regardless of whether members of the professional and parent communities are able to consider findings that run counter to long-held clinical or subjective beliefs, there exists a need for future research to clarify the scientific status of assumptions that have forged and guided professional practices and policies within the LD field.

This type of research could have a positive effect on the development of the field's knowledge base, particularly if the inquiries lead to reassessments of the efficacy of commonly used diagnostic and teaching practices. For example, one basic assumption underlying current identification practices is that learning-disabled children manifest a significant discrepancy between their potential, as reflected in IQ scores, and their academic achievement. Tacitly engrained within this assumption is the notion that learning-disabled children can attain levels of achievement commensurate with their IQ if they are assessed and taught properly. However, both the assumption of discrepancy and the implicit message that it connotes stand on shakey conceptual and logical grounds.

Many samples of learning-disabled children are selected for study on the basis of a discrepancy between the Performance IQ derived from the WISC-R and measures of academic achievement. Unfortunately, the Performance IQ, and even the Full Scale IQ, bear little psychometric relationship to measures of academic achievement, particularly in the oral language, reading, and written language domains, thus negating the predictive power attributed to discrepancies between measures of nonverbal intelligence and school learning. Of greater interest and concern, however, is that we do not know whether psychometric discrepancies tell us anything of value about how children respond to instruction and apply what they have learned across settings. For example, do learning-disabled students, selected on the basis of aptitude–achievement discrepancies actually differ from slow learners and mentally retarded students in their rate of learning in deficit areas and their ability to generalize information? One way to address this specific question, as well as the efficacy of the discrepancy concept, would be to match children from different diagnostic categories (e.g., LD, EMR, slow learners) according to the type and severity of academic deficits and determine whether significant group differences exist in response to, and in generalization of, instruction. If not, the concept of discrepancy, and the assumption of "potential," at least as assessed by IQ measures, should be carefully re-examined.

The fact tht there is a need to objectively question the scientific and clinical merit of concepts so dear to the field as "discrepancy" and "potential" should not cause concern. Recognizing and overcoming conceptual shortcomings are necessary if the field of LD is to survive and flourish as a clinical science. What is distressing is that a significant number of researchers, clinicians, and policymakers resist a careful reexamination of the tenets underlying present conceptions of LD and, in fact, continue to develop policies, procedures, and programs on the basis of assumptions that simply cannot be supported by the data (Lyon & Vaughn, in preparation). Although such practices may make for good religion, they impede significantly our ability to understand and teach those who are not successful at achieving the expectations of academic, social, personal, and vocational life. Clearly, it behooves the research community to promote within itself a critical mass of thinkers who can objectively seek out and address the conceptual shortcomings inherent within the assumptions upon which the field of LD rests. As Magee (1973) has pointed out ". . . no one can possibly give us more service than by showing us what is wrong with what we think or do; the bigger the fault, the bigger the improvement made possible by its revelation" (p. 39).

CONCLUSIONS

The views presented in this chapter have been developed and written within a context of respect for the ideals that the pioneers in LD sought to promote and for those who strive to understand and teach persons who fail to profit from typical forms of instruction. However, I am hopeful that the positions represented here reflect a genuine concern that we have gone beyond our extant data base in formulating definitional statements, identification criteria, and educational policies and practices for those who come to be viewed as learning disabled. I have attempted to use a tone that is appropriate both to the problems and challenges that we face and the directions and changes that we need to consider. Before significant improvements can be made in the research and clinical domains, we have to confront the possibility that many practices used in the field of LD may reflect a benign neglect for the principles of common sense and clinical science. Could it be that our penchant for folklore outweighs our quest for truth? To put this last question in an appropriate context, it might be wise to reflect on a quotation by the pre-Socratic philosopher Xenophanes.

> "The gods did not reveal, from the beginning, all things to us, but in the course of time through seeking we may learn and know things better. But as for certain truth, no man has known it, nor shall he know it, neither of the gods nor yet of all the things of which I speak. For even if by chance he were to utter the final truth, he would himself not know it: for all is but a woven web of guesses", (quoted in Popper, 1972, p. 78).

Perhaps, by directing at least some future research efforts toward the development of a theoretically driven taxonomy of LD that reflects continuities of development as well as valid assumptions, the probability of making better guesses as well as obtaining and understanding hard facts may be increased.

RESPONSE

Kenneth A. Kavale

Was this simply another pessimistic piece denouncing LD research? This was my initial reaction to Lyon's chapter. It soon became apparent, though, that the old adage "you can't judge a book by its cover" was true. After reading the chapter, I came away with a sense of optimism. Although problems in LD research were noted, Lyon went beyond banal critiques and offered instead a blueprint for change. The chapter provided a comprehensive outline about what and how we should be doing research in LD.

Lyon first presented several reasons why the LD field faces so many problems. He rightly pointed to the forces that hinder development. While its young chronologic age certainly imposes constraints, it is important to note that the history of the LD field transcends the 11 years noted. I have argued elsewhere that this history exerts considerable influence in the form of paradigmatic assumptions that are no longer valid. Consequently, LD has become a victim of its own history and must break the bonds of its past if it is to advance (Kavale & Forness, 1984, 1985b).

Perhaps the most telling point made by Lyon is that the many academic disputes and political machinations associated with LD will not simply go away. Time will not heal our wounds, and it becomes interesting to speculate on why we are not doing what we should be doing. Are we perhaps really more comfortable with our present chaotic state? In such a state, it is far easier to be simply a critic who decries the situation but offers little productive remedy. Lyon is correct; we must take objective stock of where LD research has been, where it is going, and where it wants to end up. In its present form, LD research can offer little encouragement. For example, Kavale and Nye (1981), in a survey of 307 experimental research studies, found that 50% selected LD subjects on the basis of previous classification where the antecedent criteria were not specified. This makes it difficult to determine the extent to which the subjects matched standard LD criteria and introduces an inherent vagueness. The resulting sample raises the vexing question: Who are we talking about? With such a question, the fundamental elements of generalization and replication are almost impossible to achieve.

Lyon then presents three research needs in an effort to point the LD field in the right direction. His first suggestion is for increased emphasis upon developmental longitudinal research. The case presented is compelling, and the LD field would do well to heed his suggestion, even with the many pragmatic difficulties associated with longitudinal research. In a recently completed review (Kavale, in press), I was taken aback by how much we do not know about the long-term consequences of LD. What little information we do have available is typically confounded by methodologic difficulties. It was, therefore, refreshing to see Lyon call for more longitudinal research. In many respects, this suggestion parallels my suggestion for "research programmes" (see Chapter 2), which represents ontologic and methodologic "dos" and "don'ts" for studying the entire LD phenomenon. The primary advantage to be gained is the elimination of a priori assumptions about LD. With no presumptions about LD, the data obtained would be neutral and we would be in a position to interpret findings in a value-free manner.

Lyon next calls for increased attention to taxonomic efforts in LD. He presents a strong rationale for taxonomic research in terms of both theoretical and clinical benefits. His own research ably demonstrates these benefits by showing the theoretical usefulness of empirical classification in reducing heterogeneity and the clinical significance of basing intervention upon a subtype X treatment interaction. In addition to the components necessary for effective taxonomic research described by Lyon, I would add another: more commonality and consensus in measurement and methodology for LD subtype research. Subtype research currently appears to be a series of relatively independent efforts that would probably produce more powerful outcomes if the efforts were pooled to produce a single classification scheme for LD (Kavale & Forness, in press).

Lyon's final suggestion about the need to examine some basic assumption about LD is, in many respects, the heart of his chapter. We simply have too much "conventional wisdom" in LD that is neither conventional nor, certainly, wisdom. Lyon forcefully and persuasively alerts us to the fact that what we believe to be true is often- "ain't necessarily so." Having alerted us to the fanciful thinking that abounds in LD, Lyon then dares to suggest that we are either very impatient or possess a penchant for folklore. This is a strong indictment but, in all probability, it is a valid criticism that hopefully will prod us into a more productive stance.

Lyon is to be congratulated on a significant contribution to this volume. The LD field cannot improve its status unless there is a significant change in the manner by which it thinks about and goes about its research activities. Lyon has presented the foibles inherent in LD research but has also provided a framework for positive change in LD research. The question now becomes: Are we willing to heed his advice?

REFERENCES

Achenbach, T.M. (1974). *Developmental psychopathology.* New York: Ronald Press.

Achenbach, T.M. (1978). *Research in developmental psychology: concepts, strategies, methods.* New York: The Free Press.

Achenbach, T.M., & Weisz, J.R. (1975a). A longitudinal study of relations between outer-directedness and IQ changes in preschoolers. *Child Development, 46,* 650–657.

Achenbach, T.M., & Weisz, J.R. (1975b). Impulsivity, reflectivity and cognitive development in preschoolers: A longitudinal analysis of developmental and trait variance. *Developmental Psychology, 11*, 413–414.

Adams, K.M. (1985). Theoretical, methodological, and statistical issues. In B.P. Rourke (Ed.), *Neuropsychology of learning disabilities: Advances in subtype analysis.* New York: The Guilford Press.

Belmont, I., & Belmont, L. (1980). Is the slow learner in the classroom learning disabled? *Journal of Learning Disabilities, 13*, 496–499.

Everitt, B. (1980). *Cluster analysis.* London: Heinemann Educational Books.

Fletcher, J.M. (1985). External validation of learning disability typologies. In B.P. Rourke (Ed.), *Neuropsychology of learning disabilities: Advances in subtype analysis.* New York: Guilford Press.

Fletcher, J.M., & Morris, R. (1986). Classification of disabled learners. Beyond exclusionary definitions. In S. Ceci (Ed.), *Handbook of cognitive, social, and neuropsychological aspects of learning disabilities.* Hillsdale, NJ: Erlbaum.

Kavale, K.A. (in press). Long-term consequences of learning disabilities. In M.C. Wang, M.P. Reynolds & H.J. Walberg, (Eds.), *The handbook of special education: Research and practice.* Oxford, England: Pergamon Press.

Kavale, K.A., & Forness, S.R. (1984). The historical foundation of learning disabilities: A quantitative synthesis assessing the validity of Strauss and Werner's exogenous versus endogenous distinction of mental retardation. *Remedial and Special Education, 6*(5), 18–24.

Kavale, K.A., & Forness, S.R. (1985a). *The science of learning disabilities.* San Diego: College-Hill Press.

Kavale, K.A., & Forness, S.R. (1985b). Learning disability and the history of science: Paradigm or paradox? *Remedial and Special Education, 6*(4), 12–23.

Kavale, K.A., & Forness, S.R. (in press). *The far side of heterogeneity: A critical analysis of empirical subtyping research in learning disabilities. Journal of Learning Disabilities.*

Kavale, K.A., & Nye, C. (1981). Identification criteria for learning disabilities: A survey of the research literature. *Learning Disability Quarterly, 4*, 383–388.

Keogh, B., Major-Kingsley, S., Omori-Gordon, H., & Reid, H. (1982). *A system of marker variables for the field of learning disabilities.* Syracuse, NY: Syracuse University Press.

Kirk, S.A., & Kirk, W.D. (1983). On defining learning disabilities. *Journal of Learning Disabilities, 16*, 20–21.

Kuhn, T.S. (1970). *The Structure of scientific revolutions,* (2nd ed.). Chicago: University of Chicago Press.

Lerner, J. (1985). *Learning disabilities: Theories, diagnosis and teaching strategies.* Boston: Houghton Mifflin Co.

Lyon, G.R. (1983). Learning disabled readers: Identification of subgroups. In H. Mykelbust (Ed.), *Progress in learning disabilities,* (Vol. 5). New York: Grune & Stratton.

Lyon, G.R. (1985a). Educational validation studies of learning disabled readers. In B.P. Rourke (Ed.), *Neuropsychology of learning disabilities: Essentials of subtype analysis.* New York: Guilford Press.

Lyon, G.R. (1985b). Identification and remediation of learning disability subtypes: Preliminary findings. *Learning Disabilities Focus, 1,* 21–23.

Lyon, G.R., Rietta, S., Watson, B., Porch, B., & Rhodes, J. (1981). Selected linguistic and perceptual abilities of empirically derived subgroups of learning disabled readers. *Journal of School Psychology, 19,* 152–166.

Lyon, G.R., Stewart, N., & Freedman, D. (1982). Neuropsychological characteristics of empirically derived subgroups of learning disabled readers. *Journal of Clinical Neuropsychology, 4,* 343–365.

Lyon, G.R., & Vaughn, S. (in preparation). Assumptions Underlying Learning Disabilities: An Analysis of Support.

Lyon, G.R., & Watson, B.L. (1981). Empirically derived subgroups of learning disabled readers: Diagnostic characteristics. *Journal of Learning Disabilities, 14,* 256–261.

Magee, B. (1973). *Popper.* Glasgow: William Collins Sons and Co., Ltd.

McKinney, J.D. (1984). The search for subtypes of specific learning disability. *Journal of Learning Disabilities, 17,* 43–50.

McKinney, J.D. (1987). Research in conceptually and empirically derived subtypes of specific learning disabilities. In M.C. Wang, H.J. Wallberg & M.C. Reynolds (Eds.), *The handbook of special education: Research and practice.* Oxford: Pergamon Press.

McKinney, J.D., & Feagans, L. (1984). Academic and behavioral characteristics of learning disabled children and average achievers: Longitudinal studies. *Learning Disability Quarterly, 7,* 251–264.

McLeod, J. (1983). Learning disability is for educators. *Journal of Learning Disabilities, 16,* 23–24.

Mercer, C.D. (1979). *Children and adolescents with learning disabilities.* Columbus, OH: Charles Merrill Publishing Co.

Popper, K.R. (1972). *Objective knowledge: An evolutionary approach.* Oxford: Oxford University Press.

Rourke, B.P. (1985). *Neuropsychology of learning disabilities: Advances in subtype analysis.* New York: Guilford Press.

Satz, P., & Fletcher, J.M. (1980). Minimal brain dysfunctions: An appraisal of research concepts and methods. In H. Rie & E. Rie (Eds.), *Handbook of minimal brain dysfunctions.* New York: Wiley-Interscience.

Satz, P., & Morris, R. (1981). Learning disability subtypes: A review. In F.J. Pirozzolo & M.C. Wittrock (Eds.), *Neuropsychological and cognitive processes in reading.* New York: Academic Press.

Satz, P.; Taylor, H.G.; Friel, J.; & Fletcher, J.M. (1978). Some predictive and developmental precursors of reading disability: A six year follow-up. In A. Benton & D. Pearl (Eds.), *Dyslexia: A critical appraisal of current theory.* Oxford: Oxford University Press.

Senf, G.M. (1981). Issues surrounding the diagnosis of learning disabilities. Child handicap versus failure of the child–school interaction. In T.R. Kratochwill (Ed.), *Advances in school psychology,* (Vol. 1). Hillsdale, NJ: Erlbaum.

Senf, G.M. (1986a). LD research in sociological and scientific perspective. In J.K. Torgeson & B. Wong (Eds.), *Psychological and educational perspectives on learning disabilities.* New York: Academic Press.

Senf, G.M. (1986b). *Sample selection.* Paper presented at the Division for Learning Disabilities/Utah State Symposium on Future Directions and Issues in Research for the Learning Disabled, Salt Lake City, Utah.

Skinner, H.A. (1981). Toward the integration of classification theory and methods. *Journal of Abnormal Psychology, 90,* 68–87.

Torgeson, J.K. (1986). *Thinking about the future by distinguishing between issues that have answers and those that do not.* Paper presented at the Division for Learning Disabilities/Utah State Symposium on Future Directions and Issues in Research for the Learning Disabled, Salt Lake City, Utah.

Torgeson, J.K., & Dice, C. (1980). Characteristics of research on learning disabilities. *Journal of Learning Disabilities, 13,* 531–535.

Tucker, J., Stevens, L.J. and Ysseldyke, J.E. (1983). Learning disabilities: The experts speak out. *Journal of Learning Disabilities, 16,* 6–14.

U.S.O.E. (1968). *First annual report of the National Advisory Committee on Handicapped Children.* Washington, DC: U.S. Department of Health, Education, & Welfare.

Wilson, B.C., & Risucci, D.A. (1986). A model for cinical-quantitative classification. Generation I: Application to language disordered preschool children. *Brain and Language, 27,* 281–309.

Ysseldyke, J.E., & Algozzine, B. (1983). LD or not LD: That's not the question. *Journal of Learning Disabilities, 16,* 29–31.

Ysseldyke, J.E., Algozzine, B., & Epps, S. (1982). *A logical and empirical analysis of current practices in classifying students as handicapped* (Research Report No. 92). Minneapolis: University of Minnesota, Institute for Research on Learning Disabilities.

CHAPTER 6

Learning Disabilities as Sociologic Sponge: Wiping up Life's Spills

Gerald M. Senf

This territory is vast and primitive.
There is money here, growing investments, and political interests.
We must protect these investments so that the area can prosper and grow.
–Attributed to Lew Wallace, Governor of New Mexico, c. 1881.

From anonimity and social disinterest to the most prevalent handicapping condition in this country—all in less than 25 years—learning disabilities (LD) must be doing something for someone. But repeated "backlashes" suggest that labeling one as LD can cause serious fiscal and political problems. In the first part of this chapter, I describe what I believe the sociologic function of LD to be: I see it as a sponge to wipe up regular education's spills and cleanse its ills. But used as such, LD becomes an unsound basis for research.

Although the focus here is on research rather than on policy, believing the two to be disparate has created social fiction and self-deception in research practice. Consequently, I will spend little space on the means by which the LD concept cleans up messes—which it does! I shall devote more space to research issues—both problems and some potential solutions.

THE SPONGE THAT ABSORBS PROBLEMS

What did we do in education before the concept of LD took force? Those with a few more years than I tell stories about teaching in the basement, next to the boiler, or, as one most credible source delights in telling, in the "boy's room." With organized parental support, legislative initiative and influence, and resulting legal mandate, LD were accepted as a legal handicapping condition under PL 94-142. Most states followed with similar legislation.

So from lavatory to sometimes lavishly appointed resource rooms, LD became the handicap of the 1970s and early 1980s. There were and will continue to be struggles defining LD as a "true" handicap akin to blindness, where sensory disorder is unquestionable, or to Down's syndrome, where central nervous system involvement is clearly apparent. Some benchmarks reflecting ambivalent support include (1) the lack of funding for the initial year following passage of the Learning Disabilities Act (1969) and the trivial subsequent funding (Senf, 1973); and (2) the widely waged federal campaign to limit LD incidence, first, by including LD in PL 94-142 only with an arbitrary 2% cap imposed and, finally, by admitting it only after a hard-fought battle to require a measured discrepancy between potential (IQ) and achievement (USOE, 1976, 1977a, b). The IQ–achievement dictum became "recommendation" under a storm of both scientific and advocacy protest (Danielson & Bauer, 1978), but field opinion was swayed and generally accepted the discrepancy model (Kirk, Senf, & Larsen, 1981). More recently, sister professions, displaced by LD, are reclaiming their territory—reading specialists and speech pathologists in particular. Most recently, a so-called regular/special education initiative represents a further ringing out of a previously ever-expanding LD sponge.

Although I may have skipped a meaningful ebb and flow in LD's alleged bloatedness, the tidal shifts have, though minor, been undeniably present during this short history. Viewing LD as a sponge, we can use this metaphor to reconcile the administrative demands of practice and those of research. (I am less concerned here that basic research typically *follows* policy or that results which contradict government policy are typically ignored. I am bothered more by the fact that the very administration of policy (lacking policy research) fills the LD sponge with flotsam and jetsam, miscellany prohibitive to the acomplishment of sensible research.) I shall describe the effect that powerful variables have on the size and contents of the sponge— effects dwarfing the most authoritative research study.

Before continuing, allow me to delimit my use of the sponge metaphor in the hope that others will seize upon related implications:

1. Although living and growing, the sponge is an immobile animal, growing by repetition of similar cells, not by increased cell specialization.

2. The living sponge is composed of cells of non- or low-communicative ability. They cling for support to the dead skeletal structure (the part we recognize as the bath sponge) and other lifeless elements. The metaphor asks explicitly whether each of us is part of the skeletal structure or a live resident? (It also asks implicitly which of these two roles one views as more favorable!)

3. The living sponge draws sustenance by extracting nutrition drawn through it. This process can be left unquestioned for the sponge. But for LD-related professionals feeding within the system, we subject ourselves to ethical scrutiny: "Who should be processed through the system? Who should benefit?"

The sponge metaphor prompts other issues, of course, but here I will point out only those factors that puff and pout the sponge. I shall then relate the impact of this analysis to the research endeavor.

What Causes the Sponge to Expand or Contract?

Remember the days when professionals argued the LD prevalence from 2% to 50% or so? (Kass & Myklebust, 1969; Tucker, Stevens, & Ysseldyke, 1983). No one could or can agree! While scientifically a nuisance, popular disagreement on such a large scale is seldom simply semantic. Vested interest—not necessarily bad—comes into play in many forms. We all know them but I will name a few; all readers may not recognize how these factors can influence research. My scenario is that what the administrative sponge wipes up becomes the research sample when the sponge is squeezed. As a defensible research sample, no such LD sponge qualifies. A chunk of the nation's LD sponge survives biologically like any sample served up by the local school. But what does this ringing out have to do with LD when conceived of in a scientific framework? Not much, I fear!

Were I to bet, I would wager that most persons concerned with LD believe that a certain specific percentage of the population is learning disabled at any given time and that misdiagnosis both excludes and, more likely, overincludes persons labelled as learning disabled. Within a scientific framework, a concept such as LD requires diagnostic reliability. Many of the field's most widely known proponents have repeatedly stated their respective definitional perspectives. (See *Journal of Learning Disabilities*, 1983 for a comprehensive review of many position statements.) These perspectives derive from a blend of clinical and research knowledge achieved over decades, beliefs as to what LD "truly is," and a sensitivity to a second major process in any field's formation—concensus.

Widely discrepant prevalence figures belie concensus. In the place of concensus has been administrative pragmatics, LD being a grey area between "normalcy" and other handicapping conditions. (See Senf, 1981 for an alternative model). Administrators have not necessarily, however, had their way designating who would or would not be served as LD; but the realities over which they preside and more or less control have enormously affected the make-up of LD samples from site to site.

The arguments regarding the pragmatics of classification are not new. Factors such as fiscal resources of parents, program availability, local professional acceptance of the LD concept, parental pressure (both individual and organized), competitive services provided by allied fields, and other forces shape and size the sponge (Senf, 1976a, 1976b, 1981; and 1986 for a detailed development of this sociologic perspective). The inevitable result of the "come one, come all" mentality is heterogeneity on a host of dimensions. With all good intentions, service professionals want to provide for those struggling in the regular program; and those teaching the "normals" often encourage special "placement" for the allegedly "problem" child. This *foilie a deux* is well documented (Ysseldyke & Algozzine, 1983) and likely introduces the single largest diversity into the LD group. Whether or not these "problem" children are "truly learning disabled" is a semantic issue but is seldom recognized as such.

Combatting Heterogeneity

It is not just the research community that abhors heterogeneity. The practitioner faced with pedagogically relevant variance among pupils sensibly seeks assistance. With nurturant conditions, the LD sponge grows; the LD group's heterogeneity increases while the heterogeneity in the regular education class diminishes somewhat. (Please recognize the self-deception in such assertions if not viewed relativistically. Does one really believe that the 90% of students termed "normal" are more homogeneous than the 4% termed learning disabled? It is likely that the normals *are* more homogeneous on such variables as behavioral control, individual work habits, and cognitive skills. But if one were to consider the teaching skills necessary to maximize each child's potential, it would be preposterous to claim more commonality for the 90% termed "normal." [See Senf, 1981 for a discussion of individual variation and child potential maximization.])

Lacking evidence, I must guess that it is not LD heterogeneity but sheer numbers that upset the service side of the LD profession. However, it is this same bloated service population that is used to comprise research samples, making the constitution of the service population relevant here. It should be noted, however, that all aspects of the field remain conscious of both absolute numbers labeled and their diversity—this latter concern being voiced as a definitional issue, "Who truly is learning disabled?"

Research must be aware of attempted solutions by its service-minded counterparts if it continues to view children labeled learning disabled as its supraordinate population. Debate has been the most visible tool in forging a conceptually coherent and functional definition. Whether in the public forum of conference presentations, organizational board meetings, classroom lectures, or legislative conference committees, discussions are heated, complexity overwhelms, and concensus (and some think truth) slips away. But could one expect much different outcomes given the free thought provided in conference presentations and to the academicians who so typically are the "speakers." Board meetings of organizations often forge solutions, but one must realize that any resultant position paper is a compromise of individuals, none of whom may agree with the total document. Further, there exists multiple organizations engaged in the same pursuit of definition, and then there is a joint committee, an organization of organizations, bent on concensus that they could not reach even among the representatives, let alone among each organization's members.

Learning Disabilities is a Sociologic Sponge!

There will never be concensus regarding the definition of LD because its meaning is embedded not in empirical fact but in the philosophy of education, the aspiration of parents for their children, the status of each profession and professional (on a variety of dimensions), personal well-being, and the deep-seated beliefs of each and every person involved as to what "should be." The LD sponge grew so fast because it was able to absorb a diversity of educational/behavioral/socioemotional problems irrespective of their cause, their stabilization, their remediation, or their prognosis. LD consequently serves a social function, that being to define itself *sufficiently ambiguously*, placing the power of service provision in the hands of those who rule the diverse educational resources. In short, if one has power, it is better to have a flexible sponge than a rigid pigeon hole (with all deference to Benjamin Franklin whose pigeon holes served the U.S. Postal System—which he founded—exceedingly well). LD is that flexible sponge that lives in the region between alleged normalcy and alleged handicap, expanding and contracting with a myriad of external events only a fraction of which concern the state of the individual so labeled.

OBTAINING RESEARCH SUBJECTS BY SQUEEZING THE SPONGE

Here, we return to the issue of the impact that the LD sponge has when researchers try to use it to constitute research samples. With reliability of selection, a prerequisite condition for the establishment of valid correlates of any condition, the variation in LD membership across time, geographic location, and sociologic conditions severely jeopardizes the research effort. However, in a "publish or perish" atmosphere and being embedded in the broader discipline of education, not known for its demanding standards, self-examination, or intellect, researchers might easily accept for research whatever is rung from the sponge.

"We're Totally Lost but Making Good Time!"

At the risk of sounding indelicate, I unequivocally contend that a research sample squeezed from a public school LD sponge would be a heterogeneous mess, containing subjects conforming to few knowledgeable persons' concept of LD. The same regrettable state of affairs would hold true for samples drawn from the university clinic, hospital, private practice offices, and other sources such as private schools and tutorial services. Each of these other potential sources of samples are influenced by the same set of confounding variables as those operating in the public sector described previously. And, of course, public sector samples vary widely from one location to another, vary over time as a result of changing conditions, and vary in conjunction with socioeconomic status, especially as it is confounded by ethnicity (Dunn, 1968).

It has been my observation that researchers do not accord sample selection the scientifically relevant role that it deserves. Instead, sample selection proceeds atheoretically, based principally on convenience, that is, the nearest "sponge." Too often, the researcher compounds the problem created by thoughtless sample selection by excusing marginally significant results as being paused by the heterogeneity of the sample. Once it is recognized that all samples are heterogeneous with respect to a host of variables, failure to find a predicted outcome derives either from a lack of reliability in sample constitution or invalidity of the hypothesis. (This simple logic was first explicated by Zigler and Phillips in 1961 and has been applied to LD researchers in papers of my authorship in 1976a, 1976b and, 1986).

The rate at which research papers are produced claiming to have found some character or behavior pattern common to the learning disabled is frightening. LD samples can generally be counted on to act differently than samples from "normals." But the overlap in outcome measures with comparison samples is typically in the range of two-thirds standard deviation (Weener, 1981; Weener & Senf, 1981), suggesting that the hypothesis does not apply to all learning-disabled subjects or that the independent variable is a weak predictor. Here the researcher often commits one of two errors: finding statistically insignificant outcomes, the cry is "Heterogeneity!" A statistically supported hypothesis results in approbation for all of the sample's subjects, whereas even the most cursory examination of the data would prove such a conclusion false or misleading. At this point—not uncommon in even published research—the researcher's training and/or integrity and certainly the utility of the given data and more generally of our research models must be called into question.

The central problem appears to be our lack of understanding of the population from which our subjects are drawn. Consequently, we are unable to generalize findings. This problem, based on a principle from elementary statistics, is generally ignored. (See Senf, 1986 for an extension of this argument of sample selection into the realm of suprapopulations and theory utilization.) The amassing of studies that defy integration has caused some researchers to suggest that we rely more on single cases, either of the traditional case history variety or through utilization of the various single-subject research designs. The obvious problem with case histories is that the knowledge derived is inductive and, hence, subject to various interpretations. Hypothesis generation is enhanced, but proof by deduction, which we now seek, is absent (Meehl, 1973).

The single-subject designs are of an entirely different order. While focusing on a single case, they seek to isolate empirically the factor(s) controlling the outcome measure(s). Such studies have their place in this context but often run afoul in their inability to generalize findings. The problem, again, is simply that we do not know the population from which the subject was drawn and, even if drawn randomly, whether the subject was representative. To select a subject "at random" guarantees nothing. Rather, random selection is an abdication of control of subject characteristics and certainly no guarantee of representativeness. Hence, replicated single-subject experiments from a known population would appear to deserve closer consideration. However, the population must be well known and a stratified sampling technique must be used to ensure that one is not saddled with Billingsley's (1977) results: In eight replications of a single-subject crossover design, two subjects performed best under self-imposed reward contingencies, two performed best under externally imposed contingencies, with the remaining four showing no preference.

Another alternative approach, derived from biologic science (Sokal & Sneath, 1963) cluster analysis, has been applied to LD samples (Lyon, 1983, 1985; Lyon & Watson, 1981; McKinney, 1984; Rourke, 1985; Senf, Luick, & Larsen, 1976). A collection of somewhat different mathematical algorithms (Anderberg, 1973) cluster analysis divides one's sample into subsamples defined by the patterning of the scores entered. Each subject's pattern of scores is statistically compared with that of all other subjects so that within-pattern similarity is maximized. (In actuality, there exists a number of mathematical algorithms, some stressing profile "elevation," others within-score variation, and so on. Ultimately, the virtue of one's chosen algorithm lies with the correlates that the resultant set of profiles or clusters embodies.) The resultant set of clusters can vary from one, that is, the sample itself, to N, the number of subjects in the sample. Both extremes are obviously self-defeating; some size compromise between the single sample and the number of single subjects is sought. This compromise in-and-of itself is directed by mathematical concerns and, in some cases, by the subjective analysis of the researcher. In any case, the reduction of sample heterogeneity on the classification variables will result, each cluster possessing less within-cluster variance than that between it and any other cluster.

Achieving stable clusters is certainly important and is why I have recommended large samples, holding out large portions of the sample for cross-validation before subjecting clustered subjects to further experimental analysis—both for the subject's and researcher's sake (Senf, 1986). The argument put forth by Zigler and Phillips (1961), discussed previously, that reliability of classification must naturally proceed validation, holds for profile types as well as for the entire sample when compared with a contrast group. The real power of the cluster analysis approach is just now bearing fruit as, for example, in the work of Lyon (1985). The key ingredients to successful work in this vein are twofold: Selection of scores to be clustered based on some viable theory, and the subsequent use of the clusters as predictor variables in accord with the tenets of the theory. (Lyon, 1985; Senf, 1986).

The Paradox of Smaller Sponges

It would seem that a careful, theoretically determined selection of dimensions would enable one to squeeze more meaningful samples for study, one's whose increased relative homogeneity promises more valid (and useful) corelates. Although I concur with this projection, the logical "downside" of the diminished sponge size must be acknowledged—decreased generalization of findings. Experimentalists have long understood that the fewer constraints one places on sample selection, the more generalizable the findings, that is, generalizable to the population from which one sampled. As one decreases the definitional domain, generalization similarly decreases. Smaller, more homogeneous "sponges" squeeze samples with more useful correlates (if one's theory generating sponge composition is good and one asks the "right" questions). To paraphrase a political aphorism of Barry Goldwater, "Extremism in the selection of one's sample is no vice. Moderation in one's principles is no virtue." However, getting the "public" to agree to a more narrow research agenda, in favor of finding high-level correlates, over a broad-based approach, which has yielded only what one would expect, generalities, has been difficult to achieve.

The resistance to researching LD as separate syndromes may derive from numerous sources, such as a fallacious belief that the group so-named was homogeneous (with respect to meaningful variables); a slavishness to, deference to, or unwitting trust in administrative definitions of LD; or simple laziness or poor thought on the part of researchers (Senf, 1986). In any case, LD as sociologically constituted has none of the qualities necessary to comprise a viable research population. Before closing, I feel obliged to mention two other approaches to the heterogeneity problem and comment on them. One is rationale subgrouping, the other the use of marker variables (Keogh et al., 1982).

McKinney (1984) discusses the use of rational (clinical) groupings as a basis for reducing heterogeneity in the interest of finding meaningful/useful information about the group so isolated. This procedure has dominated medical science and can only be said to be a solid and viable alternative. Its strength is the clinical observation, insight, and integration with theoretical concepts used in group (cluster) construction. Its faults lie in subjectivity and typically weak theoretical models, the first of which might be amelioriated by using statistical cluster algorithms in conjunction with clinical acumen.

The issue of marker variables is a complex one, which I hope Barbara Keogh has addressed in Chapter 1. My only concern lies with the prompted use of such variables, one that in the reporting stage of one's research can easily be misconstrued. There is no question that knowing that the alleged LD sample derives from a hospital clinic versus one from an inner city school is useful information. Other distinctions could be made that would require the sensible scientist to report all aspects of the samples used. Here a dilemma is encountered: Recall that the more specifically that the sample is delimited, the less generalizable the results. What then is one to do? Collect exhaustive data on all subjects only to have the study incomparable with any other study? Or does one "discard" the correlative data? Or fail to collect it? And if one decides to collect a very large set of "markers," knowing that such is impractical anyway, which markers are included?

Some resolution to these pondersome questions may lie in the utilization of marker variables. If one were to collect a host of marker variables and not use them as either independent or dependent variables, one would logically suffer the limitation on generalization of findings previously discussed. Even if the marker variable may neither theoretically nor from prior research be related to the dependent variable, the generalization of the findings is limited by the marker. However, if one were to use the marker variable as an independent variable only to find it insignificantly related to the dependent variable(s) (especially over a series of similar studies), the restriction on generality vis-a-vis that marker would become moot. Those marker variables found to be related to dependent variables could be considered independent variables in future research or, particularly if theoretically relevant, could become entries in a cluster analysis aimed at isolating more homogeneous, predictive subgroups.

SUMMARY

Not withstanding the sincerity and integrity of those who believe that they know a learning-disabled child when they see one, or those who have devised specific identification procedures, the fact remains that those children termed learning disabled are a varied lot. They do not conform to any set of reliable classification principles. The result is that reliability places low limits on our research effort's ability to find meaningful correlates of LD as defined in clinical practice. The burden is, therefore, shifted to the researcher to identify samples for study that are defensible from psychometric and theoretical perspectives. Abdication of this responsibility results in a needless waste of time for subject, system, and researcher. Squeeze the sample from the LD sponge: If a reasonably pure color appears, conduct the experiment. If the water is cloudy, so likely will be your results. Respect everyone's time: reread, rethink, and then start over.

Barbara K. Keogh

Senf's notion of LD as a "sociologic sponge" is an interesting one. Indeed, like the sponge, the LD rubric captures a vast array of "real" problems as well as considerble flotsam and jetsam. In this sense, the heterogeneity within LD mirrors that of the sponge in its natural surround. Russo and Olhausen note that "Many sponges harbour commensal worms, brittle stars, barnacles, shrimp, crabs, copepods, and amphipods...Over 13,000 animals representing 19 species were found in a single Caribbean sponge (p. 56). For the thoughtful reader of research in LD, this sample description may seem familiar. Some might argue that shrimp, barnacles, crabs, and brittle stars more accurately describe the researchers than the subjects of research. Yet the sponge metaphor underscores the variability within LD. It also emphasizes the need for careful and meaningful distinctions within the field. Perhaps the most important distinction is between the concept of LD as a vehicle for delivery of services and the concept of LD as a topic for scientific inquiry. While not mutually exclusive, they represent very different perspectives and deserve belief discussion.

Senf (1986) is probably correct when he argues that there cannot be consensus in the definition of LD because LD has emerged from social and political pressures and needs rather than from an empirical and scientifically defensible data base. For the most part, the forces that have molded our ideas about LD have been directed at securing services. Because there is only limited consensus about the kinds of services needed (e.g., medication, behavior therapy, psychotherapy) and because professionals as well as parents become invested in their own positions, the field has taken many directions. A number of somewhat different definitions have emerged and definitional arguments continue. As I have expressed in other papers (Keogh, 1983, in press), I have ceased to be troubled by the definitional problem, as I am convinced that definition has meaning only when it is tied to purpose. Because there are multiple purposes in the LD field, there will continue to be multiple definitions. The problem comes when we mix definitions and purposes, as is the case of research conducted with preselected ("system identified") subjects rather than subjects selected according to study-relevant criteria. The sponge that sops up pupils for instructional purposes may contain a substantial number of subjects who are inappropriate for a given study. This is not to negate the validity of the instructional need sponge. Most pupils referred for special services as learning disabled have demonstrated histories of problems in school. For a variety of reasons, the regular education system has not served them effectively. In a sense, then, the number of identified learning-disabled pupils might be interpreted as an indictment of regular education programs. From this perspective, it is a reasonable supposition that the number of learning-disabled pupils would decrease if the quality of regular programs improved.

The problem is not quite that simple, however, and it is unlikely that LD will disappear even in the presence of good pedagogy. There appear to be a number of pupils whose personal characteristics preclude adequate achievement without specialized instruction. These pupils represent a range of conditions and a continuum of severity. In my view, they are legitimate targets of study if we are to understand LD. They can be variously grouped and subgrouped, depending upon the organizing variables and the purposes of the grouping. As Senf has reminded us, however, sample homogeneity and generalizability of findings are a tradeoff. He also reminds us, and I emphasize, that issues of heterogeneity-homogeneity and of generalization are functions of the questions asked, that is, of the purpose of the research. I am in full agreement with Senf that current subject selection practices, common to most research in the field, do not provide powerful insights into the nature of LD and do not allow generalizations to other samples or populations. I am, perhaps, more optimistic than he that the quality of findings can be improved through more precise research practices, especially sampling considerations.

Statistical and descriptive approaches to subject selection have been widely discussed (Keogh, 1987; McKinney, 1984, 1987) and are touched upon by Senf in his contribution to the present volume; thus, I will not elaborate here. Instead, in relation to the topic of sampling, I wish to comment upon the distinction between theory testing and contextual research. This distinction is at the core of subject selection and, thus, is central to our interpretive problems. Experimental research within academic psychology has, for the most part, had a theory-testing orientation. (See early learning theorists such as Thorndike, Tolman, and Hull or contemporary cognitive or information processing researchers such as Newell, Simon, Craik, and Shiffrin.) In order to test particular theories or constructs within a theory, researchers adopt stringent sampling criteria—the less unaccounted for sample variance, the better. Thus, laboratory animals from the same genetic strain, computer-simulated subjects, or college sophomores are appropriately used. The results of these studies help build and test psychological theory but do not necessarily have direct and immediate generalization to educational practice.

It might be argued that theory testing is not the goal in most research on learning disabilities. Rather, in the majority of studies, the goal is to describe and understand a clinical condition in order to improve services. Thus, these studies are properly focused on persons and systems within Senf's "sociologic sponge." Whether planned or not, such research has a contextual base. But as Senf has noted, "LD as sociologically constituted has none of the qualities necessary to comprise a viable research population," especially if we employ methods that are based on assumptions about consistencies of subject attributes, that is, on methods developed for theory testing. This presents an interesting dilemma that requires both conceptual and methodologic response. Senf has reminded us that from the sampling perspective, part of the research task is to specify and test classification principles that are reliable and that allow the identification of meaningful correlates. I suggest that another part of the task is to understand how individual attributes that determine class membership interact with or are influenced by the social context in which LD is expressed. Stated in a different way, the context necessarily becomes a variable to study.

Finally, lest I be accused of adopting an anti- or atheoretical stance, I emphasize that although there is a difference between theory testing and theory-guided research, we need both. Most of our work in LD may not be theory testing, but it is imperative that our research be theory guided. Too many of our journals are filled with findings that cannot be tied to any theoretical perspective and, thus, are ungeneralizable and uninterpretable. Such studies represent the single case, their only excuse for being that the subjects were available and were (somehow) presumably exemplars of LD. Such imprecise reasoning and blatant empiricism has, indeed, clouded the water we squeeze from the sponge. A final observation may be in order. Recall that sponges are found to be a relatively primitive branching off from the major evolutionary tree.

REFERENCES

Anderberg, M.R. (1973). *Cluster analysis for application*. New York: Academic Press.

Billingsley, F.F. (1977). The effect of self- and externally imposed schedules of reinforcement on oral reading performance. *Journal of Learning Disabilities, 10*, 549–559.

Danielson, L.C., & Bauer, J.N. (1978). A formula-based classification of learning disabled children: An examination of the issues. *Journal of Learning Disabilities, 11,* 163–176.

Dunn, L. (1968). Special education for the mildly retarded: Is much of it justified? *Exceptional Children, 35,* 5–24.

Kass, C.E., & Myklebust, H.R. (1969). Learning disability: An educational definition. *Journal of Learning Disabilities, 2,* 377–379.

Keogh, B.K. (1983). Classification, compliance, and confusion. *Journal of Learning Disabilities, 16*(1), 25.

Keogh, B.K. (1987). Learning disabilities: Diversity in search of order. In M. Wang, M. Reynolds, & H. Walberg (Eds.), *The handbook of special education: Research and practice.* Oxford, England: Pergamon Press.

Keogh, B., Major-Kingsley, S., Omori-Gordon, H., & Reid, H.P. (1982). *A system of marker variables for the field of learning disabilities.* Syracuse, NY: Syracuse University Press.

Kirk, S.A., Senf, G.M., & Larsen, R.P. (1981). Current issues in learning disabilities. In W.M. Cruickshank & R.G.A. Silver (Eds.), *Bridges to tomorrow* (pp. 1–16), Syracuse, NY: Syracuse University Press.

Lyon, G.R. (1983). Subgroups of learning disabled readers: Clinical and empirical identification. In H.R. Myklebust, (Ed.), *Progress in learning disabilities* (Vol. 5). New York: Grune & Stratton.

Lyon, G.R. (1985). Identification and remediation of learning disability subtypes: Preliminary findings. *Learning Disabilities Focus, 1,* 21–35.

Lyon, G.R., & Watson, B. (1981). Empirically defined subgroups of learning disabled readers: Diagnostic characteristics. *Journal of Learning Disabilities, 14,* 256–261.

McKinney, J.D. (1984). The search for subtypes of specific learning disability. *Annual Review of Learning Disabilities, 2,* 150–163.

McKinney, J.D. (1987). Research on conceptually and empirically derived subtypes of specific learning disabilities, in M. Wang, M. Reynolds, & H. Walberg (Eds.). *The handbook of special education: Research and practice.* Oxford, England: Pergamon Press.

Meehl, P. (1973). *Psychodiagnosis: Selected papers* (Chap. 13, pp. 225–302). Minneapolis: University of Minnesota Press.

Rourke, B.P. (1985). *Neuropsychology of learning disabilities.* New York: Guilford Press.

Russo, R., & Olhausen, P. (no date). *Pacific intertidal life.* Berkeley: Nature Study Guild.

Senf, G.M. (1973). Learning disabilities. In H.J. Grossman (Ed.), Symposium on learning disorders. *Pediatric Clinics of North America, 20*:3, 607–640. Philadelphia: W.B. Saunders.

Senf, G.M. (1976a). Future research needs in learning disabilities. In R.P. Anderson & C.G. Holcomb (Eds.), *Learning disability/minimal brain dysfunction syndrome: Research perspectives and applications* (pp. 249–267). Springfield, IL: Charles C. Thomas.

Senf, G.M. (1976b). Some methodological considerations in the study of abnormal conditions. In R. Walsh & W.T. Greenough, (Eds.), *Environment as therapy for brain dysfunction.* New York: Plenum Press.

Senf, G.M. (1981). Issues surrounding the diagnosis of learning disabilities:

Child handicap versus failure of the child–school interaction. In T.R. Kratochwill (Ed.), *Advances in school psychology* (Vol. 1, pp. 88–131). Hillsdale, NJ: Erlbaum.

Senf, G.M. (1986). LD research in sociological and scientific perspective. In J.K. Torgesen & B.Y.L. Wong (Eds.), *Psychological and educational perspectives on learning disabilities* (pp. 27–53). New York: Academic Press.

Senf, G.M., Luick, A.H., & Larsen, R.P. (1976). *Consistent screen performance profiles isolated among first graders with school problems by using cluster analysis.* Paper presented at Association for Children with Learning Disabilities International Conference, Seattle (March).

Sokal, R.P., & Sneath, P.H.A. (1963). *Principles of numerical taxonomy.* San Francisco: W.H. Freeman.

Tucker, J., Stevens, L.J., & Ysseldyke, J.E. (1983). Learning disabilities: The experts speak out. *Journal of Learning Disabilities, 16,* 6–14.

U.S. Office of Education. (1976). Education of handicapped children: Proposed rulemaking. *Federal Register, 41,* 230.

U.S. Office of Education. (1977a). Education of handicapped children: Implementation of Part B of the Education of the Handicapped Act. *Federal Register, 42,* 163.

U.S. Office of Education. (1977b). Assistance to States for Education of Handicapped Children: Procedures for evaluating specific learning disabilities. *Federal Register, 42,* 250.

Weener, P. (1981). On comparing learning disabled and regular classroom children. *Journal of Learning Disabilities, 14,* 227–232.

Weener, P., & Senf, G.M. (1981). Learning disabilities. In H.E. Mitzel (Ed.), *Encyclopedia of educational research.* New York: Macmillan.

Ysseldyke, J.E., & Algozzine, B. (1983). LD or not LD?: That's not the question! *Journal of Learning Disabilities, 16,* 29–31.

Zigler, E., & Phillips, L. (1961). Psychiatric diagnosis: A critique. *Journal of Abnormal and Social Psychology, 63,* 607–617.

PART III

Eligibility

CHAPTER 7

Eligibility: Back to Basics

Harold J. McGrady

O ur long-term goal is to understand the phenomenon of learning disabilities (LD). Discussions at the DLD/Utah Research Symposium indicated that we need to bring a more scientific approach to our study of LD. If this is to happen, we need to be more theoretical, conceptual, and sophisticated about our research efforts. We need to apply the most appropriate research strategies, techniques, and methodologies that currently exist in the behavioral sciences, and, most importantly, we will need to ask the appropriate research questions.

Conference discussions highlighted the fact that current research in the field is fragmented. If we are to meet our goal of understanding LD, we must develop appropriate mechanisms to organize and bring together all available resources and data. This means encouraging additional conferences, generating more funding and research institutes over extended periods of time, and finding ways to facilitate continuing communication among behavioral scientists interested in solving the riddles of LD.

The stated task during the 3 days of the conference was to determine the primary issues and questions regarding various aspects in the field of LD. In our conversations, it was inevitable that we would deal with one of the most exasperating and yet most pervasive problem areas in the field of LD: eligibility.

THE CONCEPTS OF ELIGIBILITY AND IDENTIFICATION

One Webster definition of *eligible* is "qualified to be chosen." The term *eligibility* refers to whether a person satisfies a particular set of criteria. A test of eligibility may be required if a person is to receive certain services. For example, school-aged children with LD must meet the federal, state, and/or local regulations promulgated for dispensing monies or receiving services.

In contrast, when we use various forms of the term *identify,* we are making a statement. We are saying that the person is identified as "a certain category" (in our concerns, learning disabled). Identification is a more conceptual rubric. To "identify," according to Webster, is "to determine the taxonomic position." This term used in its purest sense applies to biologic classification. However, it may be used in behavioral sciences to determine whether a person fits the sum total of characteristics of a specific category or class. Thus, to identify a person as "learning disabled" implies that he or she possesses the sum total of characteristics that constitute that class. Such a person would fit the conceptual or theoretical model of LD.

Research issues regarding eligibility for LD are influenced by the relationships between two overlapping subsets of persons: (1) those who qualify for given services, according to a list of arbitrarily defined criteria, and (2) those who would be *identified* in a scientific sense as learning disabled, according to another set of criteria. It is the interaction between these two concepts, eligibility and identification, that is the core of most research issues in LD.

To raise significant research questions in the realm of eligibility, researchers must explore the relationships between these two subsets: identified LD and eligible LD. Are there children who are excluded from services, even though they would be identified as learning disabled in a taxonomic sense? Are there children who are included in services for LD, even though they would not be so identified? What are the commonalities and distinguishing characteristics among these subsets?

CLASSIFICATION

Words are interesting tools of thought. They may help us to organize our experience and communicate with other humans. The words we have chosen in the classification of LD may at times have been more confusing than enlightening. Our mixing of the terms *eligibility* and *identification* is an excellent example. Our confusions in the uses of these two terms have contributed to problems in labeling and classification of LD.

Barbara Keogh (Chapter 1) has described two types of classifiers in the field of medicine: "lumpers" and "splitters." Those who attempt to identify shared characteristics are the lumpers; those who identify the distinctive characteristics are the splitters. We will need both types of researchers if we are to learn about the phenomenon of LD from our studies of eligibility factors. Research designed to identify the essences and commonalities across all LD may be contrasted with that research which searches for subtypes within the overall category.

Misclassification in the Schools

There are many children with pseudo-LD who are treated as though they were truly learning disabled in public schools throughout the United States. Conversely, there may be children who are learning disabled but are not being treated because they do not qualify under particular eligibility criteria.

The federal government, together with various state and local agencies, has expressed concern about the former error: overinclusion. This creates unnecessary expenditures of vast amounts of special education dollars. Conversely, parent groups have reacted to the latter type of error: underinclusion. They are anxious that their children may not be receiving appropriate LD assistance.

Need for Clarification

One of the key areas of research in the field of LD will continue to be a clarification of eligibility versus identification. We need to conduct a national search for the *true* LD! We need to be more scientific than merely reverting to the intuitive notion that "I know one when I see one." Although there is considerable disagreement in attempts to define LD, everyone purports to know it when they see it. This author has stated elsewhere: "While dozens of special task forces, blue-ribbon commissions, state legislatures, state divisons of special education, and others continue to disagree on suitable legal and operational definitions of learning disabilities, thousands of teachers and psychologists practice, daily, the identification and teaching of such children" (McGrady, 1980, p. 510).

Labels

Everyone seems to have his or her own concept of what a LD is. Labels are arbitrary, but they may have a functional commonality of meaning if appropriately defined and described. In such cases, the label can be useful. In the term *learning disabilities*, we have created a label that is at one time useful and another time useless.

LD is a sociopolitical entity (McGrady, 1980). The term grew out of a need to provide special educational services to a population of youngsters who were being underserved or neglected. Thus, the creation of the term has served a purpose, that is, to bring monies, funding authorizations, and services to persons who were not at that time receiving such benefits. Use of the term also created a greater degree of awareness among the general public.

The label *learning disabilities* may be useful. As is used in current practice, however, it should not be considered as synonymous with the category LD in a taxonomic sense. The term *learning disabilities* is used today in general practice to denote eligibility, not true categorical identification. This is the seat of much of our confusion in research practice and the contradictory conclusions drawn from various studies.

Category Abuse

A key problem is that the rubric has been abused. The term *learning disabilities* has been misued: sometimes overused, sometimes underused. Nationwide we are guilty of category abuse. But, there does exist a phenomenon that led early leaders in the field to create the term. One of the primary tasks for future researchers in the field of LD should be to capture that essence. There may be many imposter LD out there, but there are also many true LD. LD is composed of a heterogeneous population, one that includes various age levels, severities, and subtypes of disability.

The Research Task

Our job as researchers is to sort out these categories. We need a taxonomy that is conceptually sound, theoretically testable, and pragmatically useful. Through research, we need to hypothecate, describe, and eventually define LDness in its many forms and variations. Our research task is to systematically determine the essences of LD from the totality of characteristics and variables that present themselves to us. The following research questions may be posed.

What are the distinguishing characteristics common to all types of LD? Is it the presence of a significant degree of intraindividual difference among specified abilities (discrepancy)? Is it deficiencies in certain key abilities? Is it the presence of certain underlying mental processes dysfunctions? Or, is it some yet-to-be-identified factor(s)?

What are the characteristics that distinguish among the various subtypes of LD? Is there a suitable classification system for LD that has relevance to intervention, that is, can intervention programs be based on a reliable LD classification system? Is the label *learning disabilities* useful? If so, are the appropriate uses for the term *learning disabilities* in school and clinical practice?

THE DECISION-MAKING PROCESS

A helpful clue in determining answers to the aforementioned questions is to review how classification has been accomplished in the past. Traditionally, a clinical model (sometimes called a medical model) has been used. Clinicians and researchers have observed various behaviors and noted aspects of "differentness." They have tried to identify syndromes or groups of symptoms that together made an identifiable entity. They have tried to relate the deficient and/or discrepant behaviors to the subject's neurologic condition, and they have tried to derive psychoneurologic correlates.

It is the author's contention that future research must concentrate on the underlying logic of the decision-making process. If researchers are to obtain a true understanding of the phenomenon known as LD, they must use and examine that logic and process.

Diagnosis by Exclusion

The clinical approach generated a certain decision-making process. This process was usually initiated by determining what the learning-disabled person was *not*. This approach is sometimes referred to as *diagnosis by exclusion*. If we could say that a youngster was:

1. Not learning normally
2. Not sensorially impaired (vision or hearing)
3. Not mentally handicapped (generalized learning disorder)
4. Not seriously emotionally handicapped
5. Not environmentally deprived (as a primary condition)

he or she would then be classified as having a LD. The implication was also understood that a LD is related to some underlying central nervous system dysfunction.

We inferred that the person had a specific LD by ruling out all other logical conditions that might have caused him or her not to learn. This phase of the decision-making process is fraught with problems. Because of the high correlation among many of these factors, the unavailability of adequate assessment techniques and other problems, the exclusionary phase of the decision-making process is often given short shrift in practice.

Determining What He or She *Is*

Notwithstanding the difficulties inherent in attempting to rule out the effects of various conditions, the exclusionary phase has not been most difficult aspect of the decison-making process. Rather, the most difficulties have been experienced in specifying what he *is*. This is exemplified by the various disagreements about what domains to include: academics, processing, verbal, nonverbal, social, perceptual, and so on. The federal definition, together with various psychometric constraints and social factors, have led to the current prevailing practice of considering LD to be primarily *school*-learning problems, particularly reading disabilities.

Concepts Underlying the Decision-Making Process

Conceptually, the decision-making process for determining LD is simple. In its barest form, there are three phases to the process:

1. Someone must decide that the child *might* have a learning disability (referral).
2. Other conditions that might lead to learning failure must be identified (exclusions).
3. Characteristics must be identified that clearly indicate the presence of a LD (inclusions).

The details of how this is accomplished, the criteria for each element, and who bears responsibility for the decision-making process are open to disagreement and subject to wide variations in professional practice. The current federal definition is consistent with most of the historic concepts for LD. Our analysis of that definition (McGrady, 1980) indicates four major concepts to be operationalized:

1. There must be a *specific*, not a general, LD.
2. There must be a *discrepancy* among abilities, not merely deficits.
3. The discrepancies must be in certain *designated* areas.
4. *Exclusionary factors* must be ruled out.

The federal definition does not address the assumption that the condition is of neurologic origin. Thus, the accompanying regulations do not require any proof of the presence of such conditions.

RESEARCH RELATED TO THE DECISION-MAKING PROCESS

The decision-making process and underlying concepts for LD may have a certain face validity. However, the practices driven by these concepts have been extremely divergent. This has led to extreme differences of opinion as to the ultimate validity of these concepts or the decision-making processes. My own studies at the University of Arizona (McGrady & Anderson, 1974), the studies of Ysseldyke and associates at the University of Minnesota Learning Disability Institute in the late 1970s and early 1980s (Ysseldyke et al., 1983), and Chalfant's (1984) recent review of national practices in identifying learning-disabled students, supply ample evidence of the national confusion and the divergence of practice in the arena of eligibility and identification for LD.

University of Arizona Studies

Our studies at the University of Arizona assessed how consistently the underlying concepts of LD were being implemented in the decision-making process for declaring students eligible for LD services (McGrady & Anderson, 1974). We were interested in knowing how accurately professionals were following the commonly accepted conceptual models for defining LD at that time. It is important to note that this study was completed prior to the advent of Public Law 94-142.

As part of a national effort, 38 LD model demonstration centers from throughout the United States participated. The data consisted of information from questionnaires, on-site interviews, and review of pertinent operational materials. With this information, we carried out a thorough systems analysis and determined the decision-making process for each project. We then created a flow chart describing the entire process. From these charts and other information gathered, we classified each system as to which elements of LD concepts were actually used in declaring students eligible for LD services. Our study concentrated on the exclusionary and inclusionary factors used in such decisions. The results pointed very graphically to the national divergence in the practice of decision making for LD eligibility.

Exclusion Decisons

There was anything but unanimity in the consideration of exclusionary factors. Only 31 of the 38 projects (82%) even verified the presence of average or better intelligence as a condition for acceptance into their LD programs. Thus, one basic premise of LD, the lack of a generalized LD, was not even considered in the decision-making process of 18% of the projects. Following is a list of the percentages of projects that considered each of the other exclusionary factors: emotional disturbance (40%), visual handicap (29%), hearing handicap (29%), motor handicap (16%), or environmental disadvantage (5%). These percentages are startlingly low.

Inclusion Decisions

The projects were also divergent in their application of inclusionary decisions. We looked at two parameters of inclusionary decisons: type of disability (deficit and/or discrepancy), and ability area affected (academic and/or processing). Any one or a combination of these factors could have been used in decision making. With our research data, we asked the question: "Are children in the United States classified as LD primarily because of deficient performance (e.g., underachievement or other interindividual differences), or because of intraindividual discrepancies? The answer was equivocal. Both discrepancy criteria and deficit criteria were used. However, when a choice was made between the two, the result was predominantly to select discrepancies, (intraindividual differences) in the decision-making process for LD eligibility.

Selecting students primarily based on intraindividual differences has been reinforced by the operational interpretation and implementation of current federal regulations. LD has become synonymous with academic discrepancy in today's public schools. This has spawned a number of attempts to create discrepancy formulas for LD. Although the statistical sophistication of some measurements and comparisons have been improved, the ultimate test will have to be whether valid parameters are being assessed. Sephisticated measurement of invalid factors will lead only to additional types of invalid identifications.

When we examined the degree to which academic performance and psychological processes were considered, the lack of concurrence among projects was even greater. There was virtually no agreement among the 38 projects concerning how to use these factors in the LD eligibility decision-making process.

Conclusions

The findings from the University of Arizona study were so divergent that we concluded: "the only safe generalization is that there is little consistency regarding how children are operationally defined as LD" (McGrady & Anderson, 1974, p. 13). Furthermore, "our varied criteria for decision-making regarding eligibility for LD services, may explain much of the confusion in this country regarding placement and intervention for LD children. It may be the prime reason that we have an extremely heterogeneous population of children throughout the United States being served under the single rubric: Learning Disabilities." (McGrady & Anderson, 1974, p. 17).

University of Minnesota Studies

More recently, Ysseldyke and associates at the University of Minnesota have studied the decision-making process for LD eligibility in the late 1970s and early 1980s (Ysseldyke et al., 1983). By that time, Public Law 94-142 was being implemented. Consequently, most decisions were driven by attempts to be in compliance with the federal law and its associated regulations. This resulted in an emphasis on the determination of placement and a concern for establishing academic discrepancy as the major qualifying characteristic to determine eligibility.

Somewhat in agreement with our Arizona findings 10 years earlier, Ysseldyke et al. (1983) concluded that: "the special education team decision-making process, as currently employed in public school settings, is at best inconsistent" (p. 77), and "There currently is no defensible system for declaring students eligible for LD services" (p. 79). Furthermore, they postulated that "the classification *learning disabilities* does not meet the criteria for a classification system" (p. 79). The rationale for this conclusion was that, "There are no characteristics or behaviors specific to LD; that is, there are no characteristics that students labeled LD evidence that are not demonstrated with equal frequency by NLD students" (p. 79). Consequently, they have provided numerous examples of overinclusion and underinclusion from their research.

The technical inadequacy of many psychoeducational tests is cited as one possible cause for poor decision making. However, one is largely left to conclude from the several years of research at the Minnesota IRLD that either (1) there is no such thing as LD, or (2) there is no valid method yet known to truly identify a person as learning disabled.

The Minnesota report explicitly disdains the clinical approach as a way of solving problems of identification: "Those who advocate 'clinical judgment' in making eligibility decisions about students are going to have to rethink their position" (Ysseldyke et al., 1983, p. 82). This author is in disagreement with that conclusion. The Minnesota conclusion was based on studies in which various professionals and nonprofessionals were asked to differentiate among students based only on profiles of scores and psychometric measures. This assumes they were given valid, reliable, and appropriate data to judge. This flies in the face of previous judgments that have damned the uses of the currently available psychometric information as a basis for decision making.

We cannot on the one hand claim that current psychoeducational practice is invalid and unreliable and then use that very data to conclude that LD cannot be identified through the clinical method. The clinical decision-making process involves much more than a few psychometric test results.

The Minnesota conclusions have not gone without challenge. McKinney (1983) has argued that: "The report of the Minnesota institute, however, does not accurately reflect the state of the art in the field, and the work of this research group has potential for serious misinterpretation and misapplication" (p. 129). One of the unresolved issues targeted by McKinney was classification. He also challenged seriously the Minnesota conclusion that learning-disabled students are handicapped primarily by underachievement. Rather, McKinney says: "The work of the other institutes does establish deficits in information processing and adaptive behavior that would not be evident on the psychometric measures used by the Minnesota group" (p. 137).

It is clear from this discussion that there is continuing disagreement about the determination of eligibility for LD, uncertainty about the valid identity of LD, and confusion between the concepts of eligibility and identity.

U.S. Office of Special Education Programs Sponsored Research

During the years since the advent of Public Law 94-142, there have been continuing attempts to review eligibility requirements for LD at both the state and federal levels. The most comprehensive recent national review was reported in "Identifying learning disabled students: Guidelines for decision making" (Chalfant, 1984). Several findings and conclusions from that report are of interest.

As in the previous Arizona and Minnesota studies, Chalfant noted extreme variance in the national application of eligibility rules. His survey of all states indicated that, indeed, psychological processes, exclusionary factors, and discrepancies were being considered. But, they were being applied inconsistently across states or school districts.

One of Chalfant's major conclusions was: "the entire concept of 'eligibility' for receiving special help of any kind needs to be reviewed" (p. xviii).

Chalfant's review of national practices also revealed errors of both overinclusion and underinclusion. Among the many problems contributing to such errors were the validity and reliability of currently used test instruments and impaired decision-making processes used by the multidisciplinary teams. Chalfant's conclusion from a previous Colorado study (Shepard & Smith, 1981) is that "The end result of these problems is that students who are learning disabled may not be identified or receive the special education services they need, while other students, who are not learning disabled, are often identified and placed in services which are not appropriate for their needs'' (p. xiv).

CONCLUSIONS

In this chapter, I have provided a discussion of selected research on the decision-making processes used to determine eligibility for LD services. These studies have exposed a consistent national pattern of inconsistency over several years. The genesis of this inconsistency has been a failure to appreciate the interaction between the practical decisions regarding youngsters' qualifications for special services (eligibility) and the more theoretical determination of their taxonomic classification as faulty learners (identification).

Eligibility decisions are pragmatic decisions of the moment. Those decisions help solve a problem, based on available knowledge. In contrast, identification decisions should provide a more sound theoretical basis for intervention in the long term.

When making an eligibility decision, we are asking the question, ''He or she is eligible for *what?*'' The controlling variable in this equation is what services are available, that is, what can he or she be eligible for? When making an identification decision, we are asking the question, ''What is he or she? What is his or her categorization as a faulty learner?'' The answer, if our classification scheme is valid, will direct us to the type(s) of treatment(s) desired.

Currently, that subset of the total student population that we call learning disabled (or declare eligible for LD services) does not coincide with the subset that is truly learning disabled. We have made the faulty assumption that our labels represent a valid population within a consistent system of categorization. As we have seen from the literature, this is not true.

When the day arrives that we have a complete, valid classification system for learning failure and a set of valid and reliable procedures for determining identities within that classification system, the labels and the categories will match. Eligibility will be synonymous with identification, and identification will have meaning in terms of required interventions. Our goal as researchers should be to reach that day.

Cecil D. Mercer

To accept the task of bringing some unifying thoughts and direction to the topic of eligibility in LD is, in itself, a criterion "to be chosen" for somebody's special education services. This topic includes many complex issues and a myriad of different viewpoints among professionals. As reflected in this chapter, McGrady performed the task in a scholarly and thought-provoking manner. McGrady identifies and discusses a major issue (the mismatch between eligibility and identification) in LD. My reaction primarily involves differences in emphasis concerning the major issues and subsequent directions.

Definition versus Eligibility and Identification

It is true that the criteria for identification and eligibility in LD have not been congruent, but this phenomenon may not represent the crux of the problem. Theoretically, the criteria for both originate from the definition of LD. Thus, the mismatch between the two criteria either occurs from the use of different definitions or diverse operationalizations of the same definition. Arguments can be readily made that the latter position represents a major problem in determining who, in fact, are the learning disabled. A consensus among practitioners regarding the definition of LD appears to exist. In a review of state departments of education, Mercer, Hughes, and Mercer (1985) report that 96% of the states include academic disability component, 92% include the exclusion component, and 84% use the discrepancy factor.

In a study of 761 learning-disabled children and 901 non-learning-disabled children, Wilson (1985) concludes that the 1977 *Federal Register* definition and criteria can be successfully used. He reports that the application of both the academic discrepancy and exclusion components provide an adequate framework for identifying the learning disabled. Rather than abandoning current components in favor of new ones, Wilson encourages more systematic and intensive study of the current definition. Moreover, from a literature review and a national study of prevalence rates of special education categories, Hallahan, Keller, and Ball (1986) report that "the data do argue for the conclusion that the definition and identification criteria for learning disabilities are at least as well articulated, and perhaps more so, than those for other categories in special education'' (p. 13).

Given that some consensus exists concerning basic definitional concepts, the primary problem of identification and/or eligibility criteria is one of operationalization. Operationalization involves the valid measurement of the basic parameters of LD. The literature is replete concerning the inadequacies of tests, measures, and procedures used to identify LD. As long as inadequate measures and procedures are used and treated as valid, operationalization will continue as a primary problem in identification and eligibility.

Heterogeneity

McGrady points out that the heterogeneity of LD makes it difficult to identify LD in a consistent and valid manner. Although there is some agreement concerning primary constructs used in defining LD, the federal definition leaves much room for various interpretations. Theoretically, a youngster may qualify as learning disabled by exhibiting a discrepancy between ability and achievement in one or more of the seven areas listed in the 1977 *Federal Register* and by satisfying the conditions of the exclusion clause. Thus, at one end of the continuum, a student who exhibits one academic/discrepancy problem is labeled learning disabled. On the other hand, a learning-disabled student may display a discrepancy in all or any combination of the seven academic problem areas. Thus, within the guidelines of the 1977 *Federal Register*, numerous types of LD are apparent (e.g., math group, written expression group). Moreover, many professionals agree that a much broader range of LD characteristics exists beyond those characteristics included in the *Federal Register*. Specifically, they note cognitive characteristics (Wong, 1982) and socioemotional characteristics (Bryan & Bryan, 1986; Weller, Strawser, & Buchanan, 1985) that are commonly attributed to learning-disabled persons.

Perspective

The problems of operationalizing the basic and secondary constructs that exist in defining LD are very complex. Future researchers must not repeat past mistakes by treating all subjects labeled learning disabled as accurately labeled or homogeneous. McGrady says this emphatically in his statement that ''Researchers will need to be more selective in their choices of subjects for studies of learning disabilities.'' Perhaps the guidelines for subject selection offered by Smith et al. (1984) should be considered.

McGrady's concern about the psychometric properties of tests used to determine learning-disabled subjects is extremely pertinent. It is imperative that only "state of the art" tests be considered in determining who is learning disabled. Similarly, perhaps it is time to only use "state of the art" diagnosticians and well-trained multidisciplinary teams in conducting research. Reynolds (1985) claims that a viable state of the art in assessment is emerging and now needs implementing. Curriculum-based assessment, computer-assisted assessment, availability of better tests, and a rising "consciousness" about identification perhaps will provide the impetus and know-how for an improved state of affairs.

McGrady has certainly raised our "consciousness" about appropriate practices in the identification of learning-disabled persons. It is hoped that researchers will apply the "state of the art" knowledge and improve research efforts and services to persons who, in fact, are learning disabled.

REFERENCES

Bryan, T.H. & Bryan, J.H. (1986). *Understanding learning disabilities* (3rd ed.). Palo Alto, CA: Mayfield.

Chalfant, J.C. (1984). *Identifying learning-disabled students: Guidelines for decision-making.* Burlington, Vermont: Northeast Regional Resource Center, Trinity College.

Hallahan, D.P., Keller, C.E., & Ball, D.W. (1986). A comparison of prevalence rate variability from state to state for each of the categories of special education. *Remedial and Special Education, 7*(2), 8–14.

McGrady, H.J. (1980). Communication disorders and specific learning disabilities. In R. J. Van Hattum (Ed.), *Communication disorders: An introduction* (pp. 509–561). New York: Macmillan.

McGrady, H.J., & Anderson, C.S. (1974). *Screening and identification procedures in the child service demonstration programs.* Tucson, Arizona: University of Arizona.

McKinney, J.D. (1983). Contributions of the Institutes for Research on Learning Disabilities. *Exceptional Education Quarterly: 4,* 129–144.

Mercer, C.D., Hughes, C., & Mercer, A.R. (1985). Learning disabilities definitions used by state education departments. *Learning Disability Quarterly, 8,* 45–55.

Reynolds, C.R. (1985). Measuring the aptitude-achievement disrepancy in learning disability diagnosis. *Remedial and Special Education, 5*(3), 19–23.

Shepard, L., & Smith, M.L. (1981). *Evaluation of the identification of perceptual-communicative disorders in Colorado.* Boulder, Colorado: University of Colorado.

Smith, D.D., Deshler, D.D., Hallahan, D., Lovitt, T., Robinson, S., Voress, J.,

& Ysseldyke, J. (1984). Minimum standards for the description of subjects in learning disabilities research reports. *Learning Disability Quarterly,* 7(3), 221–225.

Weller, C., Strawser, S., & Buchanan, M. (1985). Adaptive behavior: Designator of a continuum of severity of learning disabled individuals. *Journal of Learning Disabilities, 1,* 200–204.

Wilson, L.R. (1985). Large scale learning disability identification: The reprieve of a concept. *Exceptional Children, 52,* 44–51.

Wong, B.Y.L. (1982). Understanding learning disabled students' reading problems: Contributions from cognitive psychology. *Topics in Learning and Learning Disabilities, 3*(2), 15–23.

Ysseldyke, James E., Thurlow, M., Graden, J., Wesson, C., Algozzine, B., & Deno, S. (1983). Generalizations from Five Years of Research on Assessment and Decision Making: The University of Minnesota Institute. *Exceptional Education Quarterly: 4,* 75–93.

CHAPTER 8

Eligibility and Identification Considerations in Postsecondary Education: A New but Old Dilemma

Susan A. Vogel

With the passage of Section 504 of the Rehabilitation Act of 1973 and the regulations written in 1977, qualified handicapped persons acquired the right to equal postsecondary educational opportunities. During these same years, learning-disabled persons identified in the 1970s as the result of the passage of the Education for All Handicapped Children Act of 1975 were reaching college age. Before the implementation of Section 504, there were some learning-disabled adults who succeeded in earning undergraduate, graduate, and professional degrees, but their numbers were small (Rawson, 1968; Rogan & Hartman, 1976; Silver & Hagin, 1984; Simpson, 1979). They graduated in spite of their learning disabilities (LD) with limited or no assistance or modifications, and, in fact, many became prominent figures in public life, the arts, and the sciences.

As a result of improvements in identification and intervention and Section 504, growing numbers of learning-disabled adolescents and adults applied to and were accepted at a variety of colleges and universities. These learning-disabled students were able to benefit from the accommodations developed for handicapped students with visual and hearing impairments (e.g., taped texts, extended time for exams, use of tape recorders, calculators, and word processors). Other institutions responded to Section 504 by developing comprehensive model programs for the learning disabled (Mangrum & Strichart, 1984; Scheiber & Talpers, 1984; Vogel, 1982; Vogel, 1987). Demand for these special programs increased rapidly in the early 1980s, so much so that these institutions expanded their programs and other colleges followed suit. Still the number of applicants exceeded the availability of services. Institutions offering comprehensive programs advised high school students to apply in their junior year or be prepared to be put on a waiting list for a semester or even a year.

The increase in applicants to these special programs should have, but did not, alert other institutions as to the large number of learning-disabled students already accepted at their institutions who would begin demanding services and the still larger number of learning-disabled applicants. As recently as 1981, Abrams and Abrams (1981) recommended that institutions provide diagnostic testing (an expensive service to provide) since ". . .the economic viability of this course of action is assured by the relatively small number of students identified as being learning disabled" (p. 1495).

In the last 4 years, this situation has changed dramatically. A large midwestern, urban, public university of 47,000 students perhaps typifies this change. In the 1978–1979 academic year, the Office of Handicapped Student Services at this institution assisted 17 learning-disabled students per quarter. By 1984–1985, the same staff (1½ full-time equivalent) tried to meet the needs of 100 learning-disabled students per quarter. Diagnostic services previously provided were no longer available through the university. Students were referred to the Division of Rehabilitation Services (DORS) and, if ineligible for DORS, to private clinicians and evaluation centers.

These hundreds of learning-disabled college students fall into at least four categories:

1. The perspective students who identify themselves as learning disabled in the application process and inquire about or request specific accommodations.
2. Self-identified learning-disabled students who have already been accepted and have enrolled in the institution and want assistance or request certain modifications to be successful in their courses (also a proactive approach).

3. Self-identified learning-disabled students who are in academic difficulty and want assistance or modifications to salvage a situation.
4. Students who self-refer or whose families, friends, teachers, advisers, or counselors refer them because they suspect a LD is causing them to experience academic difficulty or failure in college in spite of putting forth their best effort.

In all cases, colleges and universities need to develop systematic procedures, either to corroborate the diagnosis or to do differential diagnosis, to determine whether in fact the student is learning disabled, and, if so, if the academic difficulty is due to the LD or some other factors.

The necessity to develop such procedures for corroboration and diagnostic testing was made dramatically clear by Best, Howard, Kanter, Mellard, and Pearson (1986). They reported that approximately 40% of the students served as learning disabled did not meet the later established state-wide criteria for the identification of learning-disabled students in California community colleges, even though there had been a concerted effort on each campus to identify the learning disabled according to the federal definition.

Overinclusion is not a new dilemma in the field of LD. It appears that this problem also plagues school-aged samples of children placed in programs for the learning disabled (Shepard & Smith, 1983; Ysseldyke, Algozzine, Richey, & Graden, 1982); therefore, it is not surprising that these same persons, upon maturity, misidentify themselves as learning disabled. However, when they enroll in postsecondary settings and have difficulty meeting collegiate expectations, the problems recur and become magnified because of the limitations of the present data base, appropriately trained diagnosticians and other key personnel, appropriate diagnostic instruments to use in identification and assessment of adults suspected of being learning disabled, and the scarcity of funding (Vogel, 1985).

Postsecondary institutions (PSIs) vary widely in their response to the requirements of Section 504. They vary by virtue of the fact that they themselves are so different from one another. Some of the more relevant areas of contrast include whether the PSI is a 2-year, 4-year, graduate, or professional school; whether it is a technologic school or a fine arts or liberal arts college; and whether it has open admissions or competitive admissions and, if competitive, the stringency of the specific institution's admission criteria. The ways that PSIs vary will have a direct bearing on the procedures and eligibility criteria that they develop to identify and accommodate the ever-increasing numbers of students, either self-identified or suspected of being learning-disabled, who request services and/or modifications. The purpose of this chapter is to discuss some of the eligibility questions that each PSI has to address, to provide a sampling of responses that have been made by representative PSI's, and, lastly, to suggest some tentative recommendations for consideration, bearing in mind that there is no one solution for all PSIs.

THE DEFINITION OF LEARNING DISABILITIES IN ADULTS

Eligibility criteria and identification are directly related to the definition of LD. Because the field of LD is still young, the most widely accepted definition in PSIs is still the definition formulated in 1968 by the National Advisory Committee on Handicapped Children that refers to *children* with special LD. The major underlying disorders in basic psychological processes referred to in this definition that are sometimes present in learning-disabled adults include difficulties in discrimination (e.g., in perceiving differences between two similar but unlike sounds, words, or symbols), in retaining what is heard or seen, and in expressing what one knows, especially through written expressive language (Aaron & Baker, 1980; Blalock, 1981, 1982; Johnson, 1980; Vogel & Moran, 1982; Vogel, 1985).

The 1968 definition was revised several times, notably by the National Joint Committee on Learning Disabilities (NJCLD) (January 30, 1981) to include both young children and adults. It states:

> Learning disabilities is a generic term that refers to a heterogeneous group of disorders manifested by significant difficulties in the acquisition and use of listening, speaking, reading, writing, reasoning or mathematical abilities. These disorders are intrinsic to the individual and presumed to be due to central nervous system dysfunction.
>
> Even though a learning disability may occur concomitantly with other handicapping conditions (e.g., sensory impairment, mental retardation, social and emotional disturbance) or environmental influences (e.g., cultural differences, insufficient/inappropriate instructions, psychogenic factors), it is not the direct result of those conditions or influences.

A later position paper (NJCLD, January 30, 1983) elaborated on the continuing and changing needs of learning-disabled adults in higher education, in achieving their vocational/career goals, and in adjusting to the social and emotional demands of adulthood. For these needs to be met, at least two problems have to be addressed: (1) the lack of sufficient recognition and understanding of the persistence of

LD into adulthood, and (2) the heterogeneity within the population of identified learning-disabled persons.

There is a small, but increasing data base and pool of experience that can assist decision-makers and service providers in PSIs to begin to develop sound eligibility criteria. Some of the relevant aspects of the previously cited definitions that may require clarification and/or reformulation when applied to learning-disabled adults in postsecondary settings are in the areas of level of intellectual functioning, potential-achievement discrepancy, and failure to achieve.

Intellectual Functioning

According to the most widely accepted definitions, learning-disabled persons vary in intellectual ability, as do non-learning-disabled persons, from low average to superior cognitive abilities as measured by traditional IQ tests such as the Wechsler (1981). The question to be addressed is how do PSIs predict the learning-disabled students' chances of success if the student self-identifies. Many PSIs request a recent psychoeducational evaluation, including assessment of intellectual functioning. But how much predictive validity does this information have and if it does have some, what do we know about levels of intelligence and success in a variety of postsecondary settings?

Very limited data are available on the intellectual functioning of learning-disabled college students, and published data are limited to samples of learning-disabled students at 4-year undergraduate institutions (Cordoni, O'Connell, Ramaniah, Kurtz, & Rosenshein, 1981; Gajar, Murphy, & Hunt, 1982; Gajar, Murphy, Raymond, Pelco, & Baird, 1983; Johnson & Blalock, 1987; Rogan, 1981; Rogan & Hartman, 1976; Vogel, 1986). In a summary of these studies, Vogel (1986) found that learning-disabled college students upon entrance had average and above cognitive abilities and were fairly even in their verbal and nonverbal abilities unless specific selection criteria were used. However, in the LD college graduate samples, the Verbal IQ means were higher than the Performance IQ means. These data could be interpreted to indicate that higher education has a differential effect on specific aspects of cognitive functioning or that persons with higher verbal than performance abilities are more likely to complete their undergraduate education. Until more empirical data are available from a variety of postsecondary settings, it is extremely difficult to determine and generalize guidelines from these data.

It is also important to keep in mind that cognitive strengths and deficits provide only one type of information and in no way guarantee the student's success or failure in college. There are many other intraindividual factors (e.g., type and severity of LD, motivation, psychological and physical well-being, denial or willingness to accept help) as well as intrainstitutional factors (e.g., level of expectations, core or distribution requirements, foreign language requirement, type and intensity of available support services, and willingness to accommodate the learning-disabled student) that must be taken into consideration by decision-makers (Vogel, 1987). All these factors have the potential to have a profound influence on learning-disabled students' chances of successfully completing their programs of studies and receiving their degrees. It is also important to take into account the pattern of strengths and deficits as reflected in the Verbal and Performance IQ scores as well as the hierarchy of individual and grouped subtest scores within each scale (Vogel, 1986).

Potential-Achievement Discrepancy

In younger learning-disabled students, one is eligible for LD services if there is a significant discrepancy between potential and achievement. This simple statement belies the fact that there is still limited consensuality regarding the quantification of potential and achievement and determination of severity of the discrepancy (Chalfant, 1985). These problem areas become even more complex in learning-disabled adults who after almost two decades of living with their LD have learned to compensate, have received remedial help, and have learned how to present themselves exposing only their strengths rather than their disabilities. Often these students appear to admissions officers and later to faculty as having no observable discrepancy and after having risked disclosure are denied accommodations or modifications because they do not appear to meet this criterion in the definition. To make matters worse, at times their integrity and credibility are challenged and they are accused of using LD as an excuse to obtain a "privilege" reserved for the "truly" learning disabled.

There are other reasons for the difficulty and complexity of establishing the degree of discrepancy in learning-disabled adults, namely, the scarcity of specialists trained in assessment of learning-disabled adults, the limited number of appropriate and valid diagnostic instruments for this age range, and the costliness of psychoeducational evaluation for either the individual or the institution (Vogel, 1985). More significant than any of the aforementioned, however, is the fact that we know very little about the effect of varying degrees and types of residual deficits in learning-disabled adults on performance in postsecondary settings. It is also possible that the significance of the degree of discrepancy is influenced by the learning-disabled student's educational goals, expectations, and career goals, that is, the higher the goals, the greater the likelihood that even a small discrepancy will have a significant inhibiting effect.

Failure to Achieve

One of the significant parts of every definition of LD is that the learning-disabled child fails to learn in spite of adequate intelligence, emotional stability, and educational opportunity and the absence of other handicapping conditions. This concept has been extended to postsecondary educational opportunities in some PSIs; for example, failure to achieve is a prequisite to granting a modification or waiver of a distribution or course requirement. Some classic examples of the operationalization of this part of the definition is the requirement that all learning-disabled students must attempt to meet the foreign language requirement, at least for two semesters, repeating the course at least once, before they become eligible to appeal to the dean's office for a modification or waiver of this requirement.

Sensitivity to the history and development of institutions of higher education provides understanding from another vantage point. Often the older the university, the heavier the liberal arts emphasis, with the primary goal being education in the renaissance tradition. Core distribution requirements and foreign language competence are clearly coming from within this tradition. Moreover, with the availability of universal public high school education and concomitantly (or subsequently, as some would say) lower educational standards and attainment, PSI faculty are concerned about any changes in college curriculum that might imply lowering standards. Regardless of the reason for resistance to modifying the foreign language requirement, there are multiple effects of failure on otherwise capable and successful learning-disabled college students.

First, there is the obvious effect on the students' grade point average (GPA). Not only do learning-disabled students report that their GPA is lowered by the two Ds or Fs, but because they have given so much of their time to studying for the language course, they neglect the rest of their courses, and all of their grades suffered. Some have found another way around the requirement, but not without a rather dear price. They reported transferring from the B.A. degree program to the B.S. program because it did not have a foreign language requirement; however, this move necessitated them to compromise on their choice of major, graduate school, and ultimately career choice. There is also the psychological toll that is extracted by failing yet again, reliving painful childhood memories, undermining only recently acquired and tenuous self-confidence, and fueling the self-doubt that is the legacy of every learning-disabled adult.

An alternative to this interpretation of the failure-to-achieve clause is to consider failure, modifications, or waivers in the past as sufficient evidence to warrant similar procedures in the present. Alternatively, the college or university could request corroboration from psychoeducational assessment that describes the person's developmental history, the severity and type of LD, underlying auditory and visual processing strengths and deficits, and their educational implications. Some institutions are, in fact, using such alternatives to determine eligibility for modifications of certain requirements.

Decision making and procedures vary from one PSI to another. In most cases, petitions are presented to a dean. At Ohio State University, a different model is used. The Director of the LD program presents the petition for a curriculum modification supported by the results of diagnostic testing to a committee composed of a neurologist, a professor in human services education, and a speech pathologist. This committee deliberates and makes its recommendations to the academic department involved, and the final decision is jointly made.

Dinklage (1971) was one of the first to write sensitively about the very bright, successful Harvard University students who had what he called a "foreign language disability." He used a diagnostic battery of tests sensitive to language aptitude combined with careful case history taking and developmental history to substantiate the need for a waiver. It took another 10 years before some data were to be collected on PSIs response to this dilemma.

In 1982, the McBurney Learning Center of the University of Wisconsin–Madison developed a questionnaire to determine how other universities were responding to learning-disabled students' requests to modify or waive the foreign language requirement. Approximately 60% of those institutions that responded (32 of 53) who had a foreign language requirement modified it in some way, allowed a course substitution, or waived the requirement. Some of the creative alternatives that have been recommended include substituting the equivalent number of course credits in the history, culture, or literature of the foreign country; substituting a computer language (though caution is advised because some learning-disabled adults find computer programming languages as difficult as foreign languages owing to their memory deficits); modifying the instructional method (oral input rather than visual, i.e., tape vs. text, or vice versa); or modifying the evaluation method, that is, oral rather than written examinations, take-home or final essay versus in-class objective or essay exam.

For the learning-disabled student with a math disability (the dyscalculic), statistics is frequently the hurdle course. At George Washington University, a course in oral interviewing techniques was substituted, since both addressed the objective, namely, become a better researcher and consumer of research (Scheiber & Talpers, 1984).

IDENTIFICATION PROCEDURES

Screening

Screening was designed as a pro-active, preventive approach to reduce failure. Whereas in persons 3 to 21 years of age, *federal law* mandates "search and serve" provisions to identify students in need of special education, *Section 504 (Subpart E)* mandates equal educational opportunity, not search and serve. However, two states have become aware of the need to screen universally incoming students to identify those students who lack sufficient proficiency in basic skills to profit from college-level courses. The results of testing then become the basis for recommendations into appropriate courses, including developmental/remedial courses. New Jersey is unique in having instituted state-wide assessment of basic skills of all entering college students whether they will attend a 2-year, 4-year, public or private college or university. In California, students who meet the entrance requirements of the University of California system, by far the most selective institutions in the state of California, take a similar battery of tests. Other public and private 2-year and 4-year institutions scattered throughout the United States have developed their own battery of basic skills tests. However, to date, this information has not been used to do universal screening of incoming students for the purpose of identifying learning-disabled students who may be at risk of failure because of the severity of their basic skills deficiences.

Based on currently available data on special admissions procedures and criteria for eligibility to receive support services in PSIs (Vogel, 1986), it is clear that the percentage of students who are learning disabled will vary on individual campuses. The more stringent or competitive the admissions requirements, the fewer the number of learning-disabled students accepted, the higher their potential, and the less severe their basic skills deficiencies. Conversely, in those institutions with less stringent admissions standards (and even more so for open-admissions institutions), the higher the percentage of learning-disabled students, the lower their potential, and the more severe and generalized their deficits. Perhaps it will be in open-admissions institutions that the use of information from universal screening will become the necessary first step in the identification process. To date, only one such screening program has been reported in the literature. This exceptional program is worthy of note because it was developed not only in an institution with highly competitive admissions criteria but in a professional school, namely, New York University Dental School (Parks et al., 1982), as a preventive, pro-active approach to enhance the students' chances of successfully completing their degree. In summary, with one exception, universal screening of all entering students has not been a part of the identification of learning-disabled college students in PSIs.

The Referral Process

As previously described, in institutions that have developed a special program to serve the learning disabled, the students themselves, their parents, high school teachers, psychologists, or counselors often refer them to the college's Admissions Office and/or to the special program itself. Such students are often referred to as external applications to the program. Other students, already accepted to the institution, may also be referred to the Disabled Students Services Office (internal applicants). In a survey of the California Community Colleges more than 90% of all learning-disabled students were referred by one or more of six sources (Ostertag, Baker, Howard, & Best, 1982). In rank order of frequency, the sources were: (1) faculty, (2) the high school (the individual was not specified), (3) the Department of Rehabilitation, (4) a counselor, (5) a parent or relative, and (6) the students themselves.

Intake Interview

For most respondents (94%) in the California Community College system, who were located in institutions that provided formal LD student support services, an intake interview followed referral (Ostertag et al., 1982). Details regarding this important step in the identification process were not provided. An underlying assumption is that students (external or internal applicants) who refer themselves or follow through on a referral recommendation made by one of the aforementioned persons or an agency, are in fact learning disabled. In actuality, this assumption must be verified, and the intake interview is the first step in this process. However, to progress through this process, students must understand that they have to be active participants in this process, willing to reveal confidential information, and share aspects of their lives that they have spent a great deal of time and psychic energy trying to hide from view. Such openness is often an indication of the level of motivation for college work, level of self-knowledge, and level of understanding and acceptance of the fact of being learning disabled and what the student can do about it.

The interviewer's first task is to determine the student's reason for seeking assistance (Vogel, 1985). In most instances, the student is experiencing academic difficulty or anticipates difficulty and needs information regarding available support services or procedures for requesting modifications. After providing such information, the inter-viewer's next task is to seek corroboration that the student is in fact learning disabled. Each PSI establishes its own procedures for verifying the diagnosis, depending upon resources and available expertise. These procedures vary from a review of previous psychoeducational evaluations and/or high school records to detailed case history taking and extensive diagnostic testing.

Diagnostic Testing

Further additional psychoeducational testing is frequently necessary if the student has not been previously evaluated or to supplement dated diagnostic testing. The first question that must be addressed is: "Does this student have the intellectual ability to do college-level work?" The most widely accepted measure of intelligence in adults used most consistently in working with learning-disabled college students is the Wechsler Adult Intelligence Scale Revised (Wechsler, 1981). As discussed earlier, one of the characteristics of learning-disabled college students is average or above intellectual functioning. In addition to determining the level of intelligence, intraindividual discrepancies or pattern of abilities unique to each individual can be analyzed (Vogel, 1986).

The extent of testing will vary depending upon whether or not the services to be provided include individualized instruction and remediation in addition to the use of compensatory strategies and course support. The scarcity of standardized, reliable, and valid diagnostic instruments for the assessment of learning-disabled adults requires that the diagnostician be skillful in eliciting important qualitative information during the testing. It is helpful to explain to the students that our tools are imperfect, that diagnostic testing involves a partnership, and that the value of the information will be in direct proportion to their willingness to be actively involved in the diagnostic testing process. The purpose for administering each test or group of tests and, when appropriate, how a test relates to academic achievement or everyday life functioning should be explained. Asking students to analyze why a task was difficult or easy, especially when the results seem to contradict observational data and/or case history information also provides important additional information.

Assessment should include those areas of functioning that have been observed to be residual problems in learning-disabled adults (Vogel, 1985) and that may affect success in college. Often included are measures of receptive and expressive oral and written language in the areas of semantics, syntax, and morphology; reading skills, including word attack and comprehension of single words and paragraphs read orally and silently, and reading rate; mathematics reasoning and computation; verbal and nonverbal concept formation; study habits and attitudes; and selected auditory and visual processing, including perception, discrimination, memory, sequencing, analysis, and synthesis. This latter part of the assessment provides important diagnostic teaching information for remediation, especially for the widespread and severe spelling disabilities that plague many learning-disabled adults (Vogel, 1985; Vogel & Moran, 1982).

FUTURE RESEARCH DIRECTIONS

A functional definition of LD needs to be developed for identification and eligibility in postsecondary settings that takes into consideration the developmental stages of the learning-disabled adult learner (Cohen, 1985; Polloway, Smith, & Patton, 1984) and the interaction of the residual manifestations of the LD, the demands of the PSI, and previous and currently available intervention and educational experiences. Also to be explored is how the characteristics of LD will differ in adults at different ranges of intellectual functioning (Cordoni et al, 1981). If in fact there is a significantly different pattern of symptomatology and/or cognitive abilities as has been suggested by Cordoni et al.'s preliminary study, the definition and eligibility criteria could reflect these differences.

Samples of learning-disabled students attending different PSIs representing the entire spectrum of options, type and severity of LD, and range of cognitive abilities should be carefully described, along with institutional characteristics, particularly the admissions process, identification procedures, and eligibility criteria. At each institution, the Office of Handicapped Students Services could perhaps serve as the liaison to a national center for the study of learning-disabled adults in college settings, similar to the national data banks and research institutes established for the study of non-learning-disabled college students (Astin, Hemond, & Richardson, 1982). In this way, the goundwork could be laid for long-term follow-up studies on degree completion, graduate studies, employment history, career paths, life adjustment and satisfaction, and personal effectiveness. These are the ultimate goals of all education and intervention.

James C. Chalfant

Dr. Vogel presents an accurate and insightful overview of the major considerations related to eligibility and identification of learning-disabled students seeking admission to PSIs. This chapter also highlights three significant questions or issues about postsecondary opportunities for the learning disabled:

1. How receptive are PSIs to the idea of admitting and supporting learning-disabled students?
2. What are the success capabilities of learning-disabled students in different postsecondary settings?
3. What must be done to develop effective intake procedures for the learning disabled in postsecondary settings?

The Receptivity Issue

Receptivity to admitting and serving learning-disabled students depends upon the mission and the philosophy of the PSI. The mission and philosophy will vary between 2-year schools, 4-year colleges, graduate institutions, professional schools, technical schools, and fine arts or liberal arts colleges.

These are difficult times for education at all levels, including the primary, intermediate, middle school, secondary, and postsecondary levels. Reductions in financial resources for many PSIs have contributed to changes in mission and phiolosophy. For example, confronted with reduced financial resources, it is not surprising that large universities speak of raising their standards for admission and graduation, eliminating programs that do not generate sufficient funds, emphasizing research and publications, increasing graduate programs and decreasing undergraduate programs, and becoming "research universities."

Although lip service is given to "service activities," university staff are seldom rewarded for service functions. With limited resources, it is understandable why university administrators are reluctant to invest their resources on a small population of students who are often perceived as having a high probability of failure at the postsecondary level. At this time, many postsecondary schools lack the information necessary to decide whether or not to invest their resources on learning-disabled students. In fact, this kind of program would be a new concept for many PSIs. Much education of PSIs must be done. A research base is also necessary to influence mission, philosophy, and receptivity.

The Success Capability Issue

The key to influencing receptivity for serving the learning disabled among postsecondary schools is to demonstrate that these students can meet their expectations for success with certain program modifications. This will require a definition for learning-disabled adults that will be clear for administrators in postsecondary settings. A second requirement is to develop eligibility requirements for determining which students might succeed in different postsecondary settings.

I agree with Vogel's analysis of the factors that need to be studied and refined, including the student's: (1) perception of what is seen and heard; (2) ability to retain information; (3) ability to express himself or herself through speaking, reading, writing, or mathematics; and, (4) a level of estimated intellectual potential to conceptualize and learn concepts taught at the postsecondary levels.

The Admission and Support Issue

The third issue that needs to be resolved is the establishment of effective intake and support procedures for learning-disabled students. Models need to be developed at the secondary level for the assessment of student capabilities for postsecondary work. A vocational evaluation is equally important. Both are needed to make a preliminary determination of the student's potential capability and vocational interests and skills. These kinds of information are necessary in selecting the most appropriate kind of PSI for application.

There is need to develop entrance requirements for the various postsecondary opportunities. One student might have the potential to succeed at a university, whereas another student would be more successful at a technical school.

Student service programs for the disabled need to develop models for the admission and support of learning-disabled students. Intake interviews, diagnostic programs, and student support strategies such as taped texts, extended time for exams, use of tape recorders, calculators, remediation, readers, and other course support need to be implemented and tested.

One approach to building postsecondary experiences for learning-disabled students is to initiate experimental programs. This will help develop procedures and provide a data base for making as strong an argument as possible for creating postsecondary opportunities for the learning disabled.

Vogel's analysis of the issues related to postsecondary education and the directions for future research that are suggested in this chapter present a clear outline of the work that needs to be accomplished in postsecondary education for the learning disabled.

REFERENCES

Aaron, P.G., & Baker, C. (1980). The neuropsychology of dyslexia in college students. In R.N. Malatesha & L.C. Hartlage (Eds.), Neuropsychology and cognition (Vol. 1, pp. 128–146). Augusta, GA: NATO Advanced Study Institute of Neuropsychology and Cognition.

Abrams, H., & Abrams, R. (1981). Legal obligations toward the post-secondary learning disabled student. Wayne Law Review, 27:1475–1499.

Astin, A., Hemond, M., and Richardson, G. (1982). The American freshman: National norms for fall 1982. Los Angeles: American Council on Education and University of California at Los Angeles.

Best, L., Howard, R., Kanter, M., Mellard, D., & Pearson, M. (April 1, 1986). Program standards and eligibility criteria for learning disabled adults in California community colleges. Presentation at the 64th Annual Convention of the Council for Exceptional Children, New Orleans.

Blalock, J. (1981). Persistent problems and concerns of young adults with learning disabilities. In W. Cruickshank & A. Silvers (Eds.), Bridges to tomorrow: The best of ACLD (Vol. II). Syracuse: Syracuse University Press.

Blalock, J. (1982). Persistent auditory language deficits in adults with learning disabilities. Journal of Learning Disabilities, 15, 604–609.

Chalfant, J. (1985). Identifying learning disabled students: A summary of the national task force report. Learning Disabilities Focus, 1, 9–21.

Cohen, J. (1985). Learning disabilities and adolescence: Developmental considerations. In S. Feinstein (Ed.), Adolescent psychiatry (Vol. XII). Chicago: University of Chicago Press.

Cordoni, B., O'Connell, J., Ramaniah, N., Kurtz, J., & Rosenshein, K. (1981). Wechsler adult intelligence score patterns for learning disabled young adults. Journal of Learning Disabilities, 14, 404–407.

Dinklage, K. (1971). Inability to learn a foreign language. In G. Blaine & C. McArthur (Eds.), Emotional problems of the student (2nd ed.). New York: Appleton-Century-Crofts.

Federal Register. (1977, August), 42 (163).

Gajar, A., Murphy, J., & Hunt, F. (1982). A university program for learning disabled students. Reading Improvement, 19, 282–288.

Gajar, A., Murphy, J., Raymond, M. Pelco, L., and Baird, N. (1983, April). *The learning disabled university student: A synopsis of applied research.* Paper presented at the International CEC conference, Detroit, MI [ERIC REID ED235 598 EC 152 550].

Johnson, D. (1980). Persistent auditory disorders in young dyslexic adults. *Bulletin of the Orton Society, 30,* 268–276.

Johnson, D. & J. Blalock. (Eds.), (1987). *Young adults with learning disabilities.* Orlando: Grune & Stratton.

Mangrum, C., & Strichart, S. (1984). *College and the learning disabled student.* New York: Grune & Stratton.

National Joint Committee on LD. January 30, 1981.

National Joint Committee on LD. January 30, 1983.

Ostertag, B., Baker, R., Howard, R., & Best, L. (1982). Learning disabled programs in California community colleges. *Journal of Learning Disabilities, 15,* 535–538.

Parks, A., Antonoff, S., Drake, C., Olivier, C., Sedita, J., Weiss, I., & Daddi, B. (1982). Screening for specific learning disabilities among dental students. *Journal of Dental Education, 46,* 586–591.

Polloway, E.A., Smith, J.D., & Patton, J.R. (1984). Learning disabilities: An adult development perspective. *Learning Disability Quarterly, 7,* 179–186.

Rawson, M. (1968). *Developmental language disability: Adult accomplishments of dyslexic boys.* Baltimore: Johns Hopkins Press.

Rogan, L. (1981). *Longitudinal studies of LD children.* Paper presented at the Conference on Young Adults with Learning Disabilities. Northwestern University.

Rogan, L., & Hartman, L. (1976). *A follow-up study of learning disabled children as adults. Final report.* Evanston, IL: Cove School (ERIC Document Reproduction Service No. ED 163-728).

Scheiber, B., & Talpers, J. (1984). *Campus access for learning disabled students.* Washington, D.C., Closer Look.

Shepard, L., & Smith, M. (1983). An evaluation of the identification of learning disabled students in Colorado. *Learning Disability Quarterly, 6,* 115–127.

Silver, A., & Hagin, R.A. (1984). Specific reading disability: Follow-up Studies. *American Journal of Orthopsychiatry, 34(1),* 93–102.

Simpson, E. (1979). *Reversals: A personal account of victory over dyslexia.* Boston: Houghton Mifflin.

Vogel, S.A. (1982). On developing LD college programs. *Journal of Learning Disabilities, 15,* 518–528.

Vogel., S.A. (1985). Learning disabled college students: Identification, assessment, and outcomes. In D. Duane & C.K. Leong (Eds.), *Understanding learning disabilities: International and multidisciplinary views.* New York: Plenum Press.

Vogel, S.A. (1986). Levels and patterns of intellectual functioning among LD college students: Clinical and educational implications. *Journal of Learning Disabilities, 19,* 71–79.

Vogel, S.A. (1987). Issues and concerns in LD college programming. In D. Johnson & J. Blalock (Eds.), *Young adults with learning disabilities.* Orlando: Grune & Stratton.

Vogel, S., & Moran, M. (1982). Written language disorders in learning disabled college students: A preliminary report. In W. Cruickshank & J. Lerner (Eds.), *Coming of age: The best of ACLD* (Vol. III). Syracuse: Syracuse University Press.

Wechsler, D. (1981). *Adult intelligence scale—revised*. New York: Psychological Corp.

Ysseldyke, J., Algozzine, B., Richey, L., & Graden, J. (1982). Declaring students eligible for learning disability services: Why bother with the data? *Learning Disability Quarterly, 5,* 37–44.

PART IV

Assessment

CHAPTER 9

Assessment Issues in Learning Disabilities Research

Doris J. Johnson

The purpose of this chapter is to raise several issues regarding assessment for research and instruction in learning disabilities (LD). Given the heterogeneity of the population and disciplines involved in research, it is important to consider ways of achieving replicable investigations to strengthen the scientific base in the field. The lack of consistent criteria for definition and diverse nomenclature make the task particularly difficult. Although superordinate labels such as "learning disability," "poor reader," and "language disorder" are useful for certain purposes, they fail to highlight the specific attributes of the individual. Furthermore, general terms for cognitive processes such as "perception," "coding," and "sequencing" are used differently across disciplines; thus, it is often difficult to compare findings. While the list of factors in this paper is not exhaustive, several issues related to the attributes of the subjects, experimental tests, and procedures will be discussed.

In many respects, our task as researchers, diagnosticians, and educators resembles a massive class inclusion exercise in which we are required to identify critical attributes of sets and subsets of learners. The task is exceedingly complex, not only because of the heterogeneity

of the population but also because of the multiple purposes of classification. The procedures and criteria used for screening are different
from those needed for classification and eligibility (Myklebust, 1968);
these, in turn, are different from those needed for precise remediation or research. Furthermore, the bases for grouping vary with the
theoretical orientation, questions, and background of the investigator.

It is exciting to see professionals from many disciplines involved
in LD research. Scholars from cognitive psychology, linguistics, neuropsychology, medicine, reading, developmental psychology, and
anthropology add significantly to our understanding of these complex
problems. The methodologies from these fields highlight characteristics of children, adolescents, and adults over time in different contexts. However, because terminology across discipline varies,
investigators are encouraged to provide definitions of processes and
procedures. While diversity of theory and ideas is healthy, ambiguity
may result in confusion or overgeneralizations.

POPULATION ATTRIBUTES

Most people in the field of LD recognize the heterogeneity of the
population. In fact, definitions of LD generally list several areas of
potential underachievement, including listening, speaking, reading,
writing, spelling, mathematics, and/or various areas of nonverbal
behavior (Federal Register, 1977). Disturbances in psychological
processes such as attention, memory, or conceptualization may also
be present. Numerous task force reports (Chalfant, 1985; Chalfant &
Scheffelin, 1969; Clements, 1966), marker variables studies (Keogh et
al., 1982), and research on subtypes (McKinney, 1984; Satz & Morris,
1981) all emphasize the range of symptoms observed. Yet all too often,
the term *learning disability* is used synonymously with reading problems or school failure. Such is not the case. Some, but not all people
with LD have problems reading; some, but not all, have disorders of
oral language, reading, and mathematics.

Although the definition indicates that there is a discrepancy
between mental ability and achievement, the word *achievement* does
not necessarily mean *academic* performance (deHirsch, Jansky, &
Langford, 1966; Denhoff, Hainsworth, & Hainsworth, 1971). Preschool
children may have significant discrepancies between their nonverbal
ability and language (see Case 1 in Table 9-1) or between their verbal
ability and nonverbal performance as illustrated in Case 2. Children
such as the latter may have only minimal academic problems but may
have serious difficulty with spatial orientation, facial recognition,
social perception, picture interpretation, play, and certain types of

TABLE 9-1.
Intelligence Profiles of Two Preschool Children

CASE 1

Verbal Scaled Scores		Performance Scaled Scores	
Information	4	Animal House	10
Vocabulary	3	Picture Completion	10
Arithmetic	6	Mazes	9
Similarities	5	Geometric Design	9
Comprehension	6	Block Design	12

CASE 2

Verbal Scaled Scores		Performance Scaled Scores	
Information	14	Animal House	5
Vocabulary	14	Picture Completion	9
Arithmetic	11	Mazes	5
Similarities	18	Geometric Design	4
Comprehension	13	Block Design	5

problem solving (Johnson & Myklebust, 1967; Myklebust, 1975). At the upper age levels, disorders of attention, orientation, and organization may also be overlooked if LD are perceived only as academic disorders.

Failure to recognize the range of potential problems may limit eligibility for services and/or the numbers of attributes on which subjects might be subtyped. In addition, data from experimental or diagnostic tests could be misinterpreted. For example, if decoding is assessed without considering whether the subjects might be unable to repeat words because of expressive language disorders, conclusions drawn about their reading ability may be incorrect. Similarly, if reading comprehension is assessed by retelling a passage without regard to the subject's conceptualization, auditory receptive and expressive language, as well as decoding, the final assumptions may be inaccurate. Educational recommendations may also be questionable. For example, the child in Case 2 (Table 9-1) had extended latencies on word retrieval tests not becaue of language problems, but because of picture interpretation difficulties.

Because of the heterogeneous symptoms, diagnosticians and researchers should consider the appropriateness of tasks used in experiments. Although reliable and valid measures are needed, the issue of "culture fairness" must be raised when working with atypical learners. This is obvious when testing the physically handicapped, deaf, blind, or bilingual, but it is sometimes overlooked when studying the learning disabled, in part, because of their subtle problems. One would not use auditory verbal intelligence tests with the deaf or perceptual-motor tasks with the physically handicapped. Nor would we assess intelligence of poor readers with tests that require reading. However, less obvious language, attention, perceptual-motor problems, and so on may interfere with the evaluation of mental ability and other functions. Examples of ways in which various learning problems interacted with intelligence levels of preschool children are shown in Table 9-2. Child A had a serious auditory receptive language disorder; Child B had poor expressive language but good comprehension; Child C had no language disorders but had visual processing disorders, picture interpretation difficulties, and perceptual-motor deficits.

Clinical diagnostic batteries may be extensive enough to detect such patterns of problems; however, since fewer tests are used in most research studies, it is helpful to determine whether the subjects had the prerequisite skills to perform a particular task. This may be done with either pretesting or post-testing. For example, before drawing conclusions about a student's knowledge of capitalization rules in writing, the subjects might be asked to copy letters or write them from memory to make certain that motor planning and visualization deficits were not the reasons for poor performance. In other words, the diagnostician/investigator is constantly asking questions such as "Am I really measuring reading?" "Will this procedure tell what I want to know about a particular skill?"

In attempting to respond to these questions, it is evident that most tests assess multiple functions. Consequently, they test more than they purport to measure, particularly with exceptional learners. Even tests of auditory and visual acuity assess more than hearing and vision. Measures of visual acuity require visual perception, spatial orientation, and/or the ability to name letters or pictures.

Similarly, tests of reading comprehension typically require conceptualization, background knowledge, memory, language

TABLE 9-2.

Performance of Three Learning-Disabled Children

Test	Child A	Child B	Child C
WPPSI Verbal	62	85	116
WPPSI Performance	110	92	85
Leiter	104	98	91
Binet	74	81	100
Peabody Picture Vocabulary	81	108	92

comprehension, decoding and other processes, any one of which may be deficient among the learning disabled. Oral arithmetic tests often measure auditory memory, language comprehension, and other skills as well as arithmetic. Therefore, as indicated previously, one might either prescreen or post-test for specific skills. Cohen (1983), for example, studied written language skills in normal and learning-disabled students and ruled out, by prescreening, any subjects who had oral language, reading, and visual-motor problems. Blalock (1977) post-tested the subjects in her study of causal thinking to determine whether disorders of visual perception, language comprehension, vocabulary, or verbal expression impeded their performance. The field needs more than simple comparisons of experimental and control groups, particularly in determining *why* certain subjects failed.

In general, studies should include as much detail as possible about the attributes of both the experimental and control groups, particularly if generic labels such as "good and poor readers" are used. In some studies, these terms represent students in the upper and lower quartiles of a class (none of whom may be underachieving on a standardized measure). In other studies, the subjects met specific criteria on tests; whereas in others, reading levels were estimated from performance in textbooks.

Criteria for both inclusion and exclusion of all subjects should be specified. Control groups drawn from regular classrooms often contain children with a wide range of mental ability and achievement, including the gifted. Therefore, both upper and lower levels of ability should be noted. Data regarding the number of subjects who failed to meet the criteria for an experiment also provide the reader with additional perspectives about the population, tests, and experimental measures used.

Studies that include multiple attributes of two or more groups contribute to an understanding of learning problems as well as theories of development. For example, Frith (1980) compared the spelling of (1) good readers-good spellers, (2) good readers-poor spellers, and (3) poor readers-poor spellers. Similarly, studies of attention that identified subgroups with and without LD were useful for both scientific and educational purposes (Dykman, Ackerman, & Holcomb, 1985), as were those done to detect subtypes of reading, spelling, and arithmetic disorders (Rourke, 1978).

While such projects often require more subjects and longer test batteries, eventually they provide relevant data for the field. As professionals from many disciplines become involved in LD, researchers should be aware of the entire range of problems. Those who have worked only with normal children may not realize how minor problems of input or output can influence performance and that many problems co-occur among the learning disabled.

ATTRIBUTES OF THE ENVIRONMENT

Future research will be strengthened if investigators provide descriptions of settings from which the groups were drawn. Factors such as class size, curriculum, overall make-up of the group, expectancies, type of school and home environment, socioeconomic levels, sex and race, and parents' education and occupation all add to our understanding of learning and LD.

As more studies of children in naturalistic settings are done, detailed descriptions of the physical environment, including toys, books, and other equipment, are needed to fully interpret the data or replicate the study. For example, results on studies of play will vary with the number and types of toys, degree of structure, numbers of children in the group, and so on. All variables need not be controlled, but details of the environment and available materials will aid readers of the study.

NOMENCLATURE AND TERMINOLOGY

Because of the lack of clear nosology in many fields, it is suggested that definitions, descriptions of tests, rating scales, scoring procedures, and settings be provided. Currently, studies on topics such as "auditory discrimination" or "word recognition" are confusing and difficult to interpret, since the same term is used for quite different psychological processes. For instance, "auditory discrimination" may refer to a relatively low level process, such as the perception of a vowel or consonant, or to more complex processes, including auditory sequential memory, analysis and synthesis of sounds, or production of words.

ATTRIBUTES OF TESTS,
EXPERIMENTAL PROCEDURES, AND MEDIA

To achieve a more replicable body of literature, studies should provide a description of experimental tasks, including content, formats, directions, materials, reinforcement, and other pertinent details. Test descriptions aid readers in this country and abroad who may not be familiar with the instruments. Several international scholars have said that the term *grade level* is meaningless in countries with differing levels of organization in school systems. Age level and standard scores provide a better frame of reference for interpreting the research.

In our studies, we frequently describe tests by using a system of task analysis that includes details about the nature of the input and output as well as level and type of content (Johnson, 1981). For example, spelling tests that require identification of the correct word (e.g., duty, duties) involve a visual-verbal input with a recognition response, whereas writing from dictation requires the conversion of an auditory-verbal input to a visual-motor response. Both are different from tests requiring oral spelling or typing. Subtle disturbances of input, integration, or output can alter performance.

A description of the task format and general organization of items might be noted, particularly when studying children with attention disorders. Factors such as number of items exposed at one time, rate of presentation, and opportunities for feedback and reinforcement are all relevant, even when they are not a part of the primary experiment.

The degree of structure provided should also be described, since many learning-disabled children have problems with self-organization, task comprehension, and ambiguous instructions. Behaviors surrounding the experimental tasks frequently differentiate the controls from experimental subjects. Observations of task comprehension, time needed to complete the experiment (even when time is not a variable), and number of reminders to stay on task yield data regarding learning and performance (James, 1976).

An inspection of many achievement and language tests indicates that type of foils many influence results. Again, this may be a part of the experiment, but when choosing reading tests, for example, it is helpful to note that some foils are both semantically and graphically related to the target word, whereas others are all graphically similar. Thus, depending upon the decoding or verbal skills of the person, grade levels may vary considerably.

Performance may also vary with the organization of items. For instance, on mathematics tests, subjects who have difficulty shifting a mental set may perform better if all problems are organized by arithmetic operation rather than by level of difficulty.

The number of items used to test a given rule or principle is relevant. Most standardized tests are screening measures at best and, as such, are insufficient for determining the subject's level of rule acquisition and automaticity. Diagnostic probes are often needed to determine whether conventional or idiosyncratic rules were used or whether the response was random (Alley & Deshler, 1979).

Although standardized tests as essential for both diagnosis and research, samples of performance in more natural settings provide important information about children and adults with LD (Hedley & Baratta, 1985). They are particularly important for making placement decisions. Children with mild to moderate problems may function quite well on highly structured tasks and yet perform poorly when required to apply several skills simultaneously. In addition, some children sustain near average performance for a short period of time, but because of problems of automaticity, rule application, or attention, they cannot complete lengthy assignments at school or work.

The opposite pattern may also be observed. Some perform better in natural settings with redundant contextual clues. Poor readers, for example, may be unable to read word lists but can use background knowledge and prediction for reading signs, menus, and application forms. Thus, generalizations about performance across contexts should be made cautiously.

While it may be impossible to include complete scripts and coding systems used for analyzing performance in professional journals, there should be an indication that schema were developed for purposes of reliability. Researchers who study complex processes such as discourse and adult-child interaction need theory-driven observations and data analyses as well as an understanding of unique characteristics of the population. Exceptional learners often "force" the investigator to think of new ways to present tasks or code data.

In a study of play, for example, Cable (1981) found fewer differences of pretend behavior among normal and learning-disabled children when she coded only nonverbal behavior than when she coded both verbal and nonverbal responses.

ATTRIBUTES OF INTERVENTION METHODS

Intervention studies are even more difficult to compare and replicate because of the number of potential variables to be manipulated or controlled. While there are some excellent chapters to guide research designs for reading methods (Calfee & Piontkowski, 1984), a few additional factors will be emphasized. Unless one has taught exceptional children or designed instructional research, one may not realize the problems in using a word such as *method*. In fact, few educators adhere to *a* method per se. Rather, they use general principles in a relatively systematic sequence. Or, they use methods for teaching a specific skill—not an entire area of achievement such as written language or mathematics. Yet "methods" are sometimes classified in the literature according to single attributes with little regard for other significant variables. For example, reading methods are often classified as "multisensory" because of an emphasis on auditory, visual, and tactual training. However, vocabulary, sentence structure, and sequence of activities may be very different. Thus, descriptions of significant variables such as type of vocabulary, orthography, syntax, content, degree of structure, modes of input, output, and other factors add clarity (Johnson, 1968).

Terms such as *prescriptive* or *direct teaching* also tend to be ambiguous. The reader needs information regarding the theoretical rationale, objectives, specific content, scope, sequence, forms of instruction, reinforcement, and many other variables. This information is also needed for describing instructional programs on computers.

Studies designed to explore instructional levels or competence/performance discrepancies should include descriptions of the media and types of probes used. For replicability, the rationale and plan for questioning should be specified. Although decisions are necessarily based on responses of the subjects, the objectives for eliciting data and the procedures for probing and coding information provide clarity.

In summary, future research in LD may have a stronger scientific base and greater replicability if attributes of the subjects and procedures are defined.

RESPONSE

Bernice Y.L. Wong

Doris Johnson brings to bear on the topic of assessment her wealth of clinical knowledge and insight. Interestingly, the issues she raises in her chapter have equal relevance for both the researcher and the practitioner. These issues pertain to interpretation of research data and clinical assessment data.

The first issue concerns the need for precision in definitions. To illustrate such need, Johnson highlights a very subtle ambiguity in the definitional clause of descrepancy between ability and achievement. She points out how erroneous it is to interpret underachievement exclusively in the framework of academics.

The second issue concerns validity of assessment and experimental tasks used. The importance of this issue regarding assessment and experimental data is obvious.

The third and fourth issues concern the need for more details in subject descriptions and descriptions of settings. Subsequently,

Johnson discusses issues that stem from attributes of tests, experimental procedures, and media and attributes of intervention methods. Regarding these latter issues, Johnson drives home the importance of writing for a broader audience, one that is not restricted to North America. This means that researchers should use a more cross-cultural perspective in subject descriptors, that is, describe subjects and settings in ways that are meaningful to readers from outside North America. In short, writing "reader-based prose" is insufficient. ("Reader-based prose" is a term coined by Linda Flowers, a cognitive psychologist who theorizes and researches cognitive processes in composing. It means that the writer writes with the audience in mind, thus he or she tries to write clearly for the sake of promoting readers' comprehension of the author's messages).

To conclude, the issues of assessment that Johnson raises in her chapter reveal her clinical shrewdness. These issues represent valuable pointers that may be overlooked simply because they appear so obvious. Yet neither researchers nor practitioners can afford to dismiss them, because, ultimately, they pertain to data interpretation. Assessment data confounded by inattention to the kinds of issues raised by Johnson lead the clinician to erroneous diagnosis and remedial programming. Similar confounds lead the researcher to a Type I error. These errors are simply too costly for any clinical diagnostician and researcher to commit!

REFERENCES

Alley, G., & Deshler, D. (1979). *Teaching the learning disabled adolescent: Strategies and methods.* Denver: Love.

Blalock, J. (1977). *A study of conceptualization and related abilities in learning disabled and normal preschool children.* Unpublished doctoral dissertation, Northwestern University, Evanston.

Cable, B. (1981). *A study of play behavior in learning disabled and normal preschool boys.* Unpublished doctoral dissertation, Northwestern University, Evanston.

Calfee, R., & Piontkowski, D. (1984). Design and analysis of experiments. In D. Pearson (Ed.), *Handbook of reading research.* New York: Longman.

Chalfant, J. (1985). Identifying learning disabled students: A summary of the national task force report. *Learning Disabilities Focus, 1,* 9–20.

Chalfant, J., & Scheffelin, M. (1969). *Central processing dysfunctions in children* (NINDS Monograph No. 9). Bethesda, MD: U.S. Department of Health, Education, and Welfare, National Institute of Neurological Diseases and Stroke.

Clements, S. (1966, January). *Minimal brain dysfunction in children* (Public Health Service publication No 1415). Washington, DC: U.S. Department of Health, Education, and Welfare.

Cohen, C. (1983). *Writers' sense of audience: Certain aspects of writing by sixth grade normal and learning disabled children.* Unpublished doctoral dissertation, Northwestern University, Evanston.

deHirsch, K., Jansky, J., & Langford, W. (1966). *Predicting reading failure.* New York: Harper & Row.

Denhoff, E., Hainsworth, P., & Hainsworth, M. (1971). Learning disabilities and early childhood education: An information-processing approach. In H. Myklebust (Ed.), *Progress in learning disabilities* (Vol. 2). New York: Grune & Stratton.

Dykman, R., Ackerman, P., & Holcomb, P. (1985). Reading disabled and ADD children: Similarities and differences. In D. Gray & J. Kavanagh (Eds.), *Biobehavioral measures of dyslexia* (pp. 47–62). Parkton, MD: York Press.

Frith, U. (1980). *Cognitive processes in spelling.* London: Academic Press.

Hedley, C., & Baratta, A. (Eds.), (1985). *Contexts of reading.* Norwood, NJ: Ablex.

James, K. (1976). *A study of the conceptual structure of measurement of length in normal and learning disabled children.* Unpublished doctoral dissertation, Northwestern University, Evanston.

Johnson, D. (1981). Considerations in the assessment of central auditory disorders in learning disabled children. In R. Keith (Ed.), *Central auditory and language disorders in children* (pp. 77–84). Houston: College Hill.

Johnson, D. (1968). Remedial approaches to dyslexia. In A. Benton and D. Pearl (Eds.), *Dyslexia: An appraisal of current knowledge* (pp. 397–422). New York: Oxford University Press.

Johnson, D., & Myklebust, H. (1967). *Learning disabilities: Educational principles and practices.* New York: Grune & Stratton.

Keogh, B., Major-Kingsley, S., Omori-Gordon, & Red, H.P. (1982). *A system of marker variables for the field of learning disabilities.* Syracuse, NY: Syracuse University Press.

McKinney, J. (1984). The search for subtypes of specific learning disability. *Annual Review of Learning Disabilities, 2,* 19–26.

Myklebust, H. (1968). *Progress in learning disabilities* (Vol. 1). New York: Grune & Stratton.

Myklebust, H. (1975). Nonverbal learning disabilities: Assessment and intervention. In H. Myklebust (Ed.), *Progress in learning disabilities* (Vol. 3). Grune & Stratton.

Rourke, B. (1978). Reading, spelling, arithmetic disabilities: A neuropsychological perspective. In H. Myklebust (Ed.), *Progress in learning disabilities* (Vol. 4). New York: Grune & Stratton.

Satz, P., & Morris, R. (1981). Learning disability sub-types: A review. In F. Pirozzolo and W. Wittrock (Eds.), *Neuropsychological and cognitive processes in reading.* New York: Academic Press.

CHAPTER 10

Beyond Traditional Assessment

Cecil D. Mercer

The identification of learning disabilities (LD) is a highly debated area. Both under- and overidentification of learning-disabled students cause problems. Underidentification deprives learning-disabled students of services, whereas overidentification results in inappropriate placements and takes resources from other programs and students. Chalfant (1985) reports that the rapid increase of students labeled learning disabled is becoming a national problem. Reynolds (1985) notes that uncontrolled increases in LD placements could result in the demise of LD programs altogether. Shepard and Smith (1983) studied the identification practices for 1000 learning-disabled cases in Colorado and found that overidentification of LD was widespread. Specifically, they reported that approximately 60% of the students identified as learning disabled did not match the legal definitions or definitions in the professional literature.

THE CHALLENGE OF ASSESSMENT IN LEARNING DISABILITIES

The need for the accurate and useful assessment of learning-disabled students has never been more pressing. Professionals, political groups, and parent groups are vigorously seeking improved ways of identifying and teaching the learning-disabled student. The following obstacles impede the search for better identification practices:

1. A lack of consensus regarding the definition of LD makes it extremely difficult to ascertain criteria that should be used in identification. Different definitions infer a variety of criteria. Even in an attempt to operationalize the same definition (e.g., federal definition), states vary considerbly in the specific criteria used (Chalfant, 1985; Mercer, Hughes, & Mercer, 1985).

2. The discrepancy factor, a major component in identifying LD, has been difficult to operationalize (Reynolds, 1985). Typically, the difference between ability scores and achievement scores is analyzed to determine whether a severe discrepancy exists. This analysis has resulted in the use of expectancy formulas. These formulas and the weak psychometric test data used in them have been extensively criticized (Berk, 1984; Cone & Wilson, 1981; Forness, Sinclair, & Guthrie, 1983; Reynolds, 1985).

3. Most instruments used to identify learning-disabled students are inadequate. Coles (1978) reviewed the 10 most frequently used tests and procedures for identifying LD and concluded that they all lack a sound empirical base. Shepard and Smith (1983) claim that many standardized tests used to diagnose LD lack adequate reliability and validity.

4. The heterogeneity of the learning-disabled population makes it difficult to develop a unifying set of identification criteria. One learning-disabled student may be very different from another, and, until further understanding of LD subgroups is obtained, the task of developing accurate identification criteria will remain extremely complex.

5. Many schools do not provide adequate services to low achievers or disruptive students. Moreover, regular classroom teachers are often not given the support system they need for helping low achievers and misbehaving students. In an effort to get help for both regular class teachers and low-achieving and/or disruptive students, referrals to the LD program are made. Consequently, many non-learning-disabled students (e.g., low achievers, slow learners, mildly retarded, culturally disadvantaged, and students with behavior problems) become placed in LD programs (Chalfant, 1985). When students in these situations are studied, the confusion over what is a true learning-disabled student is greatly increased.

6. In many instances, multidisciplinary team members have not been trained to make identification decisions about learning-disabled and nonlearning-disabled students. As a result of their study of multidisciplinary decision making about LD eligibility, Furlong and

Yanagida (1985) strongly encourge professionals to work on improving the reliability of team decisions. Moreover, Ysseldyke and Thurlow (1983) discuss some of the problems found in multidisciplinary team decision making.

PURPOSE OF ASSESSMENT

Salvia and Ysseldyke (1985) define assessment as "the process of collecting data for the purpose of (1) specifying and verifying problems and (2) making decisions about students" (p. 5). An elaboration of this definition is needed to recognize the overall purpose of assessment. To many, the belief that educational assessment should lead to better instruction is fundamental. In a report by the National Academy of Sciences, Heller, Holtzman, and Messick (1982) state that the "main purpose of assessment in education is to improve instruction and learning . . . [and] a significant portion of children who experience difficulties in the classroom can be treated effectively through improved instruction" (p. 72). Ysseldyke and Algozzine (1984) aptly state this belief:

> The ultimate goal of assessment is improvement of instruction for the learner. The only valid special education process is one in which assessment leads to treatments that have known outcomes. . . . To the extent that collection of assessment data leads to improvements in instruction, collection of those data is a reasonable activity. (p. 288)

Given that assessment is the collection of data for the overall purpose of improving the learning-disabled student's educational program, it is important to recognize sources of data that offer instructionally relevant information. Teachers and other school personnel offer a rich resource of viable data. Unfortunately, assessment procedures often rely too heavily on test data and omit or limit the use of consultation.

ASSESSMENT AND CONSULTATION

Recently, I was watching a championship little league baseball game. A normally excellent pitcher (whom I previously coached) was not performing well. His coach hovered around him after each inning in an effort to assess what was wrong and how to correct it. The pitcher's problems continued, and the pressure on him and the team increased. The pitcher's coach saw me in the crowd and indicated he wanted to talk. His first words to me were "Can you tell what Brett's doing wrong?" After watching Brett for several pitches, I told him I thought Brett was aiming the ball instead of throwing it in his normal style. Then he wanted to know what to do about it. I told him that I thought Brett needed to relax. As Brett approached the dugout, his coach chatted with him and told him to relax, pitch his normal way, and have some fun. Upon walking away I turned and said, "Brett, if you give up any more runs, plans are to eliminate postgame sodas and cut your arm off with a chain saw!" He smiled, I smiled, he pitched a shutout for the remainder of the game, and his team won.

The story of Brett vividly illustrates the need and function of consultation in the assessment process. Given the pressures of a championship game and a star pitcher struggling, his coach felt the need for some help from a peer coach. Implicit in this request was the need for information concerning the problem (diagnosis) and the treatment (recommended intervention). Meaningful assessment is incomplete without information regarding both the nature of the problem and recommended treatments. Consultation can provide both types of information. Through consultation, a teacher can receive extensive diagnostic information (e.g., Sam misbehaves because he gets teacher attention for it; Linda computes addition problems incorrectly because of a faulty algorithm). Likewise, the teacher can receive intervention information (e.g., for Sam, try planned ignoring of misbehavior and reinforcement of appropriate behavior; for Linda, try a low-stress addition algorithm).

In their review of consultation literature, Graden, Casey, and Bonstrom (1985) report that consultation has been successfully used to improve teachers' skills in dealing with problem learners and to reduce referral rates to special education. Moreover, Fimian (1986) notes that consultation from peers helps teachers deal with stress. In their reconceptualization of special education services to develop more effective schools, Bickel and Bickel (1986) claim that consultation services to teachers are essential to improve the progress of special education students. It is apparent that consultation has the potential to facilitate assessment during prereferral, referral, identification/placement, and program evaluation.

Educators have a need for different levels of consultation. In some cases, assistance from a peer teacher is sufficient; however, in other cases, multidisciplinary input is warranted. To provide a continuum of consultation services throughout the assessment process, a model is proposed (see Fig. 10-1). In this model, consultation services include a school-based support team, a district-level multidisciplinary team, and a regional diagnostic teaching center. Owing to the requirements of the 1977 *Federal Register*, multidisciplinary teams are already intact.

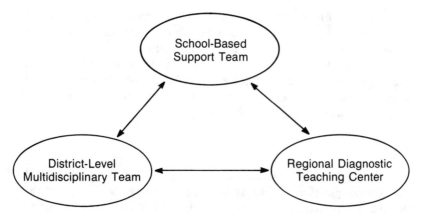

Figure 10-1. Levels of consultation to facilitate assessment practices at prereferral, referral, identification/placement, and program monitoring.

Moreover, many states and/or school districts have instituted school-based support teams. This chapter focuses primarily on the school-based support team and the regional diagnostic teaching center.

School-Based Support Team

In an effort to decrease the number of referrals to special education and improve services to students with school-related problems, more efforts need to be directed at prereferral activities (Graden et al., 1985). Teacher support teams and/or child study teams represent prereferral approaches that hold much promise. In a survey of state guidelines, Chalfant (1985) reports that 16 states provide some kind of building-based teacher support teams. These teams consist of regular teachers only or a combination of special education and regular teachers. Child study teams provide teachers with the opportunity to analyze individual student cases and determine strategies to try before making a referral to special education. Brainstorming is a key factor in the functioning of these teams. Child study teams have been found to alter the nature and rate of referrals (Chalfant, VanDusen Pysh, & Moultrie, 1979) and broaden the regular classroom teacher's tolerance for students experiencing difficulties (Gerber, 1982). Graden et al. (1985) developed and successfully tested a five-stage prereferral intervention model that features consultation and a child review team. In their discussion, they report "positive findings regarding the potential impact of the model for increasing classroom consultation and decreasing testing and placement rates" (p. 493).

The school-based support team referral process is an important but often overlooked phase in the assessment process. Careful study at the referral level can save much time, effort, and monies for the parents and school personnel involved. A well-planned referral process that yields pertinent general information (e.g., motivation factors, home situation, instructional program) makes the formal evaluation of the student a more viable and efficient proposition.

Teacher Assistance Teams

Chalfant et al. (1979) discuss a teacher assistance team model that has proved effective in helping teachers to reduce the number of inappropriate referrals and in resolving the problems of many students. Each team consists of three elected teachers, the teacher seeking help, and parents or others as needed. The referring teacher provides information concerning the student's strengths and weaknesses and what interventions have been used to help the student. The team conducts a problem-solving meeting in which the following steps are followed: (1) delineate specific objectives with the teacher, (2) brainstorm intervention alternatives, (3) select and/or refine intervention(s), and (4) plan follow-up activities.

The teacher assistance team model was evaluated in three states for a 2-year period. Of the 200 students served in the study, the teams helped the classroom teacher resolve the difficulties of 133 students, or 66.5%. Of the 116 students who were underachieving, the teams were able to meet the needs of 103 students (88.7%) without referring them to special education. Moreover, schools with Teachers Assistance Teams cut their diagnostic costs by approximately 50% (Kirk & Chalfant, 1984).

Coaching

Another school-based support team approach generating enthusiasm among educators is *coaching*. Peer coaching involves (1) the formation of a small group of teachers, and (2) peer observation. Teachers observe each other's classrooms, get feedback about their teaching, experiment with improved techniques, and receive support (McREL Staff, 1984–1985). A coaching team usually consists of three people. These teams engage in a three-phase process involving discussion and planning, observation, and feedback.

In the discussion and planning phase, the teachers focus on the improved technique or strategy that they want to learn. They outline the specific behaviors or actions that are essential for implementing the new technique. In the observation phase, teacher 1 observes teacher 2, who observes teacher 3, who observes teacher 1. It helps observation if a format (e.g., checklist, log, tape recorder) is developed that guides data collection. In the feedback phase, the observer and the teacher meet to discuss the observations. Showers (1985) reports that one purpose of coaching is to build a community of teachers who continuously engage in the study of improved teaching. The coaching process becomes a continuous cyclical process in which common understanding emerge that are essential for teaching improvement by collegial study of new knowledge and skills.

The effects of coaching are impressive. Showers (1985) reports that coaching provides the follow-up that is essential for training new skills and strategies. Also, it is more effective than lecture and demonstration in providing classroom applications (McREL Staff, 1974–1985). Coaching appears to hold much promise as a technique to help educators develop a broader repertoire of skills for meeting the diverse needs of students in mainstream settings and to reduce the number of referrals for LD programs.

District-Level Multidisciplinary Team

During the prereferral and referral stages of assessment, consultation occurs primarily among school-based staff. At the identification/placement stage, a multidisciplinary team is required to determine eligibility. This team usually consists of school-based and district personnel. Criticism of identification practices in LD is extensive. The effectiveness of multidisciplinary team functioning, standardized tests, and criteria have all been questioned (Furlong & Yanagida, 1985). Moreover, the efficacy of special education services after placement are frequently questioned (Carlberg & Kavale, 1980; Glass, 1983). School-based personnel and a diagnostic teaching center can assist placement and follow-up (i.e., program evaluations) with such activities as curriculum-based assessment, diagnostic teaching, and the delineation of local curriculum resources. These types of consultative activities offer much potential in reducing criticisms leveled at the identification process.

Regional Diagnostic Teaching Center

Rationale

In an effort to improve assessment practices and special education instructional services, the University of Florida Multidisciplinary

Diagnostic and Training Program (MDTP) was initiated in 1981. It was thought that a regional diagnostic center that stressed curriculum-based assessment had the potential to make a positive impact.

Under the rubric of curriculum-based assessment (CBA), assessment procedures are applied within the context of a local school's curriculum. Blankenship and Lilly (1981) define CBA as "the practice of obtaining direct and frequent measures of a student's performance on a series of sequentially arranged objectives derived from the curriculum used in the classroom" (p. 81). In essence, the essential feature of CBA is that the student's progress is assessed in terms of the classroom curriculum so that instruction can be better tailored to the student's needs. Marston and Magnusson (1985) report that CBA procedures have proved efficient and effective across a variety of assessment goals: screening, identification, program planning, and monitoring the progress of mildly handicapped students. Moreover, they note that CBA data indicate that special education students are learning in their special settings. Germann and Tindal (1985) report good results from using CBA to monitor academic and social behaviors. They note that CBA provides a continuous data base to help with numerous educational decisions, including problem identification, program planning, program implementation and evaluation, and program certification.

In a study of CBA, Deno (1985) concludes that achievement in basic skills can be measured in a reliable and valid manner by using the school's curriculum to generate test items. He notes that CBA holds much promise because:

1. It is *curriculum-referenced*, so that a student's competence is measured in terms of the local school curriculum.
2. It is *individual-referenced*, so that judgments can be made about an individual student's progress.
3. It is *peer-referenced*, so that the "normality" of a student's performance can be reliably determined using locally developed peer sampling.

In discussing the legal parameters of using CBA, Galagan (1985) notes that CBA, with its focus on individual needs, is capable of meeting the specific individual needs of children and, therefore, the legal requirements of the Education for All Handicapped Children Act.

Description of MDTP.

The MDTP consists of a team of professionals from neurology, psychology, language, and special education who serve children with complex medical, behavioral, and/or learning problems. Although the majority of the children are learning disabled or emotionally handicapped, students from all exceptionalities have been served by MDTP. After a child is referred, an MDTP liaison teacher visits the student's classroom for observation and consultation with the teachers. Next, the child goes to the University of Florida campus for medical, language, educational, and psychological evaluations. After the evaluations have been completed, a case conference is held with school district personnel and MDTP staff. At this conference, a diagnosis is determined and intervention plans are detailed.

It may be decided to return the child to his home school and to assign the MDTP liaison teacher to consult with local school personnel to implement the intervention plan. Or, the decision may be made to enroll the student in the MDTP diagnostic and training classroom. This class is located in the College of Education, and students may attend it for a period of from 1 to 6 weeks. Children attending the class receive intensive treatment aimed at documenting effective teaching and management strategies for the child. Data-based instruction is used to determine the effectiveness of instructional programs (e.g., reading, language, math, spelling) and management techniques (e.g., point system, contingency contracts, parent involvement). When effective interventions are documented, the child's local school teacher visits the class to observe and learn the interventions. Then the child is returned to his local school, and the MDTP liaison teacher continues to consult with the teacher to implement the intervention plan. Much emphasis is placed on designing interventions that are feasible to implement in the school districts. Peer teaching, self-correcting materials, computer-assisted instruction, instructional games, contingency contracts, parent management training, and charting progress are some of the techniques that are extensively used.

In addition to serving children with complex problems, MDTP is a valuable resource for preservice and in-service training in special education, curriculum and instruction, counselor education, speech and language, educational psychology, and medicine. Moreover, the parent training component offers services to parents and provides university students with the opportunity to be involved with parent training.

Evaluation of the Multidisciplinary Team Consultation Model

To date, more than 140 children have attended the diagnostic class and have made excellent progress in their problem areas. Data are reported in Table 10-1 on teachers, students, and parents of children who participated in the MDTP referral process and the diagnostic and training classroom during 1981 to 1984. A random sample of data on

TABLE 10-1.

Follow-Up Data on MDTP Teachers, Students, and Parents (1981–1984)

Component Evaluated	Summary of Responses	Feedback from Teachers	
		Special Education	Regular Education
Case conferences	Judged case conferences positively—to be multidisciplinary exchanges, opportunities for them to give input, useful for decision making, and a professional growth experience	88.9%	97.5%
Diagnostic classroom	Judged the diagnostic classroom observation to be a positive experience—learned about classroom management, academic interventions, and was a worthwhile learning experience	88.4%	85.2%
Educational alternatives	Found MDTP suggestions helpful and modified their teaching as a result	95%	100%
Number of new strategies tried	Attempted new strategies based on MDTP suggestions	4.4	4.5
Test results (written and follow-up)	Found the terms helpful and were useful to teachers as professionals	84.4%	87.8%

Parent Opinion	
Area Evaluated	Rate of Positive Responses to Total
Usefulness of assessments	9/10 positive
Still use techniques learned at MDTP	7/8 yes
Child still positively affected by MDTP	10/10 yes
Child doing better at home	8/9 yes
Child doing better at school	6/10 yes
Final grades this year	7/7 same or better

Student Data	
Area Evaluated	Rate of Positive Responses to Total
Absenteeism	8/11 same or positive
Standard scores	6/7 same or positive
Basal series	13/13 positive
Grades	12/13 same or positive
Conduct	8/9 same or positive

10 special education teachers, 13 regular education/Chapter I teachers, 13 students, and 10 parents was gathered based on an initial drawing of 15 persons in each category. Questionnaires were responded to anonymously by teachers and parents. Pre- and post-test scores and daily precision teaching probes taken while the students were in the diagnostic and training classroom were analyzed. Current information on students was obtained from examination of cumulative folders and parent feedback.

Teacher and parent feedback from the evaluation are very encouraging. As reported in Table 10-1, it is apparent that both teachers and parents believed that the consultations received from the MDTP staff were very helpful. The student data are also positive. Absenteeism, standardized test scores, progress in basals, grades, and conduct were examined for 13 randomly selected students who participated in the program. The results indicate that the majority of students maintained or improved from the time of referral to the present.

During the 6 weeks that these students were in the diagnostic and training classroom, pre- and post-test measures and daily data were collected on numerous interventions. For all children, substantial academic gains (e.g., reading, math, spelling) were noted as well as positive behavior change. In many instances, students acquired and/or mastered more skills in the 6-week intensive training session than they had in the previous year or years.

Data from a random sample of learning-disabled students enrolled for 6 weeks indicate positive growth. For example, the mean number of words read correctly per minute increased by 55 words for 12 learning-disabled students sampled. Moreover, grade-level reading scores as measured by the *Brigance* improved by more than 1 year (reading comprehension, 1.6; oral reading level, 1.3) for 11 learning-disabled students sampled. Improvement in rate of correct digits per minute for math facts was also very positive. The average rate gain for 13 learning-disabled students sampled was 20.7 correct digits per minute.

The evaluation data support the position that a regional diagnostic center (i.e., regional center for small districts or within-district centers for large school districts) can have a positive impact in the assessment and treatment of learning-disabled students. Parents, regular teachers, special education techers, and the students served at the University of Florida's Center report benefits, including:

1. Multidisciplinary teams can be effective in assessing the needs of learning-disabled students and in determining placements that provide appropriate educational programs. Moreover, a well-trained and effective team can serve as a model for district-level multidisciplinary teams (Hendrickson, 1986).

2. A diagnostic teaching process (e.g., 1–6 weeks) enables the team to select and validate instructional procedures for learning-disabled students who fail to improve. For example, all students in the MDTP classroom made significant progress in weak areas. The mean gain in reading recognition for learning-disabled students was 1.6 years.

3. A multidisciplinary diagnostic teaching center is able to work with school-based teachers to initiate effective instructional techniques for individual students. Moreover, these techniques often work with other students, and a positive ripple effect occurs throughout the curriculum. For example, school-based teachers report using an average of 4.5 new teaching techniques after consulting with MDTP staff.

4. A diagnostic teaching center is able to work with teachers to effect curriculum-based assessment, which, in turn, helps with identification and the monitoring of individual student progress. When local schools have teacher assistance or coaching teams, a framework for effective in-service with a regional team exists. For example, several schools who work with MDTP have set up CBA and coaching teams.

5. LD teachers in the center are continuously serving as consultants, role models, child advocates, and teachers of students with a myriad of complex medical, behavioral, and/or learning problems. In short, special education teachers need multidisciplinary expertise and a continuing support system to help with solving difficult placement and/or instructional problems. A diagnostic teaching center offers these teachers a much needed support system to help with newly placed students and previously placed students who are not progressing satisfactorily.

6. A multidisciplinary diagnostic teaching team is able to work with parents to develop a cooperative relationship with school personnel.

CONCLUSION

The major purpose of assessment is to help learning-disabled youngsters receive an appropriate education. Teachers offer a rich resource for contributing instructionally relevant information at all stages of the assessment process. With the organization of school-based support teams in many states, the foundation for teacher-to-teacher consultation is established. Teacher assistance and coaching teams provide an excellent format for teachers to help reduce referrals and improve services to students identified as learning disabled. The use of regional diagnostic teaching centers can serve as resources to school-based teachers and district-level multidisciplinary teams. The diagnostic teaching center can primarily assist schools with those complex cases in which valid identification and/or instructional approaches are elusive. Finally, the diagnostic teaching center offers a consultation support system for LD teachers.

Research concerning the assessment of LD has repeatedly identified problem areas: overidentification, inadequate instruments, questionable team decisions, and disagreement over definitional criteria of LD. Unfortunately, little effort has been made to study the assessment practices of the best diagnosticians in our field. If a person wishes to study running, he would be wise to examine the behaviors of the best runners. By randomly sampling or not controlling for competence, researchers continuously run the risk of sampling incompetence and using the data to draw conclusions such as learning-disabled students cannot be differentiated from normal peers and/or low achievers. In an effort to evaluate and improve special education's best assessment practices, it appears feasible to consider:

1. The competency level of the persons doing the assessing.
2. The use of CBA for identification and classroom progress monitoring.
3. The involvement of instructional personnel in a consultation problem-solving framework who have had *continuous* experience with the student.
4. The practices of multidisciplinary teams who have been trained in data-based decision making.
5. The use of instruments that have "state of the art" psychometric properties.
6. The study of school-based, district-level, and regional-level consultation in the assessment of learning-disabled students.

Reynolds (1985) claims that a viable state-of-the-art in assessment is emerging and now needs implementing. Curriculum-based assessment, computer-assisted assessment, availability of better tests, and a rising "consciousness" about identification, perhaps, will provide the impetus and know-how for improved assessment practices.

Samuel A. Kirk

Cecil Mercer has discussed the role of assessment in the management and remediation of children with LD. His emphasis is on educational assessment, which leads to educational programming. He has rightly de-emphasized the role of psychometric tests as the instruments for decision making, a frequent practice.

Mercer's point of view is a reaction against the excessive reliance on IQ's, mental ages, scaled scores, percentile ranks, and other indices that have in the past guided decisions about children.

But there are two purposes for assessment. One purpose is for classification. This type of assessment may have little or no relevance to education. Nevertheless, the multidisciplinary team that has been ordered by law is involved primarily in assessment for classification. This assessment determines eligibility for service. The team classifies the child as learning disabled and as eligible for service programs for the learning disabled. This procedure is no different from the procedures followed in other areas. When we send a child to an audiologist, he or she determines the child's hearing loss and reports that the child is deaf or severely hard of hearing. This assessment does not have educational relevance. It does not lead to an appropriate educational program. What it does do is help the child obtain services by declaring him or her eligible for free public education. But the child needs a different level of assessment for educational purposes.

The second kind of assessment I tend to label "diagnostic." In the field of reading, we can administer a reading test and classify the child as a first, second, or third grader. This assessment is not diagnostic. It only classifies for placement purposes. To organize an adequate remediation program for a child with a reading/learning disability, it is necessary to obtain information on formal or informal diagnostic reading tests on what the child can and cannot do. This will involve an assessment of reading errors and reading behavior. If, for example, the child is found to have excessive reversal errors, this diagnostic information leads to a program to ameliorate the reversal errors.

Assessment in education differs from assessment in medicine. Ordinarily, a family physician makes the diagnosis and prescribes and monitors the treatment. In education, we have a multidisciplinary team make the assessment, while the teacher conducts the remediation. At one time I attended a case conference manned by a neurologist, a speech pathologist, a psychologist, and a social worker. After each made his or her report about EEG's, results of psychometric tests, speech and language tests, and a social history, the decision was made that the child was aphasic and eligible for public school service in a class for aphasic children. That afternoon I visited the class for aphasic children to observe the intervention methods used. The teacher informed me that the children were sent to her with the diagnosis of aphasia. Her prescription for each child (the IEP) was formulated by her after she had assessed the language of the child. The clinic had not made educational recommendations, nor did the clinic point out what the child could or could not do.

This experience led me to believe that the person teaching the child should be the person who makes the educational assessment. Like the physician, the teacher can use ancillary help from pediatricians, psychologists, and others, but the responsibility for educational diagnosis and treatment should be the specialist in LD. This is not a new idea; speech pathologists in the schools are responsible for the assessment of speech- and language-impaired children and are also responsible for the remediation. If this point of view is correct, it will be necessary to prepare specialists in LD with the diagnostic and remedial skills to do the job. They can obtain help from other professionals, but, like a physician, they become the responsible agents for educational diagnosis and remediation.

REFERENCES

Berk, R.A. (1984). An evaluation of procedures for computing an ability-achievement discrepancy score. *Journal of Learning Disabilities, 17,* 262–266.

Bickel, W.E., & Bickel, D.D. (1986). Effective schools, classrooms, and instruction: Implications for special education. *Exceptional Children, 52,* 489–500.

Blankenship, C., & Lilly, M.S. (1981). *Mainstreaming students with learning and behavior problems: Techniques for the classroom teacher.* New York: Holt, Rinehart & Winston.

Carlberg, C., & Kavale, K. (1980). The efficacy of special versus regular class placement for exceptional children: A meta-analysis. *Journal of Special Education, 14,* 295–309.

Chalfant, J.C. (1985). Identifying learning disabled students: A summary of the National Task Force report. *Learning Disabilities Focus, 1*(1), 9–10.

Chalfant, J.C., VanDusen Pysh, M., & Moultrie, R. (1979). Teacher assistance teams: A model for within-building problem solving. *Learning Disability Quarterly, 3,* 85–96.

Coles, G.S. (1978). The learning-disabilities test battery: Empirical and social issues. *Harvard Education Review, 48,* 313–340.

Cone, T.E., & Wilson, L.R. (1981). Quantifying a severe discrepancy: A critical analysis. *Learning Disability Quarterly, 4*, 359–371.

Deno, S.L. (1985). Curriculum-based measurement: The emerging alternative. *Exceptional Children, 52*, 219–232.

Fimian, M.J. (1986). Social support and occupational stress in special education. *Exceptional Children, 52*, 436–442.

Forness, S.R., Sinclair, E., & Guthrie, D. (1983). Learning disability discrepancy formulas: Their use in actual practice. *Learning Disability Quarterly, 6*, 107–114.

Furlong, M.J., & Yanagida, E.H. (1985). Psychometric factors affecting multidisciplinary team identification of learning disabled children. *Learning Disability Quarterly, 8*, 37–44.

Galagan, J.E. (1985). Psychoeducational testing: Turn out the lights, the party's over. *Exceptional Children, 52*, 266–276.

Gerber, M. (1982, October). *Reconceptualizing the referral process: A levels of response approach to the identification and assessment of learning disabled students.* Paper presented at the annual meeting of the Council on Learning Disabilities, Kansas City, MO.

Germann, G., & Tindal, G. (1985). An application of curriculum-based assessment: The use of direct and repeated measurement. *Exceptional Children, 52*, 244–265.

Glass, G.V. (1983). Effectiveness of special education. *Policy Studies Review, 2*, 65–78.

Graden, J.L., Casey, A., & Bonstrom, O. (1985). Implementing a prereferral intervention system: Part II. The data. *Exceptional Children, 51*, 487–496.

Heller, K.A., Holtzman, W.H., & Messick, S. (1982). *Placing children in special education: A strategy for equity.* Washington, DC: National Academy Press.

Hendrickson, J.M. (1986). *The University of Florida Multidisciplinary Diagnostic and Training Program: A team with nobody on the bench?* Manuscript submitted for publication.

Kirk, S.A., & Chalfant, J.C. (1984). *Academic and developmental learning disabilities.* Denver: Love.

Marston, D., & Magnusson, D. (1985). Implementing curriculum-based measurement in special and regular education settings. *Exceptional Children, 52*, 266–276.

McREL Staff. (1984–1985, Winter). Coaching: A powerful strategy for improving staff development and inservice education. *Noteworthy*, pp. 40–48.

Mercer, C.D., Hughes, C., & Mercer, A.R. (1985). Learning disabilities definitions used by state education departments. *Learning Disability Quarterly, 8*, 45–55.

Reynolds, C.R. (1985). Measuring the aptitude-achievement discrepancy in learning disability diagnosis. *Remedial and Special Education, 5*(3), 19–23.

Salvia, J., & Ysseldyke, J.E. (1985). *Assessment in special and remedial education* (3rd ed.). Boston: Houghton Mifflin.

Shepard, L.A., & Smith, M.L. (1983). An evaluation of the identification of learning disabled students in Colorado. *Learning Disability Quarterly, 6*, 115–127.

Showers, B. (1985). Teachers coaching teachers. *Educational Leadership, 42*(7), 43–48.

Ysseldyke, J.E., & Algozzine, B. (1984). *Introduction to special education.* Boston: Houghton Mifflin.

Ysseldyke, J.E., & Thurlow, M.L. (1983). *Identification/classification research: An integrative summary of findings* (Research Report No. 142). Minneapolis: University of Minnesota Institute for Research in Learning Disabilities.

PART V

Intervention

CHAPTER 11

Intervention Research in Learning Disabilities

Samuel A. Kirk

T he field of learning disability (LD), originally associated with severe problems in learning resulting from a neurologic deficit, has in practice become primarily concerned with academic underachievement at the school-age level. This practice has led to an unprecedented increase in enrollment, which now constitutes 42% to 45% of children assigned to special education (Eighth Annual Report to Congress, 1986, p. 5).

There are many reasons for academic underachievement. Figure 11-1 describes the factors influencing underachievement (Kirk & Chalfant, 1984). It lists two major reasons for academic underachievement: (1) extrinsic or environmental factors, and (2) intrinsic or internal factors. It will be noticed from Figure 11-1 that the extrinsic or environmental factors include economic disadvantage, cultural disadvantage, lack of opportunity to learn, and inadequate instruction. The intrinsic factors, on the other hand, include mental retardation, sensory handicaps, serious emotional disturbances, and LD.

Surveys of children placed in public school classes for LD have demonstrated that approximately half of the children assigned to these classes are underachievers, but they are not necessarily learning

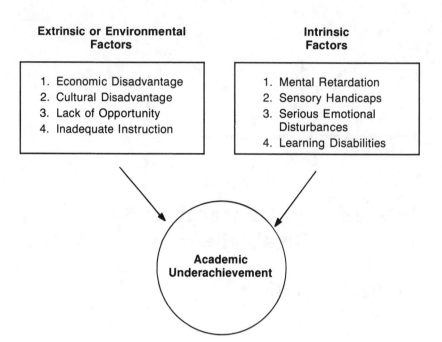

Figure 11-1. Factors influencing academic underachievement: From: Kirk & Chalfant (1984). *Academic and development learning disabilities.* Denver, CO: Love, p. 7.

disabled (Shepard & Smith, 1983). For example, a child who lacked the opportunity to learn would not be expected to be reading at the age of 9, 10, or 11 years without instruction or exposure to reading materials. The child may be of normal intelligence but, on tests, exhibits significant discrepancy between achievement and potential. Such a child is not necessarily learning disabled because the method of instruction will follow the same pattern as would be used with normal learning children. This kind of child does not need any special remedial procedures, only an adequate opportunity to learn. A mentally retarded child could have a discrepancy between age and academic achievement but would not be considered learning disabled unless an intrinsic developmental disability is found that is depressing scores on both intelligence tests and academic achievement. Many children mistakenly classified as mentally retarded on the basis of psychometric tests have been found to have normal abilities in some areas and highly depressed abilities in other areas, thus classifying these children erroneously as mentally retarded.

In this chapter, methods of intervention will deal primarily with children who are learning disabled rather than with underachieving children whose underachievement may be the result of extrinsic or environmental factors. The concept of LD as used in this chapter involves an intrinsic disability within the child that has inhibited the child's ability to learn under ordinary instruction. LD at the school-age level are academic disabilities resulting from one or more developmental disabilities such as memory, perception, attention, thinking, or language. These developmental disabilities occur at the preschool level and later manifest themselves as disabilities in reading, spelling, handwriting, written expression, and mathematics. The intervention for such a child will require remediation that ameliorates the developmental deficit during the process of teaching the academic subjects. A child who has not learned to read and has a marked attention deficit, for example, requires an environment that will control attention while the child is obtaining remediation in reading.

INTERVENTION MODELS

Intervention procedures with learning-disabled students can be classified into two broad subdivisions. The first subdivision may be called ecologic or organizational and deals with the environment or delivery system in which the child is remediated. The second subdivision deals with specific strategies of instruction adapted to the difficulties inherent in the child being remediated.

Research on Ecologic Intervention

Public schools provide delivery of services to learning-disabled school-age children through (1) self-contained classes, (2) resource rooms, (3) consultation with regular grade teachers, and (4) a combination or adaptation of these three.

A *self-contained class* allows one teacher to teach 12 to 15 children for all or most of the day. This kind of intervention requires the teacher to offer children a total curriculum. This organization has evolved because of its administrative feasibility and the tradition of teaching children in groups. Most of the classes contain some children who are underachieving in all subjects and, in practice, includes many slow-learning children.

Resource rooms have been designed to give some help to a large number of children. In this kind of organization, a teacher accepts one to three children an hour for the whole day, thus serving 15 to 20 children from different classes. This is called a pull-out method, wherein the child is taken out of the class for a short period to attend the resource room and to receive special help from a LD specialist.

The *consultation model*, on the other hand, requires that a specialist in LD diagnose children in the regular classroom and advise the teacher on how to teach the child. This is an ongoing program in which the consulting teacher can consult with teachers and deal with a large number of children.

A series of studies are needed to determine the efficacy of these service delivery models.

One research problem in ecologic intervention could ask, "What kinds of children are best assigned to self-contained classes, to resource rooms, or to a consulting teacher?" Presumably these different delivery systems are used because of the differences found among learning-disabled students.

It has been alleged that self-contained classes are most suitable for children who are underachieving in all school subjects. The self-contained class, then, teaches the child reading, writing, arithmetic, social studies, and so forth during the day. These children may be at different levels of accomplishment, but since the class is small, the teacher can gear the teaching and assignments to each child's needs. Children assigned to a resource room presumably have a specific LD. Such a child may be achieving in arithmetic at his or her age level but may be deficient in reading and spelling, in which case the child would remain in the regular classroom for most of the day but be pulled out for one period to receive special help in a resource room with one or more other children having the same problem. Children assigned to a consulting teacher are usually children with minor problems who can be helped by the regular teacher if she is given help in adapting instruction to each child.

Investigations of the assignment of children to the various delivery systems will require a thorough study of the characteristics of these children and history of success in dealing with them. Until such studies are conducted, we will not know whether the assignments of children to the different types of programs are a result of the characteristics of the children, the availability of the service in the school, or the bias of the multidisciplinary team.

Another area of research that is needed is to compare the rate of learning of children in self-contained classes with the rate of learning of learning-disabled children in resource rooms, or with children obtaining one-to-one remedial instruction. It has been hypothesized that a highly trained LD specialist can probably produce better results in one-to-one remedial instruction during a one-semester period than can be produced in a self-contained class during the whole year. If this hypothesis is correct, a teacher of the learning disabled can remediate 10 to 12 children a year under one-to-one remedial instruction, similar to the teaching of 10 to 12 children in a self-contained class for the entire year. This is the kind of research we need on a controlled basis to determine which delivery system is most effective as measured by the progress children make.

It is unfortunate that we continually organize and deliver remedial instructions to children without knowing what results we are obtaining and whether our procedures are economically feasible. Funds and effort devoted to the evaluation of delivery systems will bear beneficial results.

Research on Instructional Strategies

During the last century, psychologists have specialized in research on learning. They have delineated the factors that enhance human learning. When we survey the literature on learning, we find many principles of learning that can be used effectively in remediation. None of these principles is a complete remedial system in itself, but every set of programmed instructional materials must include sound principles of learning or sound principles of teaching based on research on the science of human learning.

Basic psychological research on learning is generated from theory and is designed to unfold the rules of human behavior. Educational research is more like engineering research, the applications of physical principles for research on machines, bridges, or spaceships. Educational research, or research on teaching, uses the principles evolved from research on learning and applies them to research on teaching. Educational researchers and theorists have attempted to apply the results of human learning research to teaching in general. Notable among these researchers are Madeline Hunter (1985), Berliner (1985), and with LD, Schumaker, Deshler, and Ellis (1986). In addition, the U.S. Department of Education funded grants to five universities to conduct research on LD. Two of these institutes dealt with intervention strategies. The Teachers College Institute studied instruction for elementary-aged learning-disabled students (Connor, 1983). The University of Kansas Institute made major contributions to the application of human learning principles to adolescent learning-disabled students (Schumaker, Deshler, Alley, & Warner, 1983).

Ordinarily, research on teaching involves a complex set of principles applied to an educational task. Research problems needed in intervention could include some of the following:

1. *Are special education teachers using special methods of teaching?* Children have been assigned to teachers who presumably

have specialized in the application of special remedial methods for learning-disabled students. Observation of many teachers has indicated that they are not using special remedial methods but are continuing the ordinary methods used with normal learning children. Special education has been defined as "distinguished by some unusual quality; uncommon; noteworthy; extraordinary; additional to the regular; extra; utilized or employed for a certain purpose in addition to the ordinary" (Kirk, 1962, p. 29). A necessary research project would observe a representative sample of special education teachers in self-contained classes or resource rooms or in one-to-one instruction to determine how many and what kinds of special education methods are being used with the different learning-disabled students.

2. *Are special education teachers using known strategies of teaching?* An associated problem would be to determine by observation whether or not teachers are using known instructional principles. Such research might encompass videotaping a large number of lessons and analyzing the results to determine the mode of communication, the use of advanced organizers, the use of minimal changes in materials, revisions and checks, student monitoring, adequate feedback, and so forth. The cause-and-effect relationship between the teacher's utilization of adequate principles of instruction and the rate of progress of the students could then be assessed.

3. *What interventions motive learning?* One commonly cited problem with learning-disabled students is lack of motivation (Adelman & Taylor, 1983). All authorities agree that intrinsic motivation is preferred over extrinsic motivation, but the question is how to develop intrinsic motivation in nonmotivated learning-disabled students. It is alleged that learning-disabled students are not interested in school and tend to avoid activities that could ameliorate their disability. The research question here is what interventions can motivate learning. Will extrinsic rewards result in adequate intrinsic motivation? One factor that should be tested is the effects of successful remediation on motivation. One hypothesis implies that children are unmotivated because they have failed, and, consequently, they avoid that which is uncomfortable for them. Successful remediation helps to develop a good self-concept and could led to intrinsic motivation. Data base for this hypothesis is needed.

METHODS OF RESEARCH

A number of procedures for research have been used in the behavioral sciences: quantitative research, single-subject research, qualitative or ethnographic research, and case studies.

Quantitative research is most commonly used by researchers to evaluate various intervention procedures. This research approach is adequate when sufficient subjects are available and the design can conform to the scientific assumptions required. With learning-disabled children, some of the problems are unique to an individual, and a sufficient heterogeneous sample is difficult to obtain. For this reason, single-subject research has been used.

Single-subject research is used when the problem lends itself to using the subject as her or his own control. Single-subject research tends to study and isolate variables, sometimes reducing the problem to very small proportions. Dealing with one variable at a time is not the same as dealing with the science and art of teaching, which uses a number of principles in sequence.

Qualitative research deals with observation of characteristics of situations or behavior. It watches children in their own naturalistic settings. It can involve counting as well as observing without counting. Much of the research that observes teachers and students interacting attempts to objectify the procedure through the use of video tapes. According to Kirk and Miller (1985), qualitative research has validity but lacks reliability. Nevertheless, if we are to understand the nuances of the teacher/student interaction in a remedial situation, it is necessary to study the efficacy of student/teacher interaction in different intervention settings.

Case studies have generally been avoided by researchers on a longitudinal basis because they believe that generalizations are difficult to make from case studies. Longitudinal case studies cover a span of many years. Often researchers do not have the time or the funding to conduct longitudinal case studies that take years to complete. In addition, these studies cannot be readily controlled, and interventions change over time. On the other hand, some have claimed that a thorough case study with a clear description of the characteristics of the subject and the intervention can lead to a generalization that the intervention will work on another person with the same characteristics. This is the procedure used by clinicians and teachers on an informal basis. A teacher may ignore a child who is hyperactive and has difficulty staying on task and pay attention to this child when he or she is on task. If it works, the teacher uses the same procedure with another hyperactive child. Whether the more acceptable behavior will last over time and whether it will generalize to other tasks are concerns that must be dealt with in longitudinal studies.

It is possible that many insights into interventions will evolve from longitudinal case studies. Avoiding case studies as unscientific may be depriving use of essential facts and theories. We should remember that Piaget evolved his theories from the study and observation of his three children, and that the classic study of the *Wild Boy of Avignon* by Itard has withheld the test of more than a century.

In summary, research on intervention is more complex than experimental research on a single variable in human learning. Intervention research involves many variables that must function congruently and in unison, including the special education teacher, the time allotted for intervention, the class setting, the home, the peers, and other agents. Among the crucial research studies that are needed are (1) a comparison of the rate of learning for learning-disabled children in the various service delivery systems—self-contained classes, resource rooms, consultation system, and one-to-one remedial intervention; and (2) research on instructional strategies and the determination of their use by special education teachers. These studies require various research methods, including quantitative and qualitative research as well as single-subject research when applicable. Longitudinal case studies of learning-disabled children, not commonly reported, may give us needed information on effective intervention as well as valuable hypotheses for more controlled studies.

RESPONSE

Edwin W. Martin

Samuel Kirk's chapter, "Intervention Research in Learning Disabilities," provides a clear and basic introduction to the subject cited. It is instructive that Kirk begins by discussing his concept of LD, since much of our research assumes that there is one "thing" called LD and that we are all in agreement about its nature. Given the heterogeniety of the phenomena that interests us, it is not surprising that our research results are sometimes confusing.

"Learning disabilities at the school-age level are *academic disabilities* resulting from one or more developmental disabilities such as memory, perception, attention, thinking or language." (emphasis added). This definition is interesting in contrast to the federal definition in the Education of the Handicapped Act, which was based on a definition developed by the National Advisory Committee on Handicapped Children in 1968, which Kirk chaired. That earlier definition, in which Kirk's thinking was a major ingredient, although similar in many respects, read in part, ". . .those children who have a disorder in one or more of the *basic psychological processes* involved in the understanding or in using language, spoken or written which disorder may manifest itself in imperfect ability to listen, think, speak, read, write, spell, or do mathematical calculations. . ." (emphasis added).

The contrast in these definitions helps emphasize Kirk's position that, as he states, "The field of learning disability (LD), originally associated with severe problems in learning resulting from a neurologic deficit, has in practice become primarily a problem of academic underachievement at the school-age level."

It is interesting to see the subject of LD and the research on the topic continue to evolve in the direction of academic performance. I recall a conversation with Richard Masland, then Director of the National Institute of Neurological Diseases, concerning the Advisory Committee's definition cited previously, which was then being developed. A few years earlier, the Neurological Institute had published a thoughtful monograph on Minimal Brain Dysfunction, which gave that terminology great currency in some circles. Masland, however, had no difficulty with the emergence of the term *learning disability*. As he told me then, he was not sure that the phrase minimal brain dysfunction had any practical value for educational treatment and he thought that a term which focused on the actual learning and classroom behavior of the children would be more useful in focusing attention and research interest.

Given the continuing change in emphasis, if not fundamental assumptions, that Kirk's new definitions suggest, Kirk goes on to affirm that our field is sorely lacking in "intervention research," that is, (1) studies of the environment in which the "child is remediated," and (2) the specific strategies used by instructional staff.

It is a point similar to that made by Semmel, Lieber, and Peck (1986), who state, "policy issues related to the effects of mainstreaming, identifying least restrictive environments, and other problems concerned with the effects of specific types of educational environments on child outcomes will not be successfully resolved without a shift in conceptual and methodologic approaches to analysis of special education environments" (p. 184).

As an example of an intervention research topic from an ecological perspective, Kirk suggests, "What kinds of children are best assigned to self-contained classes, to resource rooms, or to a consulting teacher?" It is instructive that the question is not the one that has been so frequently asked, by others: "What environment—special class or regular one—is the best for children with (fill in the disability)? One reason why research reviews are not able to report consistent findings of research designed to test whether one setting or another is "best" is because this type of question again assumes various kinds of homogeneity. Kirk's question assumes heterogeneity and the possibility of different answers for different children. I would go further and suggest adding, "and for what kinds of learning?" (e.g., social or academic).

Kirk continues to be interested in "What is special about special education?" and suggests as a research topic, "Are special education teachers using special methods of teaching?" This approach to what has been called "process" research is consistent with his overall message that LD are academic disabilities. Analyses of the teaching-learning process may be instructive not only about what is, in fact, happening in the classroom but also about the nature of LD. I have one reaction, however, and that is the study of *process* by itself, independent of *outcome* can be a nice academic pursuit. I would be interested in trying to determine what is happening in situations that, by whatever criteria feasible, may be judged successful. I am not as interested in Kirk's question, "Are special education teachers using special methods?" as I am in the question, "Are successful teachers using special methods?"

In all, Kirk has written a deceptively simple chapter that demonstrates once again that he is still leading our thought after more than 50 years on that task.

REFERENCES

Adelman, H.S., & Taylor, L. (1983). *Learning disabilities in perspective.* Glenview, IL: Scott, Foresman and Co.

Berliner, D.C. (1985). Effective classroom teaching: The necessary but not sufficient condition for developing exemplary schools. In G. Hustin & H. Garber (Eds.), *Research on exemplary schools* (pp. 127–154). New York: Academic Press.

Connor, F.P. (1983). Improving school instruction for learning disabled children: The Teacher College Institute. *Exceptional Education Quarterly*, 4(1), 23–44.

Eighth Annual Report to Congress on the Implementation of the Education of the Handicapped Act, Vol. 1. (1986). *To assure the free public education of all handicapped children.* Washington, DC: U.S. Department of Education.

Hunter, M. (1985). Knowing, teaching, and supervising. In G. Hustin & H. Garber (Eds.), *Research on exemplary schools* (pp. 170–192). New York: Academic Press.

Kirk, J., & Miller, M.L. (1985). *Reliability and validity and qualitative research.* Beverly Hills, CA: Sage Publications.

Kirk, S.A. (1962). *Educating exceptional children* (1st ed.). Boston: Houghton Mifflin.

Kirk, S.A., & Chalfant, J.C. (1984). *Academic and developmental learning disabilities.* Denver: Love.

Schumaker, J.B., Deshler, D.D., Alley, G.R., & Warner, M. (1983). Toward the development of an intervention model for learning disabled adolescents. The University of Kansas Institute. *Exceptional Education Quarterly,* 4(1), 45–74.

Schumaker, J.B., Deshler, D.D., & Ellis, E.S. (1986). Intervention issues related to the education of L.D. adolescents. In J.K. Torgesen & B.Y.L. Wong (Eds.), *Psychological and educational perspectives on learning disabilities* (pp. 329–365). New York: Academic Press.

Semmel, M.I., Lieber, J., & Peck, C.A. (1986). Effects of special education environments: Beyond mainstreaming. In C.J. Meisel (Ed.), *Mainstreaming handicapped children: Outcomes, controversies and new directions.* Hillsdale, NJ: Erlbaum.

Shephard, L.A., & Smith, M.L. (1983). An evaluation of the identification of learning disabled students in Colorado. *Learning Disabilities Quarterly,* 6(2), 115–127.

CHAPTER 12

Conceptual and Methodological Issues in Interventions With Learning-Disabled Children and Adolescents

Bernice Y.L. Wong

I ntervention research* involving learning-disabled students is an important topic because treatments of their academic problems based on empirically validated instructional approaches provide a sounder rationale and more confidence. Within the learning disabilities (LD) field, one discerns the nascent development of a body of empirical data from intervention research. With the influence of research on thinking skills and strategies among congnitive psychologists and intervention research in instructional psychology and reading, intervention research in LD will likely increase in the future,

---

*Intervention research refers to instructional research in which the researcher induces a skill or a strategy to promote learning. The experimental design, instructional procedures, and data analyses parallel any experimental research study in terms of subject randomization to treatment groups, manipulation of variables, and so on.

thereby expanding the body of empirical data. It seems timely now to examine certain conceptual and methodologic issues in intervention research with the learning disabled.

CONCEPTUAL ISSUES

The conceptual issues discussed are diverse. They range from the issue of developmental framework in intervention research, to the respective roles of deficient knowledge base, process problems, and affective variables in intervention research, and the issue of individual versus group instruction. Together, they represent some serious conceptual deficiencies in current intervention research with the learning disabled. More important, unless they are redressed, these conceptual deficiencies would stymie our progress in intervention research.

The Need for an Acquisitional/Developmental Frame in Intervention Research

In intervention research with learning-disabled students, we are always trying to induce some cognitive skills or a strategy that promotes learning. The underlying assumption is that, unlike the successful learners, learning-disabled students have not attained the skill or strategy targeted for training. The intervention study typically proceeds from either a hypothesized deficiency or an empirically substantiated deficiency in the learning disabled that is reported in a prior study. What appears to be lacking is a development framework with which to conceptualize the intervention research study. Specifically, LD researchers engaged in intervention research may profit from asking a question of acquisition. "How do successful learners acquire that cognitive skill or particular strategy that learning-disabled students lack?"

One may ask: Why should we consider such an acquisitional question? Does it not suffice to continue with well-designed intervention studies? After all, the success rate of intervention studies to date have reached a reasonable batting average! The justification and importance of developing an acquisitional frame to analyze and guide intervention research is that it provides a broad and sound conceptual basis for intervention. Specifically, an acquisitional frame ensures that we include, on the one hand, cognitive-developmental variables and, on the other hand, instructional variables and their interactions. Moreover, an acquisitional frame in intervention integrates our instructional research with theory and research in developmental and cognitive psychology. One does not decry the usefulness of the intervention studies in LD. At issue is whether we should continue to use a conceptually shallow, shot-gun approach in LD intervention research. For (to repeat), the existent intervention studies have been generated on either a hypothesized skill or strategy deficiency or on empirically observed deficiencies. Effective but devoid of a developmental or acquisitional frame, the variables manipulated in these intervention studies may in retrospect be fragmentary and isolated. Hence, we need to rethink intervention in light of the aforementioned acquisitional question.

The Role of Trainees' Deficient Knowledge Base

Trainees' knowledge base deserves more attention from intervention researchers. To elaborate, it is common practice to pull main-streamed learning-disabled children out of class for daily academic remediation when they are not involved in language arts (reading) and math instruction. Often, classroom teachers release them in periods of social studies. When these learning-disabled children get into the upper elementary grades (e.g., grades 6 and 7), they tend to have a cumulative deficiency in social studies knowledge. My questions are: (1) How does deficient domain knowledge in, for example, social studies affect students' subsequent learning in high-school social studies? (2) How does deficient domain knowledge in any subject affect learning-disabled students' learning strategies that are designed to promote content learning?

Research in reading has amply demonstrated the role of prior knowledge in comprehension and new learning. We should address the role of deficient knowledge on learning-disabled students' subsequent new learning in any academic area and in their subsequent learning of learning strategies. At present, we know that deficient knowledge base seriously impairs a child's ability to learn a strategy. Chi (1981) found that when a child's knowledge base is well established and stable (e.g., the child knows the names of her classmates well), she could learn to use a new strategy for retrieving the names. Prior to introduction of the new strategy, alphabetization (recalling classmates' names in alphabetical order), the child had used the classroom seating arrangement as her retrieval strategy. When she had to learn a list of unfamiliar names (names that do not belong to her friends), however, the same newly acquired strategy of alphabetization was not as facilitative in retrieving the names.

The relevance of Chi's (1981) study concerns how learning-disabled students' deficient knowledge base in subject areas impedes their learning and applying inculcated strategies designed for use in those areas. For example, learning-disabled students in lower intermediate grades who have consistently been released from mathematics classes for reading remediation, might, in time, across the grades, develop a deficient or weak knowledge base in mathematics. This deficiency, for example, in multiplication concept and procedures, could in turn impede their learning of division and fractions. Moreover, if they were given training in the use of strategies to tackle division, for example, estimating the correct answer to a long division sum, they may have difficulties in learning to apply the strategy because of a weak foundation of multiplication concepts and procedures. Chi's findings and others (Miyake & Norman, 1978; Voss, 1982) attest to the interdependence of knowledge and strategy use and suggest that intervention research in LD needs to consider the variable of knowledge base.

How Do Process Problems Interact with a Given Intervention?

Where do process problems fit into intervention research? Process problems are an integral part of the conceptualization of learning-disabled children, adolescents, and adults. Yet in LD intervention research, researchers have not controlled for this dimension of subject variables, by including subgroup(s) with processing problems that may interact with the given intervention. For example, in an investigation of effective strategies to aid story recall in learning-disabled children, it would be instructive to have one trained group of learning-disabled children with adequate memory functions and another with severe memory problems. Together with a nontrained learning-disabled group and the parallel comparison groups of non-learning-disabled children, the investigators would have been able to map out the strategy's specific effects on the three groups of learning-disabled children with variable memory functions. The value of such intervention data is self-explanatory.

We need to include such subgroups if we are serious about testing the efficacy of our interventions. As seen in the example, subjects with processing problems help specify the conditions under which the tested intervention has worked and when it needs modifications, as well as suggesting what kinds of modifications it needs. These suggestions in turn can lead to fruitful follow-up investigations.

But what kinds of processing problems should we focus on for inclusion in intervention research? To begin with, let us capitalize on Torgesen's systematic and methodologically impeccable work on memory-processing problems in learning-disabled children. Torgesen and Houck's (1980) study highlighted both strategic and more deepseated, structural memory-processing problems in learning-disabled children. What is disappointing is that no one in intervention research has capitalized on Torgesen's work and investigated how learning-disabled children with mild and severe short-term memory-processing problems respond to differential instructional methods. By asking researchers to consider how their instructional techniques fare on learning-disabled subjects with processing problems, I hope that we shall see intervention studies that include a subgroup with identified processing problems that may interact with the intervention. Such inclusion would net data that enriches our understanding of the conditions that provide for efficacious interventions.

The Neglect of Affective Variables in Intervention Research

Consistent characteristics noted in learning-disabled children are their lack of motivation to learn and their passive learning style (Licht & Kirstner, 1986; McKinney & Feagans, 1984; Pearl, Donahue & Bryan, 1986; Torgesen, 1977). In intervention studies designed to promote their learning of skills and strategies, it appears remiss not to include this affective dimension. Indeed, LD intervention research has focused on "cold cognition" (Zojonc, 1980). This criticism needs redressing.

I submit that we need to show how learning-disabled children and adolescents' self-efficacy changes progressively as a function of successful intervention. We also need to document their continued motivation to learn after the cessation of intervention. Since they have experienced success in learning during the intervention, they should engender motivation to learn. Unless we document concomitant affective aspects of intervention, our research is incomplete. More important, unless we induce motivation to learn in the learning disabled, we may not obtain sustained maintenance of what we train them in our interventions.

I should point out that the affective dimension of attribution has been manipulated in intervention research, notably in reattribution training. In point of fact, Borkowski, Johnson, and Reid (1985) and Palmer and Goetz (1985) have proposed recent intervention models that integrate metacognition (metamemory in the case of Borkowski et al.) and attribution. As an exam`e of affective variables, I use measurement of self-efficacy simply because it seems to me that we should not be tied to one aspect of affective variables, such as attributions.

The Issue of Individual Instruction Versus Small-Group Instruction

Empirically and in practice, learning-disabled students learn well in one-to-one instructional settings. The problem concerns the expense in providing one-to-one instruction, both in intervention research and in school practice. One recalls Bloom's "Two sigma" problem. Bloom (1984) found that average students who were tutored individually achieved about two standard deviations above the average of their non-tutored peers. Put differently, the tutored students surpassed 98% of the nontutored students. Bloom's view is that we should find ways of bringing about such academic achievements in all students under more practical, more cost-efficient conditions. Accomplishing such achievements in students through individual tutoring is simply too costly for society. This is what he calls the "two sigma" problem (Bloom, 1984, p. 6). how can we resolve this problem, especially in this day of budget crunch?

I would like to invite you to consider the feasibility of cooperative learning conditions in intervention research. The research on cooperative learning versus competitive learning indicates that students function better in the former learning condition. In the cooperative learning condition, handicapped children were found to interact more with nonhandicapped children. They felt that they were helped more in this situation and were more cohesive with their nonhandicapped classmates (Johnson & Johnson, 1982). However, in cooperative learning groups involving less able students, more able students fared less well when the learning outcome was less successful. Nevertheless, Bryan, Cosden, and Pearl (1982) found that learning-disabled children can be trained successfully to function well in cooperative learning groups with non-learning-disabled children.

It seems to me that stratified cooperative learning groups involving bright, average non-learning-disabled and disabled children present a new and potentially illuminating research variable. Hitherto, intervention studies have compared learning-disabled with non-learning disabled students. Yet, in the mainstreamed classrooms, learning-disabled children and teenagers have to work alongside and sometimes with non-learning-disabled peers. It would be informative to find out how interventions may work when we mix learning-disabled and non-learning-disabled students. Of course, we may have to spend time pretraining them to work together cooperatively. But that seems a small price to pay.

METHODOLOGIC ISSUES

Like the conceptual issues, the methodologic issues raised are diverse. They point to problems in research methodology that explain, at least partially, failures or ambiguities in intervention outcomes. Intervention researchers must attend to these methodologic issues, since they cannot afford to waste time, energy, and research funds in experimentally flawed research.

Developmental Nature of Intervention

Sometimes researchers report failed interventions without realizing that they forgot to build up from more basic components or steps to the intervention procedure used. In short, they need to attend to the developmental nature of certain kinds of interventions. The more complex the intervention, the more important it is to attend to this issue.

The developmental nature of interventions is readily appreciated in the case of improving written composition in learning-disabled students through word-processing on the microcomputer. The intervention researcher here must consider building sufficient typing skills, providing writing prompts, inducing knowledge of genre of writing (e.g., narrative vs. expository), and so on. In short, the intervention researcher has a long way to go in building up support skills before he or she can move on to test the efficacy of increasing learning-disabled children's composition through word-processing on the microcomputer.

The Packaging of General and Domain-Specific Strategies

Thus far, intervention researchers in LD have focused on inducing general strategies that enhance learning in learning-disabled students. It seems opportune to reflect on the issue of inducing domain-specific strategies. Researchers in cognitive psychology and instructional psychology have been concerned with the role of domain-specific knowledge (Chi, 1981; Voss, 1982; Larkin's reference work on physics problems), and Cook and Mayer (1983) have advocated research on domain-specific strategies in aid of specific content learning.

Because secondary curricula focus on specific content areas (e.g., math, social studies, English, and science), the notion of designing domain-specific strategies to facilitate learning-disabled adolescents' content learning appears to be appealing. Yet these adolescents still need to learn general strategies such as self-monitoring their reading comprehension. The pertinent research issue appears to be mapping out an optimal combination of general and domain-specific strategies and investigating their comparative efficacy in promoting content learning in learning-disabled adolescents.

Sustained and Programmatic Interventions

The existent intervention studies in LD tend to be one-shot studies. Although the findings are instructive, they would have been even more instructive if they had been programmatic. It appears that what is needed are intervention studies that systematically try out various parameters of particular instructional procedures and learning strategies over the same population of learning-disabled subjects as well as different groups of learning-disabled subjects. For example, it would be instructive to research the effects of building successive strategies in the same group of learning-disabled students, to see how the increasing strategic repertoire enhances academic learning. Specifically, such sustained and programmatic research would allow us to see:

1. How trainees invent new strategies, given a base of sufficient strategic repertoire.
2. The evolution of trained strategies—how trainees modify the learned strategies to suit their purposes: how student use over time enables a simple strategy to evolve into a more sophisticated one.

These factors are important because the ultimate goal in intervention research is to enable learning-disabled students to be self-regulated successful learners. (For an elaboration on these questions, see Wong, 1985a.)

The Issue of Ecological Validity

In intervention research, one needs to use training materials that are ecologically valid, preferably, school curricula and approximation to school operations or routines. However, a caveat here appears necessary. In striving toward ecological validity, intervention researchers must maintain perspective as rigorous researchers. To illustrate this issue, let me cite an example. In an intervention study designed to enhance reading comprehension, the researchers gave the treatment group a particular vocabulary training. For the control group, the researchers used the classroom teacher's teaching approach in vocabulary training. In doing so, the researchers thought that they were attaining ecological validity in their study; however, the classroom teacher did not use the same vocabulary words as the experimenters with the treatment subjects. Moreover, the post-test targeted vocabulary items that were covered in the training given only to the treatment subjects.

In thinking that they were meeting the criterion of ecological validity, the intervention researchers inadvertently built in a serious experimental confound in their study: They had unwittingly biased the treatment in favor of the treatment subjects, thereby committing a Type I error. To avoid a Type I error, they should have included an additional group in which the subjects received the same vocabulary training approach as the first group, with the vocabulary items being the same as those used by the classroom teacher. This example is used to support the case for more perspective (or more balance, more thoughtfulness) in intervention researchers' attempts to be ecologically valid in their research studies.

Maintenance and Transfer

More than one maintenance test is required, because consolidation of learning may take time.

Frequently in instructional research, the investigators seldom measure trainees' learning progress during training. Moreover, they tend to use only one post-test. To thoroughly measure the viability of training effects, the researchers need to measure progressive performance changes in the trainees during acquisition. Also, they must use more than one post-test or maintenance test. These tests, used during acquisition and maintenance, must involve different materials than those used in training (Palincsar, 1982; Wong, 1985a;b).

The justification for spaced, successive measures of trainees' learning during acquisition and maintenance lies in accommodating the trainees' consolidation of learning. Such consolidation of learning takes time. Thus, only successive measures placed at well-considered intervals would enable researchers to get a clearer picture of the nature of the trainees' learning and by reflection, the efficacy of their training.

The fact that consolidation of learning takes time appears well illustrated in Figure 12-1, which depicts data from Nolte and Singer (1985). Nolte and Singer trained 9- and 10-year-old children by a process of active comprehension. The children were taught through experimenter-modeling to generate questions throughout reading. As shown clearly in Figure 12-1, training effects began to emerge from the seventh test onward. Thereafter, the between-group differences in experimental and control subjects widened progressively and strikingly. If Nolte and Singer only had one or two tests, they would have reached a very different conclusion regarding their training procedure.

Meaningful transfer tests: Do we need "far transfer" as a post-test? In instructional research, the investigators often include near and far transfer tasks in their post-tests (Palincsar, 1982). Near transfer tasks are those that differ from the training tasks in surface features. However, solving them requires that the subjects use the same cognitive processes as those involved in the training tasks. Far transfer tasks, on the other hand, should differ in both surface features and underlying cognitive processes in the training tasks. For example, let us suppose that the experimenter investigated two methods of teaching addition of 2-digit sums with regrouping. In addition to a post-test, she used a near transfer test of 3-digit sums with regrouping, and, for

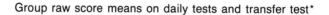

Group raw score means on daily tests and transfer test*

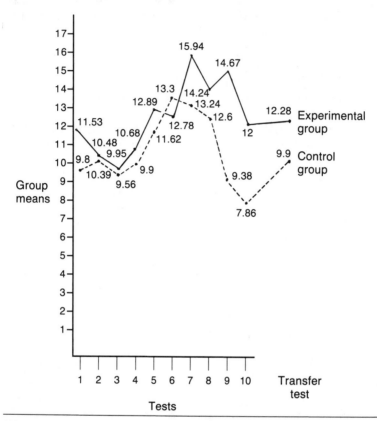

Tests

*Means for raw scores are indicated. The results could also be depicted in the form of standard scores. The graph would look about the same, but differences would be exaggerated.

Figure 12-1. Data from Nolte and Singer (1986). Figure reproduced with permission from both the *Reading Teacher* and the authors.

a far transfer test, she asked the children to perform 4-digit subtraction items with regrouping.

The nature of far transfer tasks should give us pause, since it poses interpretational problems for instructional researchers who use them in their studies. Because the researchers have not trained their subjects on the far transfer tasks, if positive findings on the far transfer tasks occur, how could the researchers interpret them apart from muttering that they had bright subjects?

It seems opportune to consider the meaningfulness of using far transfer tasks in instructional research. We should not blindly perpetuate research paradigms without periodically reviewing the underlying rationale and the meaningfulness of using them. In light of the above, I submit that we may consider abandoning far transfer tasks in future instructional research studies.

Interpretations of Intervention Effects

Component analysis: One major criticism of intervention studies is that the training package often involves multiple components or sub-skills. Thus, although the training package is successful, the critical components have not been isolated (Wong, 1985b).

Indeed, if one cannot isolate the components that play a causally critical role vis-à-vis the positive intervention outcome, one would not be able to explain clearly what causes the outcome. Such weakness in explanatory mechanism impairs the theoretical framework that originally generates the instructional research.

Counter-argument to component analysis: Despite the persuasiveness of the need for component analysis of training packages, there is a counter-argument to it. There may be conditions in which a component analysis of the positive intervention outcome appears infeasible. These conditions exist when (1) all the components within the intervention package are necessary, but each by itself is insufficient; and (2) the components within the intervention package exert a reciprocal effect on one another. In support of (1) is the doctoral study by Hutchinson (1986). Using a cognitive task analysis, she decomposed the skill of solving algebraic word-problems into two steps: (1) teaching learning-disabled adolescents correct representations of the algebraic word-problems, and (2) teaching them the solution. Hutchinson (1986) found that instruction of *both* steps was necessary to effect mastery of the algebraic word-problems in learning-disabled adolescents. Neither representation nor solution instruction per se was sufficient.

Clearly, as instructional researchers, we need to always be mindful of possibilities other than the one view that predominates our current thinking. Awareness of the other side of the coin, so to speak, on the view of component analysis of intervention outcomes may increase our ability to explain the psychological mechanisms that mediate effective interventions.

Nitty-Gritty Issues

Processing Time Allowed Subjects in Intervention Studies

There is a tendency among LD instructional researchers to use rigid training procedures without due consideration for the consequences on the trainees. To illustrate, one intervention researcher

reported giving her learning-disabled and non-learning-disabled subjects 3 minutes to process a passage before testing. There was no accom-
modation for subjects who did not finish reading the passage in the
set time limit. All subjects had the passages removed from them after
3 minutes and were promptly given a test.

Elsewhere I have discussed how insensate it is to have such
thoughtless adherence to rigid experimental procedure (Wong, 1985a).
If subjects were not allowed sufficient processing time, regardless of
whether the outcome is positive or negative, the resultant data are
meaningless. This problem is particularly serious when learning-
disabled subjects are involved. Because of the decoding and reading
comprehension problems, denying learning-disabled subjects sufficient processing time in assimilating a prose passage during training
is to introduce a serious confound into the data. The uselessness of
the intervention is obvious.

Mastery of Skills and Strategies Prior to Post-Tests Being Given

Many instructional researchers neglect to designate a priori a
training criterion in their studies. The reader has no assurance that
the learning-disabled and non-learning-disabled trained groups were
trained to criterion before they were given post-tests. When trainees
are tested prior to their demonstrating clearly that they have mastered
the skill or strategy targeted for training, the probability is high that
the researcher would not find positive intervention effects. She or he
then laments the time, money, and effort spent. (Plus no publication!)
Such lament is of course premature. After all, the trainees have not
yet had enough training. Such a study (in which mastery of trained
skill or strategy in the trainees was not ascertained prior to their being
tested) basically has not given the designed intervention a thorough
testing (Wong, 1985a).

EPILOGUE

In this chapter, I have shared my thoughts on instructional research
in LD. Some of these thoughts are new, and some are not quite new.
But all of them have occupied my mind in the last few months. I have
wrestled with them, but I have not answered all of them. Some of these
issues are simply too difficult for one head to solve. But by sharing
them with you, in particular, with our esteemed senior colleagues in
the field, I know that we will ultimately resolve these difficult conceptual and methodologic problems in instructional research in LD.

G. Reid Lyon

Bernice Wong's analysis of the conceptual and methodologic issues surrounding educational interventions with disabled learners is a timely piece of work. I gravitated to much of what she had to say in her chapter primarily because I believe that a very complicated task confronting researchers is to understand the instructional factors that have to be considered when teaching students with special needs. Hopefully, when all is said and done, the field of LD will be judged on how effectively it has developed and tested hypotheses concerning how to teach concepts to persons who do not acquire them by standard instructional methods. The emphasis on instruction and learning seems reasonable since the population that professionals in LD seek to help consists of persons who, for at least part of their day, are not learning information in a manner that allows them to understand it, remember it, and generalize it to other contexts. As such, it is refreshing to read Wong's views on how we can best conceptualize research frameworks that guide the investigation of teaching practices and procedures to aid learning-disabled students.

Within the context of delineating conceptual and methodologic issues in intervention research, Wong has identified a series of objectives for inquiry that will allow us to better understand *what* we should teach to learning-disabled students, *how* we should teach them, and *why* we should study teaching and its outcomes according to designated guidelines. More specifically, Wong's suggestion that we investigate the effect of inducing both general and domain-specific learning strategies is a compelling one and addresses, in part, the question of *what* to teach disabled learners to increase the probability of success in the classroom. Data from studies conducted by Wong (Wong, 1979; Wong, 1985a, 1985b; Wong, Wong, & Foth, 1977) and others (Deshler & Schumaker, 1986; Schumaker, Deshler, Alley, & Warner, 1983) clearly underscore the importance and applicability of research in learning strategies.

Appropriately, Wong then takes us beyond our typical tendency to be satisfied with addressing only the *what* to teach question by arguing that we must strive to answer such questions as *How* do successful learners acquire skills and strategies? *How* do processing deficits affect response to various forms of intervention? *How* do we

teach concepts and learning strategies to students such that comprehension, acquisition, retention, and generalization are fostered. In my
mind, Wong's call for conceptually and methodologically sound
research in these *"how"* domains focuses attention on one of the
greatest challenges facing educational researchers today, that is, how
do we represent classroom tasks to learning-disabled students so that
individual learning characteristics are accounted for and the new information being taught is related to existing learner knowledge. Recent
advances in the cognitive sciences (Farnham-Diggory, 1980, 1986 for
relevant reviews) have led to a growing literature that indicates that
both the structure and content of school tasks can be modified and
presented in ways that facilitate a student's ability to establish relationships between new and stabilized knowledge domains (Mastropieri
et al., 1985; Scruggs et al., 1985).

Wong's discussion of methodologic guidelines for intervention
research clearly addresses several *why* questions related to research
on teaching. For example, *why* intervention sequences need to be constructed within a developmental framework, *why* interventions need
to be carried out over a sustained period of time, and *why* our training
materials and tasks must be characterized by robust ecological validity.
Unless we adhere to Wong's suggestions for rigor in these areas, the
probability of developing a greater understanding of both what and
how to teach will be seriously compromised.

I must admit, however, that I came away from Wong's paper with
a sense of incompleteness and wanting. Neither Wong nor the rest of
us have adequately addressed the need to create and construct research
designs that are robust, flexible, and dynamic enough to study the
ongoing instructional decision-making process that teachers engage
in as they impart concepts to students. Most of us who teach children
and/or adults would agree that we constantly strive to get our points
and ideas across to our students. Most of us would also agree that there
is a larger purpose to teaching that goes beyond the straightforward
inculcation of concepts, that is, inducing students to abstract information across settings, problem-solving situations, and time. How do
successful teachers teach these things? In particular, how do they teach
them when the student does not initially acquire the information or
generalize it?

Understanding how "good" teachers decide upon different
representations of concepts for different students, monitor and adjust
the number of conceptual elements being presented, routinely induce
strategies for learning, inspire students to invest themselves in the
instructional unit, and perform all of these behaviors simultaneously
or in quick combinations is as important as determining whether
learning-disabled and non-learning-disabled students differ in

response to different phonics approaches—maybe more so. This is because no matter how well designed, defined, and sequenced an intervention method or material may be, such conventions are static and linear. It is the teacher who carries the method or material to the student, and the means and style of delivery vary among teachers. It is possible that this type of variance is highly related to student outcome.

Clearly, what is being addressed here cannot be studied easily or well by traditional methods. How and why teachers make instructional decisions reflects a complex and multivariate process that is not generally amenable to pre- and post-test and/or experimental/control group designs. Possibly, theoretically and conceptually based ethnographic observational methods may help us capture and study the exceedingly complicated instructional process that teachers engage in on a routine basis. Regardless of the particular approach, there is a need to augment the research procedures as discussed by Wong with methodologies that are as dynamic and flexible as the teaching process itself. Isn't this what we mean by "ecological validity?"

REFERENCES

Bloom, B.S. (1984, May). The search for methods of group instruction as effective as one-to-one tutoring. *Educational Leadership*, 4–17.

Borkowski, J.G., Johnston, M.B., & Reid, M.K. (1985). Metacognition, motivation, and the transfer of control processes. In S.J. Ceci (Ed.), *Handbook of cognition, social, and neuropsychological aspects of learning disabilities*. Hillsdale, NJ: Erlbaum.

Bryan, T., Cosden, M., & Pearl, R. (1982). The effects of cooperative goal structures and cooperative models on learning disabled and non-disabled students. *Learning Disability Quarterly, 5*, 415–421.

Chi, M.T.H. (1981). Interactive roles of knowledge and strategies in development. In S. Chipman, J. Segal, & R. Glaser (Eds.), *Thinking and learning skills: Current research and open questions* (Vol. 2). Hillsdale, NJ: Erlbaum.

Cook, L.K., & Mayer, R.E. (1983). Reading strategies training for meaningful learning from prose. In M. Pressley & J.R. Levin (Eds.), *Cognitive strategy research: Educational applications* (pp. 87–131). New York: Springer-Verlag.

Deshler, D.D. & Schumaker, J.B. (1986). Learning strategies: An instructional alternative for low-achieving adolescents. *Exceptional Children, 52*, 583–590.

Farnham-Diggory, S. (1980). Learning disabilities: A view from cognitive science. *Journal of Child Psychiatry, 19*, 570–578.

Farnham-Diggory, S. (1986). Commentary: Time, now, for a little serious complexity. In S. Ceci (Ed.), *Handbook of cognitive, social, and* neuropsychological aspects of learning disabilities. Hillsdale, NJ: Erlbaum.

Hutchinson, N. (1986). Teaching learning disabled adolescents algebraic word-problems through correct representation and solution. Ph.D. thesis, Simon Fraser University, B.C., Canada.

Johnson, R.T., & Johnson, D.W. (1982). Effects of co-operative and competitive learning experiences on interpersonal attraction between handicapped and non-handicapped students. Journal of Social Psychology, 116, 211–219.

McKinney, J.D., & Feagans, L. (1984). Acadmeic and behavioral characteristics of learning disabled children and average achievers: Longitudinal studies. Learning Disability Quarterly, 7, 251–265.

Mastropieri, M., Scruggs, T., Levin, J., Gaffney, J., & McLoone B. (1985). Mnemonic vocabulary instruction for learning disabled students. Learning Disability Quarterly, 8, 57–63.

Miyake, N., & Norman, D.A. (1978). To ask a question, one must know enough to know what is not known. Journal of Verbal Learning and Verbal Behavior, 18, 357–364.

Nolte, R.Y., & Singer, H. (1985, October). Active comprehension: Teaching a process of reading comprehension and its effects on reading achievement. The Reading Teacher, 24–31.

Palmer, D.J., & Goetz, E.T. (1985). Selection and use of study strategies: The role of the studier's beliefs about self and strategies. Unpublished manuscript, Texas A & M University.

Pearl, R., Donahue, M. & Bryan, T. (1986). Social relationships of learning-disabled children. In J.K. Torgesen & B.Y.L. Wong (Eds.), Psychological and educational perspectives on learning disabilities. Orlando: Academic Press.

Schumaker, J.B., Deshler, D.D., Alley, G.R., & Warner, M.M. (1983). Toward the development of an intervention model for learning disabled adolescents. Exceptional Education Quarterly, 3, 45–50.

Scruggs, T., Mastropieri, M., Lewin, J., McLoone, B., Gaffney, J.S., & Prater, M.A. (1985). Increasing content-area learning: A comparison of mnemonic and visual-spatial direct instruction. Learning Disabilities Research, 1, 18–31.

Torgesen, J.K., & Houck, G. (1980). Processing deficiencies in learning disabled children who perform poorly on the digit span task. Journal of Educational Psychology, 72, 141–160.

Voss, J.F. (1982, March). Knowledge and social science problem-solving. Paper presented at AERA meeting, New York City.

Wong, B.Y.L. (1979). Increasing the retention of main ideas in learning disabled children through the use of questions. Learning Disability Quarterly, 2, 43–47.

Wong, B.Y.L. (1985a). Self-questioning instructional research: A review. Review of Educational Research, 55, 227–268.

Wong, B.Y.L. (1985b). Issues in cognitive-behavioral interventions in academic skill areas. Journal of Abnormal Child Psychology, 13(3).

Wong, B.Y.L., Wong R., & Foth, D. (1977). Recall and clustering of verbal materials among normal and poor readers. Bulletin of the Psychonomic Society, 19, 375–378.

PART VI

Public Policy

CHAPTER 13

Learning Disabilities and Public Policy: A Role for Research Workers

Edwin W. Martin

S everal public policy issues are now being raised that will have a large impact for children and adults with learning disabilities (LD). These issues must be faced by those of us who have a professional interest or responsibility for such persons. At their most significant level, public policy decisions may substantially alter the education of hundreds of thousands of children by redefining the population considered to be learning disabled.

LEGISLATION AND THE LEARNING DISABLED

One simple way to begin to feel the impact of public policy is to imagine for a moment that you are a national or state legislator and have it within your power to introduce legislation that will result in changes you wish to see for children and adults with LD. What would you propose?

To carry this exercise a little further, think for a moment about some actual legislation that has affected children with LD. For example, in 1966, the author had the privilege of working for the House of Representatives and helping to draft the first Education of the Handicapped Act. Its main features were to begin a program of grants to the states to initiate, expand or improve educational programming for children with disabilities, and create the Bureau of Education for the Handicapped (BEH) and a National Advisory Committee on Handicapped Children.

The definition of "handicapped children" in that law included children who were mentally retarded, hard of hearing, deaf, speech impaired, visually handicapped, seriously emotionally disturbed, orthopedically impaired, or otherwise health impaired. You may note that there was no mention of children with LD. This omission meant that the states were not free to spend any of the federal funds they received on classes or other programs for children so identified. Some states and local districts got around that prohibition by classifying the children as "other health impaired," that is, neurologically impaired.

The exclusion of children with LD in the first Education of the Handicapped Act was not accidental. Parents of such children had petitioned the Congress for their inclusion, but a few advocates for other groups of children viewed the new category as a threat and as competition for limited funds. They convinced key Congressional staff persons that the definition of LD was so broad that it could include any economically disadvantaged child whose circumstances resulted in educational problems. They argued that such children, already assisted by the Congress through Title I of the Elementary and Secondary Education Act, would use up all the resources needed by children who were, in fact, disabled.

Efforts to include children with LD under the provisions of the Education of the Handicapped Act continued after 1966. In 1970, partial progress was made. Children with LD were included in Amendments to the Education of the Handicapped Act, which provided for legislation authorizing grants for teacher training, research, and a new program of model service projects. Basic participation in the grants to states program was still not approved. Key to the acceptance by Congress of the category of LD in the 1970 legislation was a definition of children with LD for special educational purposes that was developed by the National Advisory Committee on Handicapped Children working jointly with the Bureau of Education for the Handicapped. The Congress used that definition in framing the new law.

When the Congress passed Public Law 94-142 in 1975, it was possible to successfully advocate for the inclusion, finally, of children with LD in the basic federal law. *If that public policy had not been changed, the more than 1.5 million children currently identified as requiring special education as a result of LD would not now be participating under Public Law 94-142.* By then there were widespread programs for persons with LD operating under local and state law, and opposition was minimized. One sign that opposition still remained, however, came when a Senate staff member insisted on letting the 1970 LD model projects legislation expire since the category was now part of the larger law.

Another example of resistance by public policymakers toward including those labeled as learning disabled in federal policy occurred within the Vocational Rehabilitation Administration regarding the acceptance of persons with LD as qualified for vocational rehabilitation services. As Assistant Secretary for Special Education and Vocational Rehabilitation, the author needed to put extreme pressure on the colleagues of the rehabilitation agency to include persons with LD. They finally agreed after discovering that medical references were including the category "learning disabilities" as a medically recognized syndrome. For awhile, it seemed that it might be necessary for advocates to sue the Rehabilitation Services Administration under the provisions of Section 504 of The Rehabilitation Act, which prohibits discrimination against persons with disabilities, an irony indeed, since that is the Act which the agency is charged with administering.

POLICY ISSUES FACING PRACTITIONERS AND RESEARCHERS

What policy issues now face practitioners and researchers interested in LD? There are many, but perhaps the most critical is still the issue of identifying which children are indeed disabled. Are children who do not have LD being identified and educated as learning disabled? Are they harmed by that process? Is it wasteful of public funds? What responses will local school officials make, or how will legislative bodies respond?

A recent survey of more than seven hundred readers of two trade newsletters, *Education Daily* and *Education of the Handicapped*, illustrates this issue. To the question "Is overplacement happening in your (school's) jurisdiction?", 34% of the respondents answered "yes." Fifty-six percent thought that overplacement was also happening in other jurisdictions. To the question "In what category is overplacement the biggest problem?", 85% answered "learning disabilities." Of the people making this response, 51% saw the "overburdening of regular education teachers" as the primary cause for overplacement, and another 30% believed that the cause was poorly trained pesonnel (*Education of the Handicapped*, 1986). Although these opinions were gathered from a small sample, they probably represent prevailing attitudes.

Most importantly for the research and professional community, will the governmental decision-makers have good data on which to base their decisions or will they have to act on popular opinion? Even if it is not possible to offer research information to policy makers, can the professional community (and parents) offer well-thought-out positions with reasonably broad scientific support that might be the basis for policy judgments? As was shown in the Congressional acceptance of the National Advisory Committee definition, such consensus positions often carry considerable weight. The Congress and other legislative bodies tend to rely on expert opinion when they can get it in reasonably consistent and understandable form.

Two recent examples demonstrate the potential power of public opinion. One was a lengthy article highlighted by a front-page headline in *Newsday*, a major metropolitan New York newspaper with a circulation of more than 600,000. The story's opening paragraphs contain the following statement:

> "The growth in the number of learning disabled children has led certain educators to question whether too many youngsters are being channeled into special education, when some of them might be better served by a remedial program or another less stigmatizing approach" (Marks, 1986, p. 5).

This article, carefully written with no bias against special education, presents a common, but undocumented, belief that many children currently in special education classes are not appropriately placed. Unfortunately, information like this will play a role in public debate and, perhaps, in generating public policy in New York. Public perceptions do influence public policy; therefore, the need for research and evaluation becomes critical if educational expenditures are to withstand to make their case for special education opportunities for their children.

Another example, also from the New York area, involves Mayor Koch's Commission on Special Education, on which the author served. In 1985, this group reviewed special education in New York City amidst a popular climate in which the Mayor and others had expressed concern for the rapid rise in special education enrollments and costs. The Commission heard expert witnesses claim that many children who were not disabled were being placed in special education classes because "they were the only game in town." The children could receive additional assistance only through special education because no other remedial programs were available.

The Commission asked New York University professor, Jay Gottlieb, to review the placement procedures and records of Committees on the Handicapped (the mechanisms for placement in New York City). Among other findings, Gottlieb confirmed that the children being referred for special class placements as learning disabled did in fact present more serious educational retardation than did nonreferred students (Gottlieb, 1985). While not answering all questions about the efficacy of testing this popular, if unproven, view that "too many children are in special education," Gottlieb's data did reassure those Commission members and others who, based on popular reports, feared school personnel were assigning to special education any child who was not doing well in school, a population with vast proportions in the City. School board members, legislators, and school officials need valid information, not opinions, on which to base their judgments. The point is not that Gottlieb's data provided scientific proof in response to important questions, but rather that it was a useful and persuasive tool in public policy review.

In addition to the question of identifying those students with LD, other policy issues that require attention include: What are the intersections between regular and special education? To what extent is mainstreaming an effective special education placement for children with LD? These questions are linked together because it seems that discussions about the intersection between regular and special education are growing out of concerns over the costs of special education and the growth of numbers of children identified as learning disabled.

Some years ago when the author recommended to Congress that it include children with LD among the disabled children to be protected under the Education for All Handicapped Children Act of 1975, there was concern expressed regarding the need to develop an identification process that could be used to correctly include such children. The BEH was given the responsibility for developing a Federal Regulation that would direct the assessment and identification practices under the law. Until that regulation was reviewed and accepted by the Congress, a limitation was placed on the number of children that states could identify as learning disabled for federal purposes under Public Law 94-142, a sum equal to 2% of school-age children in the United States.

This example illustrates that legislative policy decisions are frequently drawn from economic or administrative concerns, rather than based on facts about the population to be served. There was no research basis for the 2% figure. As a result, a child might have been turned away from special education because his or her state already filled its two percent "quota" and was unwilling to accept a child for whom federal reimbursement was not possible. In essence, this "capping" provision upset the protections of the basic law. (Note: A school district could not legally have rejected a child for that reason, but experience indicates that many decisions to refer or place a child are influenced by underlying fiscal considerations.)

It seems likely that much of the interest in providing more specialized education for children with LD and other disabilities in the regular classroom is motivated by cost and administrative concerns. That is not to say that there is a lack of real concern for the children's educational needs, but that the "solution" may emerge within the context of financial concerns.

Some other policy-related issues with significance for the research community include: (1) Are resource room programs effective and, more specifically, under what conditions and for whom? (2) What are the basic skills, attitudes, and so on, that teachers of children with LD should have (i.e, certification and competency standards)? (3) Do teachers, trained and certified as "noncategorical" serve learning-disabled children as effectively as so-called specialized personnel in LD? (4) What type of secondary education is needed for children with LD? and (5) What kind of vocational education and rehabilitation will increase successful job placement? One last issue that might be offered, (6) At what point in the process of early identification and programming should children be identified as having LD?

ROLES FOR RESEARCH SPECIALISTS

If these and other questions discussed in this chapter are of significance to the child or adult with LD and the professionals educated to assist such persons, what are the responsibilities, if any, of a researcher? The author's experiences with the research community suggest that some will answer in words such as, "I have a special area of research interest, and that is where my efforts must go. These may be important questions for the field in general, but that is not my concern." It is hard to argue with this position, as a specialist should have the right to follow his or her own interests—that is part of academic freedom. Others will find research in policy-related areas to be challenging, if not frustratingly difficult, and may proceed on one or more concerns of policy significance. Overall efforts may be piecemeal and nonconclusive.

It seems likely that both of these possibilities will occur. It is essential, however, that more research specialists play a role in developing new public policies. There is a need for the research specialist to help create an informed dialogue, finding areas where knowledge is reasonably sound and helping the professional and parent communities articulate positions to the policymakers.

This does not mean that making "research" presentations to the Congress or other policymakers is necessarily required or, in some cases, desirable. The author was often disappointed in the impact research workers had on the Congress. Frequently their testimony sounded like papers that had been prepared for a research convention and were filled with professional jargon, technical language, and overly cautious disclaimers as to the soundness of information presented. While those of us with a bit of familiarity with research understand the need for scientific caution in the presentation of conclusions, the net effect of this kind of testimony was too frequently to convince Congress that researchers are boring and their work unconvincing.

On the other hand, a presentation designed for an intelligent lay audience and that is able to weave together the best practices, current research impressions, and professional judgments can be enormously influencial. Policymakers, for the most part, want to do the "right" thing; they simply need supporting information presented to them in a format that allows them to understand and act upon the relevant facts and issues.

Research workers should also be active in professional and parent organizations to have an impact on public policy. Most organizations now have government affairs committees and political "networks" enlisting interested members. Helping such groups develop positions and public statements is very important. Research specialists carry a responsibility to help their accumulation of knowledge be usefully applied. It was the author's observation in more than 15 years of government service that policy decisions will go forward, based on available information, if available and persuasive, and, if those of us, as professionals, are not effectively and actively involved, the populations we seek to serve will suffer from the misapplications or from absence of attention.

In addition to efforts of research workers, the federal government should exercise new leadership in creating the opportunity for long-term research support on LD and public policy relevant to this population and other persons with disabilities. It was unfortunate that the Department of Education ended the support for the research centers in LD. The government should continue to review programs carefully to ensure that they are productive and useful, but the wiping out of all such research centers was a policy rather than professional judgment, which this author believes was in error. Children with LD represent the largest single group of children served under the federal law, and, because many serious questions remain concerning this population, research efforts in this area should be expanded, not reduced. Furthermore, research needs to be relatively long-term to show maximal sophistication and effectiveness. Individual 3-year grants, although useful, are not sufficient for comprehensive understanding of complex phenomena.

There can be no greater testament to our open society than P.L. 94-142. This legislation reflects the most humane and progressive instincts in our society. It was passed by the Congress, not because of monied special interests or huge blocks of voters, but because it met a genuine need as articulated jointly by parents and professionals. With its inclusion of individualized education plans, requirements for non-discriminatory testing and related services, including various therapies, it reflects the best of current practice in special education. That such a bill is possible, even if it may be less than perfect, is an affirmation of the fact that research workers, in concert with others, can be effective in creating better opportunities for the children and adults their research is designed to benefit.

In the next few years, more public policies affecting persons with LD are going to be developed, and they are likely to have tremendous significance for thousands, perhaps millions, of children and adults. The research community must continue to play an active and instrumental role in this evolution.

RESPONSE

Gerald M. Senf

Public policy is an elusive concept: research regarding public policy seemingly becomes merely a figment of imagination—a task in the "Twilight Zone." Not so really, if one understands first what public policy involves.

Kiesler's (1980) framework as applied to mental health is useful for LD. He defines "national mental health policy as the de facto or de jure aggregate of laws, practices, social structures, or actions occurring within our society, the intent of which is improved mental health of individuals or groups. The study of such policy includes the descriptive parameters of the aggregate, the comparative assessment of particular techniques, the evaluation of the system and its subparts, human resources available and needed, cost-benefit analyses of practices or actions, and the cause-and-effect relationships of one set of policies...to others, as well as the study of institutions or groups seeking to affect such policy." Simply substituting "learning disabilities" for the term "mental health" in this definition provides us with a clear public policy framework, the aspects of which provide fruitful avenues for empirical research. I shall mention some specific research questions later, after first describing the interplay between "guild" concerns and the ability of a field to affect public policy.

Guild or survival concerns of a field such as LD depend ultimately upon the perspective of the populus, "outcomes that are mediated by public opinion and by policy decisions that are shaped, in part, by public beliefs about the field" (Pallak & Kilburg, 1986). A field's failure to provide the populus and their representatives with accurate and persuasive information regarding their goals and societal contributions endangers itself. Excessive concern for internal affairs, such as those which plagued LD (Colarusso, 1980; Goodman, 1980; Senf, 1980; Wiederholt et al., 1980), severely weaken a field's ability to maintain, let alone increase, its credibility. Edwin Martin's chapter cites occassions in which LD has been opposed by competing service providers and had its very claim to existence challenged. He does not attribute the challenges to any particular deficiency of the LD leadership or its strategy; instead, he views the developments of the last two-plus decades in historical perspective, although it is clear that he views history with a policy perspective. For example, he cites the rejection of the LD concept in 1966 legislation as due to competing interests, the 2% cap placed on LD in 1975, and his own initiative on behalf of LD in its confrontation with Vocational Rehabilitation as examples of external pressures on the field.

Unfortunately, but understandably, Martin chose to frame his comments in an historical framework and from a personal perspective. A public policy research perspective is present but embedded, so read his words carefully. For example, he states, "most critical is still the question of identifying which children are indeed disabled." Although he does not explicitly deal here with policy research, his focus on "identifying" as opposed to "defining" followed by citation of data regarding the reasons for "overplacement" (as being due to overburdening of regular education teachers) dramatizes the importance of public opinion research in maintaining public support. In this instance, note that overplacement, which could have been viewed as empire building or any of a number of negative accusations vis-à-vis LD, is empirically relegated to the regular educators' alleged "overburdening." This information has distinct policy implications contrary to those of competing hypotheses regarding the burgeoning incidence of LD.

As one considers a field's impact, outside of its own guild or de jure interests, Martin poses the question, "Will the governmental decision-makers have good data on which to make their decisions or will they have to act on popular opinion?" Here, Martin is clearly implicating the important role of extra-guild efforts, although I find the distinction confusing: Are "good data" and "popular opinion" distinct? In the present frame of reference, so-called good data are those that predispose those in power to support a field's efforts, in large part by "public opinion" or expert testimony. Martin clearly understands that influence is not an either/or issue but an interplay between data and opinion. The bottom line can most simply be stated, ". . . support for the field. . . is dependent on policy decisions (decisions to allo- cate resources and support) that result from political processes whether at the level of a foundation, a university budget process, a state legis- lature, a state executive agency, a federal executive agency, or the Con- gress" (Pallack & Kilburg, 1986).

In this context of political influence, two remaining questions need addressing: How has and will LD fare? What public policy research might influence its cause? Space prohibits review of published information supporting the utility of LD services, although its rele- vance is crucial to LD's welfare. Martin gives us little insight into LD's fate given the recent so-called regular-special education initiative. But he does list some questions of relevance—questions posed simply as of empirical interest but that could have policy implications.

Taking the first as an example, "Are resource room programs effec- tive. . .," one can easily see the difference between a simple research issue, as posed, and one of policy. In a parallel question in psychology, one regarding the effectiveness of psychotherapy, Kiesler (1980) acknowledges the contradictory outcome studies (similar to those regarding drug intervention or perceptual training efficacy, e.g., Kavale & Forness, 1983; Mattson & Kavale, 1983). However, he further notes that the introduction of as few as two to eight psychotherapy sessions adjunct to medical intervention reduces subsequent medical utiliza- tion by up to 50% and reduces job absenteeism by similar amounts. The policy issue is not psychotherapy outcome per se. "Rather, the primary issue is the marginal utility of psychotherapy when added to an existing system." The field of LD has simply not addressed such questions in policy terms and, as a result, has presented the populus with conflicting and unnecessarily qualified results, all to the field's detriment, a point Martin makes well in his section on "Roles for Research Specialists."

Finally, to provide the reader with a better feel for policy research issues, I shall list some issues relevant to LD today. (See Kiesler, 1980 for further discussion.)

1. One could accomplish descriptive research detailing agency practices and outcomes.

2. Descriptive research outlining the parameters of the LD service and research systems as they actually function would be useful.

3. One could assess the marginal utility of various LD services, that is, services in addition to regular education (as opposed to studying various services in isolation).

4. Related to issue 3, one could seek to understand what variables make adjunct LD services useful so that the knowledge could be used as policy to effect organizational change.

5. Secondary analyses of studies, such as those cited earlier by Kavale and colleagues, certainly have policy implications.

6. Evaluation research, including cost-benefit analyses, would be most useful in the policy arena. Long- as well as short-term cost analyses might show that higher short-term costs of LD services are offset by long-term savings.

7. The field should self-consciously assess the personal and familial costs of receiving LD services over long periods of time.

8. One needs to examine the most efficient and cost-effectve mix of professionals and auxiliary personnel for various service provision in recognition that the LD teacher cannot possibly always be the sole or best treatment agent of choice.

9. What one might term *LD economics* would have enormous policy ramifications. In general, what is the impact of service cost on utilization by various socioeconomic groups? Does underutilization by the poor cost society more in the long-term through unemployability, crime, and so on? Are adjunct non-school-based services unused as a result of high cost and lack of insurance coverage, only to cost society more in the long-term?

10. What is the empirical demand for LD services as perceived by the client population, and what proportion and which members of the populus actually receive services?

While the questions posed are generic in nature, the results of any given research effort could have far-reaching policy implications. For the professional continuance of the LD field, it is necessary that its members understand its relationship to the broader matrix of health and education services and to communicate its role and knowledge directly to the populus. Policy is made based on decision-makers' "best knowledge." LD professionals must become directly involved in effecting this knowledge base; otherwise, they will face adverse policy decisions in the public arena.

REFERENCES

Colarusso, R. (1980). Future directions for DCLD? *Journal of Learning Disabilities, 13,* 184–195.

Goodman, L. (1980). The anatomy of divisiveness. *Journal of Learning Disabilities, 13,* 180–184.

Gottlieb, J. (1985). Report to the Mayor's Commission on Special Education on COH Priorities in New York City. In "Special Education in New York City's Public Schools: Making It Special in More Than Name" (Final Report to Mayor I. Koch of the Commission on Special Education, Richard I. Beattie, Chairman), Appendix B.

Kavale, K., & Forness, S.R. (1983). Hyperactivity and diet treatment: A meta-analysis of the Feingold hypothesis. *Journal of Learning Disabilities, 16,* 324–330.

Kiesler, C.A. (1980). Mental health policy as a field of inquiry for psychology. *American Psychologist, 35,* 1066–1080.

Marks, P. (1986, May 19). Special education on Long Island: System within the system. *Newsday,* pp. 5, 24–25, 27.

Mattson, D.P., & Kavale, K. (1983). One jumped over the balance beam: Meta-analysis of perceptual motor training. *Journal of Learning Disabilities, 16,* 165–173.

Pallak, M.S., & Kilburg, R.R. (1986). Psychology, public affairs, and public policy: A strategy and review. *American Psychologist, 41,* 933–940.

Senf, G.M. (1980). "Audacity," yes! "Good will," no! Alienation in the LD profession. *Journal of Learning Disabilities, 13,* 174–179.

Staff. (1986, January 8)., Learning disabled rise continues to perplex educators. *Education of the Handicapped, 12* (1), 7–10.

Wiederholt, J.L., et al. (1980). A reply from the Board of Trustees for DCLD: A factual response to April's fiction. *Journal of Learning Disabilities, 13,* 412–419.

CHAPTER 14

Research on the Identification of Learning-Disabled Children: Perspectives on Changes in Educational Policy

James D. McKinney

T he objectives of the present paper are to review the findings of a series of recent studies at the Frank Porter Graham Child Development Center that evaluated the efficacy and educational validity of new identification procedures based on the concept of IQ/Achievement discrepancy, and to discuss the implications of this research for changes in educational policy affecting learning-disabled children.

The research described in this paper was supported by grants from the Office of Special Education and Rehabilitative Services (No. G008430051), the National Institute of Child Development and Human Development (No. HD17349), and the North Carolina State Department of Public Instruction. The author is grateful to Dr. Joni Alberg for her permission to cite data based on her dissertation at the University of North Carolina. Portions of this paper were delivered at the South Carolina State Symposium on LD Research.

Background

The term *specific learning disability* (LD) was introduced in the early 1960s to describe a diverse collection of disorders that were associated with school failure but could not be attributed to mental retardation, other forms of exceptionality, or environmental disadvantage. Most definitions of LD attribute school failure to deficiencies in the "basic psychological processes" that underlie effective learning. Early research in the field attempted to link LD to a variety of specific ability deficits under the assumption that faulty neurologic functioning produced developmental lags in the growth of key abilities such as visual perception, attention, memory, or language. This research tended to focus on the study of single abilities, which gave rise to a number of "single syndrome" theories. However, research on single abilities failed to account for the broad range of learning problems within this very heterogeneous group of children (Kavale & Forness, 1985; McKinney, 1987). As a result, there has been little consensus in the field about the principal manifestations of LD and its prevalence, etiology, and appropriate treatment.

Nevertheless, professionals and parents continued to offer evidence and arguments for the existence of a group of children with significant learning handicaps who did not fit existing categories of exceptionality. To provide learning-disabled children with special education services, the federal definition incorporated into Public Law 94-142 included children who did not achieve at a level expected of their age and general ability, and eligibility for services was determined through the exclusion of other handicaps and environmental disadvantage as the obvious causes of school failure.

Policy Issue

Since the definition of LD allows students to be placed in special education without determining the exact nature of their learning handicap, it is possible to include students who fail to achieve because of social or motivational factors rather than because of some inherent defect in development. This is the case because school failure could be the result of any number of factors that negatively influence learning besides specific LD. Although we should be concerned about underachievement regardless of its cause, it is important to differentiate those students who can take advantage of mainstream instruction with minimal help from those who require special education as the most appropriate placement of choice.

The ability of professionals to differentiate learning-disabled students who require special education from other underachievers has been increasingly questioned by policymakers and many professionals in the field (Algozzine & Korinek, 1985; Algozzine & Yesseldyke, 1983; Smith, 1982). At the same time, the cost of services for learning-disabled students has risen sharply as a function of the dramatic rise in prevalence, particularly in relation to other handicapping conditions. After the implementation of Public Law 94-142, the cost of special education increased at a rate of 14% per year, which was approximately twice the increase for regular education (Keogh, 1987; Stark, 1982). Subsequent research indicated that these increases in special education costs were largely due to increases in the number of learning-disabled students identified. When Public Law 94-142 was being debated in the Congress, it was originally estimated that 2% of the school population, or 17% of the handicapped population would be learning disabled. Between 1978 and 1982, the proportion of handicapped students classified as learning disabled rose from 28% to 40% at a rate of 3% per year. At the same time, the proportion of mentally retarded students declined from 26% to 18% of the handicapped population served. In addition to the large number of learning-disabled students served, the prevalence of LD has varied greatly both across and within states. Nationally, the percentage of handicapped students served as learning disabled varies from 26% to 64% of the handicapped population across the 50 states.

As these trends became evident, policymakers and leaders in the field of special education became increasingly critical of the definition of LD and of apparent inconsistencies in eligibility criteria across states and local school districts. In 1980, the General Accounting Office issued a report to the Congress that noted these trends and concluded that many slow learners and other noncategorical underachievers were being inappropriately classified as learning disabled because of imprecision in the definition. Also, several research studies tended to verify the extent of misclassification in LD programs (Shumaker, Deshler, Alley, & Warner, 1980; Shepard & Smith, 1983; Ysseldyke, Algozzine, Shinn, & McGue, 1982).

Concept of IQ/Achievement Discrepancy

Lack of consensus on the major marker variables that define LD and the failure of psychometric and etiologic classification procedures to provide useful indices, have led to an increased reliance upon IQ/achievement discrepancy as the defining feature of LD. To reduce the number of children identified as learning disabled and to serve more severely handicapped children, many states have revised their rules and regulations to require discrepancy criteria, or are in the process of doing so. In general, most of the proposed revisions involve specifying a particular method for calculating the discrepancy and setting more stringent cutoffs for service eligibility. Although the use of discrepancy criteria does provide a more objective index of under-achievement and can be used to delimit the population of children who could be classified as learning disabled, the concept of dis-crepancy and its measurement presents a host of methodologic, theo-retical, and practical problems that are only beginning to be understood.

First, there are many ways to quantify discrepancies between actual performance and expected performance, depending upon how "expected performance " is defined and how the deviation from expec-tancy is calculated. In general, a child could be underachieving com-pared to what is expected of his or her age, grade level, or intellectual potential. Thus, to the extent that the criterion for "expectation" is defined differently across states, schools, and individual professionals, we will see great variance in both the number and kinds of children who are identified.

Similarly, variance in the learning-disabled population has been introduced because different methods have been used for calculating discrepancy. Although many methods for discrepancy have been pro-posed in the literature, four basic methods have been common in prac-tice (Cone & Wilson, 1981). In the past, the most frequently used method was deviation from grade level. This method compares achievement scores in grade equivalents to the child's grade place-ment. The second method involves the use of expectancy formulas (Harris, 1970) in which the child's age, number of years in school, and mental age (or IQ) are used in a ratio equation to calculate either an "educational quotient" or expected grade performance. In general, both the grade level deviation and expectancy formula methods have been shown to have serious limitations and are currently not recommended in practice as reliable and valid indices of underachieve-ment (Cone & Wilson, 1981).

As the result of recent methodologic studies that compared various methods (Cone & Wilson, 1981; Forness, Sinclair, & Guthrie, 1983; Shepard, 1980), there has been a trend for states to adopt either the standard score comparison method or the regression method. The former method, which is gaining popularity, involves converting achievement scores to the same standard score units used with IQ tests (e.g., M = 100, SD = 15) and simply subtracting the two measures. Although the standard score method is convenient to use in practice, it does not account for the fact that IQ and achievement scores are cor-related and thereby produces discrepancy scores that are biased by a statistical effect called *regression-to-the-mean*. The phenomenon of regression-to-the-mean refers to the tendency of extreme scores on one measure to be less extreme on a correlated measure. This is a serious limitation in the reliable measurement of discrepancy, because the magnitude of differences between achievement and IQ will vary at different points in the distribution of scores. Thus, for example, the amount of difference that would be considered to be "significant" would be different for children with lower IQs and/or higher IQs compared with those with average IQs. At present, we do not have a great deal of evidence about the extent to which regression to the mean influences the outcomes of identification procedures in actual school practice.

The final method for quantifying discrepancy is to use a regression equation to predict academic achievement for individual children from their IQ scores. The discrepancy is thus defined as the difference between predicted achievement and obtained achievement. Because this method is the most sound statistically and accounts for the correlation between IQ and achievement, it is considered to be the best available method for measuring underachievement. However, a major criticism of the regression method has been that because of its technical requirements, it is not practical to implement in typical school assessment. In order to apply this method in practice, the professional must have tabled norms for each pair of tests that are used at all age and ability levels. In order to develop such norms, it would be necessary to administer the same tests to the same children in a large randomly selected sample. Faced with the costs of such an effort, many states have adopted the standard score method as a reasonable approximation to the regression method; however, some states have developed regression based norm tables by using estimates of the population values for various tests.

To date, most of the research on the use of IQ/achievement discrepancies has been methodologic in nature and has involved the comparison of various formulas and the evaluation of different cutoff criteria (Cone & Wilson, 1981; Forness, Sinclair, & Guthrie, 1983; Shepard, 1980). In general, the aims of these studies have been to improve the measurement of discrepancy itself and to develop procedures for restricting the number of children who are potentially eligible for special education.

At the same time, there remain a number of unanswered questions that are relevant to policy decisions concerning the identification and education of learning-disabled children. For example, if IQ/achievement discrepancy were the sole criteria for eligibility and if we determined eligibility in an objective fashion that was unbiased by school referral and identification practices, what would be the estimated prevalence compared with current practice? Also, little is known about how different identification criteria will influence the nature of the population that will be served in the future, or how they will impact the nature of the population currently served. For example, what are the consequences of using different methods and procedures for determining discrepancy with respect to the denial of services for children who would qualify previously, and for the potential disclassification of children who are currently served? Will we in fact serve a population of children that is more appropriately labeled LD? Finally, what is the educational value and relevance of IQ/achievement discrepancy scores? Do discrepancy scores provide any information that is useful in educational planning, or are they merely a device to limit eligibility?

ESTIMATED PREVALENCE OF LEARNING DISABILITIES AMONG FIRST AND SECOND GRADERS

The first study was conducted as part of an ongoing research program in which we used group administered IQ and achievement tests to screen out all underachievers (regardless of the cause of their underachievement) from a sample of all first and second graders ($\underline{n}$ = 2,986) in a large school system (McKinney & Feagans, 1986). The only children excluded from the sample were those with moderate and severely handicapping conditions. We then administered individual IQ and achievement tests to a randomly selected subsample of all underachievers with average to above average IQ. Since we assessed a randomly constituted sample drawn from all children at risk for LD, we could estimate the total number of underachievers among all first and second graders in the school system who would be eligible for LD services independently of school referral and identification practices.

To identify underachievers based on group administered tests, we restandardized the total scores from both tests and then used a regression model to predict the expected achievement for all children in the sample. Residual scores (predicted-obtained scores) were standardized to provide an index of IQ/achievement discrepancy. Table 14-1 shows the results of this analysis displayed by grade and IQ level. The total sample of 2,986 children was classified into underachievers ($\underline{n}$ = 520) who scored 1 standard deviation ($\underline{SD}$) below IQ expectancy, target achievers ($\underline{n}$ = 1,986) who scored within 1 $\underline{SD}$ of IQ expectancy, and overachievers ($\underline{n}$ = 480) who scored 1 $\underline{SD}$ above what one would predict given IQ. Inspection of the data in Table 14-1 shows that the entire subgroup of underachievers ($\underline{n}$ = 520) represented 17% of the population in first and second graders in this school system. Also Table 14-1 shows that the sample contained 49 (1.6%) children who scored in the mildly retarded range on the group-administered IQ test. A total of 377 (12.6%) scored in the borderline range of IQ. The mildly retarded group represented less than 1% (0.87%) of the underachievers, and children in the borderline range represented 3.5% ($\underline{n}$ = 104). Thus, it is clear that IQ/achievement discrepancy alone does not provide an index that is uniquely characteristic of learning-disabled children.

The issue about services for children in the borderline range of IQ is complicated by a lack of consensus about the definition of a slow learner. To exclude the so-called slow learner, some states only consider children with IQs greater than 85 as eligible for LD services. On the other hand, if current policy considers IQ/achievement discrepancy as a characteristic that is common to all learning-disabled children, a case could be made for including this 3% of the population who show significant discrepancies if they conform to other criteria in the definition (e.g., the exclusionary provisions). From a theoretical perspective, slow learners would belong to a subgroup of children in the borderline range of IQ who achieve at a level that is consistent with low general ability and whose academic problem could be attributed to psychosocial or environmental factors (e.g., see subgroup B in Table 14-1).

Table 14-1 illustrates the effects on prevalence rates of the decision to either include or exclude children in the borderline range of general ability. Since children in the borderline range who are discrepant are eligible in some states but not others, Table 14-1 suggests

TABLE 14-1.
Total Sample Classified by Discrepancy, Grade, and IQ Level

Grade	(> +1 SD) Overachievers		(–1 < +1) Target Achievers		(< –1 SD) Underachievers		Total Sample	
	1	2	1	2	1	2	1	2
IQ Level								
> 130	0	0	42	43	7	6	49	49
116–130	0	0	210	203	28 (A)	18	238	221
86–115	192	218	636	626	163	168	991	1012
71–85	38	30	93 (B)	112	56 (C)	48	187	190
<71	0	2	12	9	19	7	31	18
Total	230	250	993	993	273	247	1496	1490

SD = standard deviation

that the prevalence of LD across states could vary by as much as 3.5% of the school population as the result of this factor alone (see subgroup C in Table 14-1). It might also be noted that the percentage of children in the borderline range of IQ who show significant discrepancies exceeds the original LD prevalence estimate of 2% to 3% of the population.

Because of this debate concerning the definition of "slow learners," we based our prevalence estimate on the sample in subgroup A in Table 14-1. Subgroup A contains 390 students, or 13% of the population, who were underachievers of average or above-average IQ and therefore were potentially eligible for LD services based on group-administered tests. In order to estimate the number of children who would qualify within subgroup A, we randomly selected 150 children and administered WISC-Rs and Woodcock-Johnson Achievement Tests. Classification as LD was based on the presence of significant discrepancy between WISC-R full-scale IQ and one or more areas of achievement assessed by the Woodcock-Johnson tests calculated by the standard score comparison method.

Using this procedure, we found that 30% of the random sample of 150 underachievers would qualify as having a significant discrepancy (-1 SD) in one or more areas of achievement as measured by individually administered tests. Using these figures to estimate the prevalence of LD in subgroup A of Table 14-1, we concluded that approximately 117 first and second graders would likely qualify for LD services. This number represents 3.9% of the total sample of first and second graders after eliminating children with subaverage IQs and those who were being served in special education classes for other types of handicaps.

Finally, we examined the school records of the children in our random sample of underachievers to assess the overlap between our independent classification procedures and those used by the schools to identify learning-disabled children. Within this sample, 30.8% were classified as learning disabled by the schools, approximately the same number we had classified as eligible by independent testing. However, only one half of the school-identified children were classified as discrepant by our testing. On the other hand, the schools had not identified one half of the children we classified as eligible for services based on discrepancy criteria. Since it was possible that the schools identified some children based on measures that were different from ours, or not administered in this study, the lack of agreement between our identification procedures and those of the schools does not provide direct evidence on the extent of missclassification. On the other hand, it does indicate that eligibility policies based on IQ/achievement discrepancy will not only impact the numbers of children served, but may also change the composition of LD programs with respect to the types of children who are served. This issue was explored more fully in the study reported in the following section.

EVALUATION OF CHANGES IN IDENTIFICATION CRITERIA IN NORTH CAROLINA

On January 1, 1985, the North Carolina Department of Public Instruction adopted the standard score comparison method and set a 15-point difference criterion as the index of severe discrepancy. Prior to that time, the expected grade level method was used to assess underachievement. This decision was made by a committee of professionals, parents, university personnel, and state department personnel who reviewed the available literature and the policies and procedures of other states. They concluded that although the regression method was the most sound statistically, the standard score comparison method was preferable because of ease of implementation, practicality, and cost. However, the committee also recommended that the regression method continue to be studied for possible implementation in the future. The first study in this regard was conducted by Alberg (1986).

Comparison of Prevalence Estimates

In order to compare prevalence estimates based on the North Carolina standard score method and regression analysis, Alberg (1986) obtained group-administered California Achievement Test (CAT) data from the North Carolina Annual Testing Program and IQ data from the Test of Cognitive Skills (TCS), which was administered at the same time by the schools. The research sample contained all third ($\underline{n}$ = 1,445) and sixth ($\underline{n}$ = 1,637) grade students who participated in the 1985 annual testing program. As part of this program, exceptional students are identified, and those who were classified as moderately to severely retarded, behaviorally-emotionally handicapped, and otherwise handicapped were eliminated from the sample. The elimination of these students was designed to operationalize the exclusionary provisions in the definition of LD. In order to estimate the prevalence of underachievement using the North Carolina standard score method, Alberg (1986) standardized the CAT and TCS total scores to a mean of 100 and a $\underline{SD}$ of 15 for each grade level. She then subtracted the two standard scores to calculate the discrepancy between IQ and achievement and applied the 15-point cutoff score specified in the North Carolina regulations to classify students as underachievers. The estimated prevalence of underachievement was also determined by a regression analysis at each grade level, and the discrepancy scores were then standardized. Students scoring –1 SD below the mean of the discrepancy scores were classified as underachievers.

Since the regression method is considered to be the sounder method statistically, the results of this analysis were taken as the standard for comparing the results of the North Carolina standard score method. Table 14-2 shows the percentage of the total sample classified as underachievers by each method for each grade level. This analysis shows that if a –1 SD cutoff were used, 263 children, or 17% of the sample, would be classified as underachievers by the regression method. If children who scored in the mildly retarded range were excluded, the prevalence estimate would be reduced to 254 children, or 16% of the sample. North Carolina does not now exclude children in the borderline range of general ability from LD services. However, Table 14-2 illustrates that if this were done, the prevalence estimate for underachievement based on regression analysis would be reduced to 14% of the third-grade sample.

The North Carolina standard score comparison method for the third-grade sample classified 194 children, or about 13%, as discrepant. In evaluating the data in this table, it should be noted that unlike the results with the regression method, no retarded children were identified as discrepant, and only two children in the borderline range were identified. While these outcomes might be interpreted as consistent with the State's objectives in implementing the standard score method, they actually illustrate a major methodologic flaw in this approach to calculating discrepancies.

TABLE 14-2.
Percentage of Total Sample Classified as Underachievers by Each Method at Each Grade and IQ Level

IQ Level	Grade 3		Grade 6	
	Regression	SS	Regression	SS
>130	0.70	2.28	0.85	0.36
115–129	2.75	3.67	1.53	1.03
100–114	4.11	4.43	2.69	0.73
85–99	6.86	2.90	6.47	1.10
70–84	2.35	0.14	3.85	0.37
<69	0.61	0	0.37	0

Adapted by permission from Alberg (1986).

As noted earlier, the standard score comparison method does not account for the correlation between IQ and achievement and therefore does not adjust the prevalence estimate for the phenomenon of "regression-to-the-mean." Comparison of the results in Table 14-2 for each method shows that whereas regression analysis produced proportional estimates of discrepancy across the full range of IQ, the standard score method tended to overestimate the number of underachievers in the above-average IQ range. Thus, the North Carolina method not only underidentifies students, it is also biased toward the identification of brighter students compared with the regression method.

In addition to the problem of regression effects in the North Carolina method, Alberg's (1986) data revealed another serious limitation when the two methods were compared across grade levels. Table 14-2 and Figure 14-1 show that while the regression method produced comparable prevalence estimates across grades, the North Carolina standard score method identified 13% of the third graders and only 3.6% of the sixth graders. To understand these outcomes, it is important to note that the North Carolina method considers neither the correlation between IQ and achievement at a given grade level nor the fact that this correlation is known to increase across grade levels. In Alberg's (1986) data, the correlation between IQ and achievement scores was 0.61 at grade three and 0.83 at grade six. As the correlation between IQ and achievement increases with age, achievement is predicted more accurately. As this occurs, the variability of the differences between the predicted scores and actual achievement decreases. Thus, the standard deviation of the unadjusted discrepancy scores of younger children would necessarily be greater than that for older children.

The North Carolina criteria use a 15-point cutoff for defining a "severe discrepancy" for all age groups. The use of a constant cutoff score assumes that the standard deviation of the discrepancy scores is the same as the standard deviations of the test scores used to calculate the discrepancy. However, Alberg's (1986) data show that the actual SD of the discrepancy scores varies systematically with developmental changes in the relationship between IQ and achievement. In the present study, the SDs of the discrepancy scores calculated by the North Carolina method were 13 in the third-grade sample and 9 in the sixth-grade sample. Accordingly, the use of a constant 15-point cutoff sets a more stringent standard for eligibility in the sixth grade than in the third grade. In a subsequent analysis, Alberg found that if the actual SDs of the discrepancy scores were used, the prevalence estimates for the North Carolina method would more closely approximate those derived from the regression method.

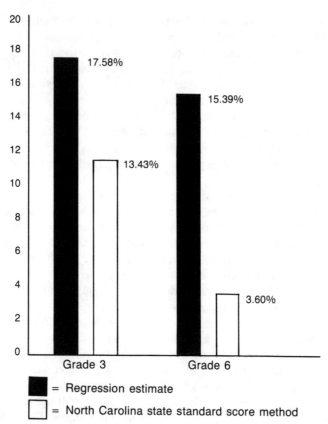

Figure 14-1. Estimates of discrepant underachievers regression vs. North Carolina state standard score method. From Alberg (1986), with permission.

Impact on School-Identified Learning-Disabled Students

Although the classification of learning-disabled students in North Carolina is based on individually administered tests, Alberg (1986) was able to illustrate the likely consequences of applying the new standard score method with group test data. When all of the school-identified learning-disabled students in the sample were identified, Alberg found that 47% of the third graders and 24% of the sixth graders would qualify by the regression method. However, only 27% of the school-identified third graders qualified using the North Carolina method and, remarkably, only 6.8% of the sixth graders qualified. Thus, for the statistical reasons just discussed, the North Carolina criteria disproportionately declassified sixth-grade children compared with the regression method. Also, the North Carolina method would probably result in the declassification of many students in the borderline range of general ability who would be more likely to qualify by the regression method.

Characteristics of Identified Children

In order to assess the probable impact of changes in the North Carolina rules and regulations on the characteristics of learning-disabled children, Alberg (1986) randomly selected three groups of 10 students each for case study analysis and examined their school records. Two of the groups were composed of school-identified learning-disabled students from the larger sample who did and did not meet eligibility criteria based on the analysis of group IQ and achievement tests. A third group was selected who met the criteria based on group tests but who were not identified by the schools as learning disabled.

In general, children who were eligible but not identified by the schools were brighter than school-identified learning-disabled children and achieved at a level that was more age appropriate but not commensurate with their ability. Both learning-disabled groups were older than discrepant children who were not identified and had a significant history of grade retention (70% in the nondiscrepant group; 80% in the discrepant group). Thus, underachievers who were not identified did not have a history of retention or other factors that would suggest an obvious learning problem, even though they were performing below their ability. Children who were identified but were not discrepant appeared to be more mildly handicapped and/or had problems in fewer areas compared with learning-disabled children who were discrepant. Classification of many of these students appeared to be based on clinical judgment rather than on discrepancy.

In conclusion, the results of Alberg's (1986) study indicated that the implementation of the new IQ/achievement criterion in North Carolina for identifying learning-disabled students would achieve a number of policy objectives. It would (1) reduce the pool of students who would be potentially eligible for special education services in the future, (2) declassify a substantial number of students identified by the old criteria, and (3) produce significant changes in the characteristics of the children who were served. However, it is questionable whether the new North Carolina method would achieve these objectives in a reliable and equitable fashion. The most serious issues illustrated by Alberg's (1986) research are the inconsistency in prevalence estimates across grades and the exclusion of students who would qualify by more statistically sound methods. Because of basic statistical flaws in the North Carolina method, it yielded unreliable estimates of prevalence that were biased against older students and students in the borderline range of general ability, although such students are not specifically excluded in the state definition. Also, because of these statistical flaws, many older children who would qualify in the primary grades would risk declassification in the upper grades upon re-evaluation. Thus, in the absence of other evidence to support their eligibility for services, the sole reliance upon the current discrepancy criterion in North Carolina is not likely to ensure that all children with LD would be served.

RELATIONSHIP OF IQ/ACHIEVEMENT DISCREPANCIES TO ACADEMIC OUTCOMES

Many important research questions about the concept of discrepancy itself have not been addressed in the literature. Perhaps the most basic issue is whether discrepancy scores actually indicate the presence of LD, and, if so, whether they can be used as an index of the severity of the condition that is useful in educational planning.

The results reported here are based on the endpoint assessment of the Carolina Longitudinal Learning Disabilities Project (McKinney & Feagans, 1984, 1986). This project began in 1978 during the period of implementation of Public Law 94-142 with a sample of 63 newly identified first- and second-grade learning-disabled students and randomly selected classmates. We were able to maintain a sample of 42 learning-disabled and 43 non-learning-disabled children that we followed over a period of 7 years until they reached the age of 11.5 years.

When the children were selected in 1978–1979, eligibility for special education placement was determined by a graduated grade-level discrepancy method. Since the criteria for the identification of learning-disabled children changed over the course of the study, we conducted additional analyses to determine the effects of alternative classifications based on age and IQ/achievement discrepancies on the characteristics and achievement outcomes of our sample (Short, Feagans, McKinney, & Appelbaum, 1986). Using the current state standard score discrepancy method, we found that at the time of identification, 38% of the learning-disabled sample would have met present criteria. Similarly, using regression methods based on the parameters obtained from the normal sample, 40% of the learning-disabled sample were discrepant for IQ, and 54% were behind for age. Surprisingly, when we applied the state criteria to the normal sample, we found that 42% were below expectation based on IQ.

In general, IQ/achievement discrepancy for the longitudinal learning-disabled sample increased over the first 3 years of the study but was quite stable for the normal sample (Short et al., 1986). Thus, by this criterion, learning-disabled students became more disabled with age in spite of special education services. This finding confirms the general conclusion reached by McKinney and Feagans (1984) for achievement scores alone. When the sample was followed to age 11 years, 47% of the children remaining in the learning-disabled sample showed significant discrepancies according to state criteria compared with 38% when they were first identified. Also, 42% of the children remaining in the normal comparison sample were discrepant; the same percentage as that found initially.

When children's initial status as discrepant or nondiscrepant during the first year of the longitudinal project was related to later achievement outcomes, we found that the academic performance of learning-disabled children remained below that of normal achievers, regardless of the child's initial status as discrepant or nondiscrepant. Status as discrepant or nondiscrepant was not a significant variable. Figure 14-2 illustrates these findings for later outcomes in reading.

Since one would expect poorer outcomes for discrepant children, these results with respect to long-term outcomes for learning-disabled and non-learning-disabled students do not support the assumption that IQ/achievement discrepancy scores index the severity of children's LD. Also, discrepancy scores do not appear to provide any useful prognostic information that is different for learning-disabled and

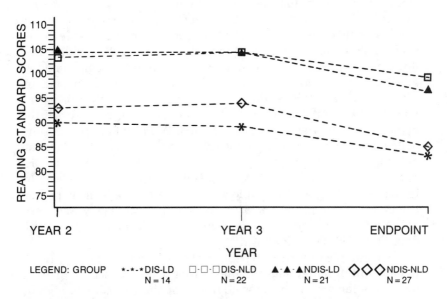

Figure 14-2. Longitudinal achievement outcomes for each group by discrepancy reading.

non-learning-disabled children. On the other hand, evidence from the same longitudinal study with respect to the analysis of LD subtypes indicated that patterns of specific disabilities in language, cognitive processing, and behavior were prognostic of later outcomes (Feagans & Appelbaum, 1986; McKinney & Speece, 1986; McKinney, Short, & Feagans, 1986). Accordingly, although discrepancy criteria may be used as one index of underachievement, and therefore establish that a child needs some kind of help, it may be of limited value to educators in deciding how much help or what kind of help is required to improve progress.

GENERAL CONCLUSIONS AND POLICY IMPLICATIONS

The evidence reviewed in this chapter illustrates a number of conceptual and methodologic problems associated with the growing trend to focus on IQ/achievement discrepancy as the principal index for determining eligiblity for LD services. These problems pose a number of serious consequences with respect to the issue of prevalence, the nature of the population served as learning disabled, and the equitable treatment of the children affected.

First, it should be emphasized that IQ/achievement discrepancy is not a characteristic that is specific to LD; rather it is only one index of underachievement that could result from any cause of school failure. Accordingly, there will always be more children who are potentially eligible by this criterion than the number of learning-disabled children who are presumed to exist theoretically. Also, it is evident that discrepancies exist for many children who might be considered as gifted as well as those who might be viewed as slow learners. Even after excluding mildly retarded children and those in the borderline range of IQ, the potential pool of eligible children may exceed the hypothetical prevalence of LD by as much as 10% of the population, depending upon the particular measures used and the method for calculating discrepancy. Moreover, our estimate of the extent of discrepancy based on a two-step screening procedure followed by individual testing with multiple measures still exceeds the hypothetical prevalence of LD by 1% to 2%. In sum, if discrepancy were used as the sole criteria for LD, there would simply be more eligible children than originally estimated.

Second, the use of discrepancy scores will not necessarily result in more uniform prevalence figures across states and school districts unless the same policy is adopted regarding the inclusion of high IQ students and those in the borderline range of general ability. In the former case, some states require additional procedures to determine whether bright students have been sufficiently stimulated or whether they appear to have genuine LD. Similarly some states exclude borderline students, whereas others do not. In the first study, it was noted that different policies regarding these subgroups could produce variances in prevalence of up to 6%, or twice the hypothetical prevalence. Thus, the assumption that an identification policy based on discrepancy per se is sufficient to produce more uniform standards is not viable unless the policy deals specifically with those students who are not now excluded by most definitions. The development of criteria for students in the higher and lower IQ ranges is complicated by the fact that their discrepancy could be due to LD theoretically. Nevertheless, it would appear that more uniform and/or less variable prevalence rates would not be obtained without consensus on the definition of a slow learner and the criteria for excluding gifted underachievers.

Third, in addition to different policies regarding the inclusion of bright and borderline children, the substantial heterogeneity of the learning-disabled population with respect to learning characteristics could continue to be a problem if states and school districts use different formulas for calculating discrepancy scores. To date, research on different methods for measuring discrepancy has focused primarily on the effects of different methods on prevalence estimates. However, Alberg's (1986) data show that different methods not only affect the number of children who would be eligible but also influence the types of children identified. Thus, unless a uniform approach is taken with respect to discrepancy measurement, a policy that merely attempts to reduce prevalence by requiring more stringent discrepancy criteria would not necessarily identify a population of children that was more appropriately labeled LD.

Accordingly, some provision should be made to ensure that children who are identified and placed based on IQ/achievement discrepancy actually display the characteristics that have been associated with LD in the literature. Because discrepancy scores provide a more objective index of underachievement, there has been a tendency in typical school practice and in the administration of special education programs to assume that a single symptom is sufficient to determine the condition. It should be remembered that discrepancy is associated with many different academic problems, just as high fever is associated with influenza in some children and meningitis in others. In the same vein, we have little evidence to suggest that discrepancy would include all the subgroups of children who have traditionally been considered as learning disabled. For example, IQ/achievement discrepancy may not be manifested in younger children with attentional disorders but may emerge later on. Similarly, discrepancy scores might be sensitive to certain language disorders but not to others, depending upon the tests that are used. Clearly, additional research in this area is needed if we are to accomplish the dual goals of both reducing prevalence and serving children who are more appropriately labeled learning disabled.

Fourth, it is questionable whether reliance on IQ/achievement discrepancy as the major criterion for LD would identify a population of students who more clearly require special education services than those identified previously. A key element in the rationale for the use of discrepancy scores is that they provide an index of educational need. Thus, it has been argued that even if we cannot pinpoint the specific cause of school failure, children who are severely discrepant are at greater risk for continued school failure than those who are not discrepant and therefore are more deserving of special education services. However, longitudinal evidence presented previously indicated that school-identified learning-disabled children's status as discrepant was not prognostic of long-term academic outcomes. Also, outcomes were not different for randomly selected normal children who were discrepant compared with those who were not discrepant. Thus, the adoption of more stringent discrepancy criteria may not decide the issue of "who should be served in LD programs."

Finally, it is clear that some methods for calculating discrepancy scores are better than others and that the use of technically inadequate methods has serious consequences for many children with respect to the declassification of those currently served and the potential denial of services for those who would qualify if better methods were used. The issue of technical adequacy is particularly troublesome when it can be shown that certain subgroups of children and/or children of certain ages are systematically excluded by biased statistical methods when such children are not specifically excluded by category in state and federal regulations. Given the urgency and critical nature of the policy issues concerning the prevalence of LD nationally and its impact on special education costs, it is perhaps understandable that decision-makers would seize upon the most direct, feasible, and cost-effective solutions; particularly if there was some preliminary evidence to suggest that the potential benefits outweighed uncertain harm. However, given the very serious methodologic issues involved in the calculation of discrepancy and the potential for errors of significant magnitude, it is critical that the best available practices are implemented. To do otherwise is to exacerbate the present problem by inviting further criticism of identification practices, and thereby further eroding public confidence in our ability to select and educate learning-disabled children appropriately.

In this regard, it is my belief that most of the methodologic problems illustrated by these studies can be overcome based on a more thorough understanding of the problems involved in the measurement of discrepancy and of the specific consequences they have for children and educational practice. The solution to these problems is within our technical and scientific capability, and this area seems to be one in which research can have a rather immediate and beneficial impact on educational policy.

On the other hand, I am less optimistic that the current emphasis on IQ/achievement discrepancy, as the major defining feature of LD, will solve the many substantive problems concerning the nature of the disorder itself and its appropriate treatment in the public schools. Although it is the case that discrepancy scores can be used to delimit the number of children who are served, determine eligibility more objectively, and distinguish a broad subgroup of underachievers who are potentially learning disabled, the problem still remains to differentiate those who are truly handicapped and provide them with the most effective forms of service. Accordingly, we must continue to pursue basic research on the nature of LD as a handicapping condition and how such children respond to different instructional options.

Nevertheless, given the pressing policy issues raised by inadequate identification procedures nationally, there is a very clear need and mandate for more precise and uniform criteria for assessing underachievement as one feature of the definition of LD. The principal thesis of this chapter has not been to question the value of present attempts to improve identification procedures, but rather to argue that we should proceed in a reflective and scientifically defensible fashion so that we do not create new and unforeseen problems that overshadow those of the present.

RESPONSE

Carol Weller

When I approached James McKinney's chapter on discrepancy, it was with a sense of alarm and trepidation. How could I respond and how could a researcher write about a subject as hackneyed as discrepancy? How could new knowledge be advanced? How could trite and banal rhetoric be avoided?

In my frustration, I conjured an image of Howard Beale (Peter Finch) in the movie *Network* (MGM, 1976). Beale's frustration was my frustration with a system gone awry. Then I read McKinney's chapter. The research was cogent, and the message was clear. In a professionally judicious and tactful style, McKinney was articulating Beale's message and my thoughts: "I'm as mad as hell and I'm not gonna take this anymore."

Since the introduction of the concept of discrepancy to the field of LD, the amount of attention paid to identification and description of severe discrepancies between IQ and achievement has been a drain on the talent pool of special education. Attempts to empirically operationalize LD with discrepancy criteria have lured numerous researchers into tedious investigation of details of psychometric procedure rather than consideration of relevant psychosocial characteristics of learning-disabled persons. Decision-makers at the state and national levels have pursued the simplistic notion that IQ/achievement discrepancy is LD—an academic disorder present only during the school years. Together, they have spent their time, money, and human resources devising definitions of discrepancy through expectancy formulas, deviations from grade level, standard score comparisons, and regression analyses. As a result, they have been left with insufficient time and energy to innovate a solution strategy and procedural design for defining LD.

If researchers and decision-makers continue to focus on definition of discrepancy rather than definition of LD, the implications for the field are staggering. LD will continue to be described as an ill-defined group of persons whose numbers continue to escalate at an alarming rate. LD will continue to be characterized as a mild school-age phenomenon that does not exist prior to school entry nor in adulthood. Variation among classification procedures will continue across the country, and service delivery options will not become universally standardized. Lack of precision in selection of research samples will persist, and adequate validation of instructional strategies and assessment tools will remain impossible.

However, if researchers and decision-makers focus their efforts toward defining LD rather than discrepancy, significant change within the field is possible. Researchers must begin anew with investigative efforts that lead to an adequate definition encompassing all parameters of LD. Laying aside memories of the recent sociopolitical debacle of the Public Law 94-142 definition and the schism within the field, they must unify to thoughtfully develop and critically examine theoretical and basic research options that account for the heterogeneity of the learning-disabled population. Without excluding preschoolers, adults, persons with English as a second language, gifted persons, handicapped persons, and nonhandicapped persons from their research samples, they must devote intensive efforts to the investigation of the psychosocial and behavioral manifestations of the LD syndrome. They must vigorously pursue empirical alternatives to delineate the characteristics of subgroups that constitute the learning-disabled population. They must not dilute their efforts to define LD with redundant investigation of discrepancy and premature description of policy issues until scientific investigation of all avenues that may define "LDness" has revealed convincing answers.

The charge to decision-makers to define LD is no less exhaustive. Before deciding to terminate, modify, or refocus the existing educational policies related to classification and definition by discrepancy, developers of policy must meticulously explore the educational and sociologic ramifications of changes proposed by researchers. They must investigate and describe the needs of systems and identify and delineate problems that underlie these needs. They must remain open to new designs for implementing new strategies while predicting defects in the designs and their implementation. They must investigate and relate outcomes of these designs to sources of support, available human and material resources, and program change activities. They must conduct their research in a timely and precise manner that advances knowledge and enhances service delivery.

It is difficult to immerse ourselves and our field in change. It is threatening to seek creative alternatives to established norms. However, whether we perceive ourselves as researchers of the definition of LD or researchers of the policies surrounding a LD definition, we should heed the premise of McKinney's chapter: We can solve the technical problems of defining discrepancy, but the solution to these problems will not resolve the problems of defining LD. Using the reflective and scientifically defensible approach suggested by McKinney, we should adopt the precept of Beale as our watchword: "The solution to the problems of the nation [LD] does not lie in government. It lies in the hearts and minds of each of us."

REFERENCES

Alberg, J.Y. (1986). *Evaluation of alternative procedures for identifying learning disabled students in North Carolina.* Doctoral dissertation submitted to the University of North Carolina at Chapel Hill.

Algozzine, B., & Korinek, L. (1985). Where is special education for students with high prevalence handicaps going? *Exceptional Children, 51*(5), 388–394.

Algozzine, B., & Ysseldyke, J. (1983). Learning disabilities as a subset of school failure: The oversophistication of a concept. *Exceptional Children, 50*(3), 242–246.

Cone, T.E., & Wilson, L.L. (1981). Quantifying a severe discrepancy: A critical analysis. *Learning Disability Quarterly,* 359–371.

Feagans, L., & Appelbaum, M.I. (1986). Language subtypes and their validation in learning disabled children. *Journal of Educational Psychology, 78*(5), 373–481.

Forness, S.R., Sinclair, E., & Guthrie, D. (1983). Learning disability discrepancy formulas: Their use in actual practice. *Learning Disabilities Quarterly, 6,* 107–114.

Harris, A. (1970). *How to increase reading abilities* (5th ed.). New York: David McKay.

Kavale, K.A., & Forness, S.R. (1985). *The science of learning disabilities.* San Diego: College Hill Press.

Keogh, B.K. (1987). Learning disabilities: Diversity in search of order. In M.C. Wang, H.J. Walberg, & M.C. Reynolds (Eds.), *The handbook of special education: Research and practice.* Oxford, England: Pergamon Press.

McKinney, J.D. (1987). Research on conceptually and empirically derived subtypes of specific learning disabilities. In M.C. Wang, H.J. Walberg, & M.C. Reynolds (Eds.), *The handbook of special education: Research and practice.* Oxford, England: Pergamon Press.

McKinney, J.D., & Feagans, L. (1984). Academic and behavioral characteristics: Longitudinal studies of learning disabled children and average achievers. *Learning Disability Quarterly, 7*(3), 251–265.

McKinney, J.D., & Feagans, L. (1986). *Bibliography of the Carolina learning disabilities project.* Chapel Hill, University of North Carolina, Frank Porter Graham Child Development Center.

McKinney, J.D., & Speece, D.L. (1986). Longitudinal stability and academic consequences of behavioral subtypes of learning disabled children. *Journal of Educational Psychology, 78*(5), 365–372.

McKinney, J.D., Short, E.J., & Feagans, L. (1985). Academic consequences of perceptual-linguistic subtypes of learning disabled children. *Learning Disabilities Research, 1*(1), 6–17.

Shumaker, J.B., Deshler, D.D., Alley, G.R., & Warner, M.M. 1980. *An epidemiological study of learning disabled adolescents in secondary schools: Details of the methodology* (Research Report No. 12). Lawrence, Kansas: The University of Kansas Institute for Research in Learning Disabilities.

Shepard, L. (1980). An evaluation of the regression discrepancy method for identifying children with learning disabilities. *Journal of Special Education, 14,* 79–80.

Shepard, L.A., & Smith, M.L. (1983). An evaluation of the identification of learning disabled students in Colorado. *Learning Disability Quarterly, 6*(2), 115–127.

Short, E.J., Feagans, L., McKinney, J.D., & Appelbaum, M. (1986). Longitudinal stability of LD subtypes based on age- and IQ-achievement discrepancies. *Learning Disability Quarterly, 9,* 214–225.

Smith, M.L. (1982). *How educators decide who is learning disabled: Challenge* to *psychology of public policy in the schools*. Springfield, IL: Charles C Thomas.

Speece, D.L., McKinney, J.D., & Appelbaum, M.I. (1985). Classification and validation of behavioral subtypes of learning disabled children. *Journal of Educational Psychology, 77*, 67–77.

Stark, J.H. (1982). Tragic choices in special education: The effects of scarce resources on the implementation of Pub. L. No. 94-142. *Connecticut Law Review, 14*(47), 477–493.

Ysseldyke, J.E., Algozzine, B., Shinn, M.R., & McGue, M. (1982). Similarities and differences between low achievers and students classified learning disabled. *The Journal of Special Education, 16*(1), 73–85.

CHAPTER 15

Providing Services to All Students with Learning Problems: Implications for Policy and Programs

James C. Chalfant

A crisis is emerging in American education. Each year our educational system is unable to meet the needs of increasing numbers of students with learning problems (Task Force on Federal Elementary and Secondary Education Policy, 1983). Three questions are before us:

1. How extensive is this increase in the number of school-age students who are failing to learn adequately from our educational system?
2. Why are we failing to adequately serve these students?
3. What changes must occur so that our educational system will be able to meet their needs?

EXTENT OF THE PROBLEM

In the 1984–1985 school year, of the 42 million young people in public schools, at least 4% or 1,845,928 were classified as learning disabled and were placed in special education programs for the learning disabled under Public Law 94-142. This number also represented an increase from the 1983–1984 school year of 34,000 students nationwide.

There is another 10% to 20% of the school population who are not in special education programs but who have mild or moderate learning problems that interfere with their education progress. The exact number of these children is undetermined and varies from one school district to another, but they are commonly described as students who are slow learners; have social, conduct, and behavior problems; possess low self-esteem; are experientially deprived; or have problems in understanding or using language (Chalfant, 1984).

It is estimated, therefore, that 20% to 30% of the school-age population, or at least 8,000,000 students, are having difficulty progressing in our schools because of learning problems stemming from social isolation, dependence, poverty, family difficulty, or other causes. Many of these students come from poor and minority groups (Barriers to Excellence: Our Children at Risk, 1985). Many of these students are not adequately prepared to enter the work force (Will, 1984). One in four students who enrolls in the ninth grade "drops out" of school before graduation (National Center for Educational Statistics, 1983).

A SYSTEM'S PROBLEM

There is a system's problem in American education. Many of our schools are functioning as though they had two separate educational systems (Bogdan, 1983). The first system is regular education, which has the responsibility for teaching all students. The regular education system is typically organized in grade levels, and instruction is delivered primarily through groups. Basic academic skills are taught at the elementary level and subject matter content is emphasized at the secondary level. Unfortunately, the present 180-day K–12 system is not designed to teach these basic skills and content to inefficient learners. Students who are unable to keep up with their peer group are often referred for special education consideration. The expected outcome is that the students will be removed from the regular classroom for at least part of the school day for specialized assistance.

The second system is composed of specialized assistance programs designed to serve students with handicaps. Over the past two decades, there has been a proliferation of legislation and federally funded "special," "compensatory," and "remedial" education programs designed to ensure educational success for these students. Such programs include special education, vocational education, rehabilitation, mental health, bilingual education, Chapter I programs for the underprivileged, and so on. "Currently there are at least 42 federal programs targeted specifically for handicapped individuals. Altogether they command budget in excess of 36 billion dollars" (Bennett, 1985, p. 11). These specialized assistance programs originate from different legislation, have different funding patterns and different rules and regulations, and represent a fragmented approach to many different but interrelated problems.

The specialized programs were designed to make achievement possible for all students. Each of these programs has contributed significantly to this stated goal and has expanded knowledge about pedagogy and technology for selected segments of the student population. For example, in the 10th year since the passage of Public Law 94-142, special education has (1) refined the concept and practice of individualized instruction, (2) reaffirmed the role of parents in the education of their handicapped child, (3) made education possible for one-half million previously unserved handicapped children, and (4) improved services for several million other persons (Will, 1986).

Yet, the complete fulfillment of the goal of meeting the needs of all students with learning problems still eludes us. In reviewing these separate specialized assistance programs, parents, teachers, and administrators agree that these programs have achieved mixed results: Some students have benefited, others have not, and many students with mild or moderate learning problems have not been served because they did not meet the state or federal eligibility criteria for these compartmentalized categorical programs. Although well intentioned, the pull-out approach has failed in many instances to meet the educational needs of all students with learning problems and has created, however well intentioned, barriers to their successful education.

Our educational system is flawed when it consists of many diverse parts never or rarely connected as a whole and fails to serve many students who need special help. To resolve this situation, we must step back, analyze our entire educational system, and identify the barriers that are obstructing assistance to all students with learning problems. Then, we must seek passages around these barriers and create a more responsive, coordinated, and effective educational system. The research community in learning disabilities (LD) must provide leadership in this effort, because the movement to place students with learning problems back in the regular classroom has many policy implications.

This chapter identifies five basic issues that have implications for future policy changes that will affect the field of specific LD. It also presents implications for needed research. These include issues concerning (1) specialized programs, (2) regular teacher intervention, (3) administrative problems, (4) categorical funding, and (5) personnel preparation. The research community in LD must provide leadership in the research efforts to resolve these issues, because the growing movement to place students with learning problems back in the regular classroom has many policy implications.

SPECIALIZED PROGRAM ISSUES

The concept of the need for special education programs for the mildly and moderately handicapped in our schools has already become a major policy issue at the federal level. The program of greatest concern seems to be services for the learning disabled. Specialized programs are gradually increasing as a policy issue at both the state and local levels.

The Office of Special Education Programs in the Department of Education has established task forces to study and address this problem. State Departments of Education are rewriting their guidelines and establishing experimental alternative programs for serving the mild and moderately handicapped student. Local school districts are seeking easier and less expensive methods for serving the mild to moderately handicapped student.

The first criticism of current special education programs is that students with learning problems must demonstrate failure in school before they can be placed in special education programs. The requirement of "demonstrable failure" has resulted in the term *pathological model* to be used to describe specialized services in the school. A comparison is often made with the medical model, which addresses patients only when their symptoms become so severe that massive and costly intervention is needed to save the patient. The use of a preventive model to make services available before failure and specialized pull-out programs become necessary is then raised as an alternative.

The second criticism is the use of criteria for determining eligibility and placement. In some cases, students are excluded from special help because they fail to meet eligibility requirements. In other cases, students who do not meet eligibility requirements are deliberately misclassified as handicapped to give them help in the absence of alternative services. The lack of specificity of the criteria, the lack of systematic monitoring, and the lack of re-evaluation procedures result in placement decisions being made that are often inappropriate and not in the best interests of the students.

The third criticism is that segregation from their classmates in specialized programs leads to stigmatization resulting in social rejection, feelings of inadequacy, low self-expectations, failure to persist on tasks, and continued failure to learn.

The fourth criticism is that specialized programs often result in adversarial relationships between the parents and the school. Parents often feel that they are not allowed in the decision-making process, and school personnel often feel that parent demands are not realistic. The end result is a series of parent-school conflicts.

Many of the criticisms that are being directed toward specialized programs consist of philosophical arguments and the casual use of catchy concepts such as "pull-out programs," "the medical model," or "demonstrable failure." These arguments often exaggerate, misrepresent, or make incorrect implications and often ignore the benefits of specialized programs. They do a disservice to these programs, which use preventive models and do not require demonstrable failure to occur before providing service. Criticisms of specialized programs are needed, but they should be accurate and well documented. It is important to state that these four major criticisms are not agreed upon by all professionals or parents.

If the criticisms being directed toward specialized programs are continued, the future support for specialized programs for the federal, state, and local levels will continue to be reduced or even eliminated.

Research Implications

The Identification Process

Research is needed with respect to the identification process. Accurate data are needed from school districts that are (1) using precise criteria for identification, (2) applying sound decision-making procedures with respect to determining eligibility, (3) monitoring, and (4) re-evaluating.

Experimental Program Alternatives

Research is needed to explore the feasibility and effectiveness of alternative programs, not only for learning-disabled students but for all students with learning problems. State departments of education, institutions of higher education, and public schools should unite to create and evaluate innovative experimental programs. This will probably require a waiver from existing rules and regulation requirements. Flexibility is needed to use existing funds from categorical programs to support experimental service programs.

Program Impact Upon Students

A data base is needed to show the impact of different kinds of service programs upon the students. Data are needed with respect to the academic, social, and emotional development of the students in specialized programs. Contrast groups of students in other programs can be used to determine whether differences in performance occur. One method for achieving such a data base is to establish experimental programs. This is discussed in the section entitled "Experimental Programs: An Approach to Change."

Parent-School Relationships

Research is needed to determine those circumstances or issues that often contribute to parent-school conflict, as well as the activities, such as the involvement and participation of parents planning their child's education, which reduce adversarial relationships.

REGULAR TEACHER INTERVENTION ISSUES

The average school year consists of 180 6-hour. Curricula is typically structured by grade levels. Students usually use the same textbooks and materials, which are taught on a fixed schedule. The structure of the school day does not provide teachers with the time nor the instructional environment to plan for and meet the needs of individual students (Sarason, 1982).

All students do not learn in the same way nor progress at the same rate, but American schools are organized as though they do (Boyer, 1983). Students who learn at a slower rate need to progress through the curriculum at a slower rate, using different or modified textbooks and materials in classes of reduced size (National Education Association, 1983). According to A Nation at Risk (1983), some schools are providing only 17 hours of instruction per week, and the average school provides only 22 hours of instruction per week.

Unfortunately, many teachers are not trained to plan or provide individualized instruction. Many view the identification and assessment procedures, including planning and special assistance for students, as the sole responsibility of special education. There is a conceptual, attitudinal, and competency problem with respect to many classroom teachers individualizing instruction.

Another serious problem in regular education is the absence of a teacher support system to help teachers (1) identify students who have learning problems, (2) individualize instruction for students who have learning difficulties but who do not qualify for special education services, and (3) meet the needs of students with learning problems who are mainstreamed in regular classes.

Policy Implications

The problems confronting classroom teachers have become so severe that concern is being expressed at local, state, and national levels. To resolve these problems, a total restructuring of regular education is likely to occur. Changes may occur in the length of the school year, school day, curricular content, teacher expectations, and teacher competencies.

The question that is being considered is "To what extent can regular classroom teachers serve students with learning problems in the classroom?" There are some who believe that nearly all handicapped students can be taught by regular classroom teachers with certain environmental modifications in the classroom and appropriate teacher training. Others believe a wider range of alternative programs other than special education will resolve the problems of the mild and moderately handicapped as well as the nonhandicapped population with problems. Regardless of which proposed approaches are implemented, the result will be changes in the scope and mission of special education services.

Research Implications

Research is urgently needed to determine (1) the extent that teachers can help students with handicapping conditions within the framework of the regular classroom, and (2) the kinds and amount of support teachers need to individualize instruction for students in the regular classroom. There is a need to develop alternative programs for nonhandicapped students with learning problems. The research community in the area of LD has expertise in the individual assessment and remedial procedures for academic and developmental disabilities. The field of LD probably has more to offer concerning the education of mild and borderline students than any other group in special education. Our research group should provide the leadership in the forthcoming effort to develop alternative programs in special education.

ADMINISTRATIVE ISSUES

There are several administrative issues that prevent school administrators from developing and delivering services to all students with learning problems. These include (1) problems created by existing rules and regulations, (2) lack of clear administrative responsibility and accountability, (3) lack of interagency coordination, and (4) lack of interest in serving low achievers.

Effective programming is often inhibited or prohibited by federal and state rules and regulations. Case loads are rigidly fixed. Any variation from the regulations requires the school district to submit detailed justification. This requires a great deal of time and excessive paperwork in explaining rationales, justifications, and explanations. The procedure discourages creative educational programming. Another problem is the amount of time and money spent in excessive record keeping. Many rules and regulations prohibit serving handicapped and nonhandicapped together and interfere with the efficient use of local resources. Special education personnel can serve only those students who have been declared eligible. To meet student needs, many administrators declare nonhandicapped students eligible for special education services. This is a natural consequence of the lack of alternative programs for the non-handicapped and the lack of flexibility of the rules and regulations.

A long-standing problem is the lack of interagency coordination of resources. Agencies are frequently funded from different sources and tend to operate as discrete administrative units. This autonomy makes it difficult to maintain communication and establish working relationships between special education, regular education, vocational rehabilitation, mental health, bilingual education, preschool services, and so on. This situation makes comprehensive programming difficult.

The gap between regular education and special education has created confusion over who has the responsibility and should be held accountable for the education of students with learning problems. Some regular administrators view special education as being responsible and accountable for all students with learning problems. This perspective is shared by some special educators.

Administrators who lack a feeling of ownership or partnership in helping students with learning problems do not try to (1) promote higher standards and expectations for students with learning problems, (2) improve levels of student performance, or (3) help these students prepare to enter the community or work force. Only seven states require school administrators to show some preparation in the education of handicapped students on either their teaching certificate or as part of their administrative certificate (Parks, 1985). If building principals do not understand the special needs of students or the services that they need, they cannot serve as school leaders or role models in creating the curricular modifications or teaching practices necessary to meet the needs of individual students.

The tendency of special educators to teach the handicapped in small, separate groups outside the regular classroom with only minimal communication with regular education staff only adds to the problem.

Policy Implications

Superintendents of schools, board members, state educational agencies, and federal agencies are becoming more confused and overwhelmed by the tangle of rules and regulations, communication problems, lack of coordination between agencies, and the confusion over who is responsible and accountable for students with learning problems: regular education or special education. When the frustration level reaches a certain point and the confusion of local, state, and federal levels becomes so great, they will be unable to see how to untangle and resolve these problems. The easiest and most direct approach is to do away with the rules and regulations, change funding sources and allocations, and create a single educational system rather than continue a separate and dual system of regular education and special education. The responsibility and accountability can then be fixed to a single person such as the building principal.

Research Implications

It is the responsibility of the research community to analyze the problems created by existing rules and regulations, the lack of clear administrative responsibility and accountability, and the lack of interagency coordination. When the nature of these interrelated problems is understood, experimental projects to eliminate these problems should be developed and field tested. Failure to help administrators and legislative bodies sort out these problems, and failure to generate alternatives will result in simplistic and sweeping changes based on political pressures.

Researchers in the LD field must extend their skills to study problems that may not be related to LD per se but will have tremendous impact on our field. We must address these problems.

CATEGORIC FUNDING ISSUE

At present, Public Law 94-142 monies are granted on a per-child basis for those students diagnosed as handicapped. The advantage of categoric funding is that small, select populations are ensured of receiving the financial support necessary to provide needed special education programs. Unfortunately, there are students with learning problems who could benefit from specialized instruction but who are not eligible for services under existing rules and regulations. Categoric funding, therefore, is viewed by many as a formidable barrier to providing services to students who need help but who are not eligible.

Another criticism leveled at categoric child-based funding is that it provides a financial incentive for local educational agencies to identify students as handicapped. This contributes to the danger that educational decisions will be based on financial considerations rather than on educational need. Another concern about categoric funding is that the rules and regulations make it practically impossible to financially support the cost of programs for students who need multiple specialized services. Finally, categoric funding is viewed as having little or no flexibility in using available monies effectively.

Policy Implications

A common alternative to categoric funding is the use of block grants. The federal or state government will provide a lump sum of money for all educational services. Historically, when funds have not been strictly allocated for the handicapped, they have been swallowed up by the regular education programs in their efforts to provide for the nonhandicapped school population. Many administrators would welcome the flexibility of block grant funding. Parents and special educators fear that block grant funding will gradually result in the withdrawal of support from special education.

Research Implications

Research studies are needed in the areas of financial support. There are a number of questions that need to be addressed:

1. What is the average cost per child for different levels of special education services?
2. What is the cost per child for mainstream alternative services, including the cost of support personnel?
3. What kinds of specialized services are not covered by categoric funding: multiple services? screening? diagnostic assessment? audiologic services? or other related services?
4. What kind of changes in the rules and regulations can be made to provide the flexibility to use available categoric funds effectively?
5. How can funding be tied to a graduated continuum of service and reimbursement options that channel funds to needed programs and services?

PERSONNEL PREPARATION ISSUES

Many special educators are unfamilar with regular classroom curricula and teaching methods. Similarly, many regular classroom teachers are unfamilar with the characteristics of the handicapped and how they are served—the different kinds of learning and behavior problems, assessment procedures, and strategies for individualizing instruction within the classroom. This is not surprising since regular educators and special educators are usually trained separately with different curricula and different field experiences. Without a common core of attitudes, knowledge, and competencies, neither regular nor special educators are familar with each other's roles or capabilities.

Policy Implications

The gap between the attitudes, knowledge, and competencies of regular teachers and special educators has great policy implications for the development of mutual policy integrated programs and their implementation in the schools, and the way that teachers are trained and certified.

Research Implications

Research is needed in the area of training special education and regular education personnel. There are a number of questions that need to be answered:

1. What kinds of student learning and behavior problems can a regular classroom teacher handle in the classroom?
2. What kinds of teaching skills must a regular teacher have to cope successfully with those problems?
3. What kinds of experiences must special educators and regular teachers have to:
   a. Understand the competencies and job descriptions of their colleagues?
   b. Communicate effectively and interact in a professional manner?
4. What core courses and experiences should be provided for both groups?
5. What kinds of "cross categoric" training of teachers is needed to serve students with mild learning or behavior problems?
6. What is the impact of competency-based in-service upon teaching performance?
7. What are the best training methods for delivering effective in-service:
   a. Local staff development centers that provide or design continuous in-service packages?
   b. Self-paced programs?
   c. Correspondence courses?
   d. Televised courses?
   e. Internships?

8. Should certification requirements be broadened from an emphasis on coursework and credit hours to competency-based certification?

EXPERIMENTAL PROGRAMS: AN APPROACH TO CHANGE

Future program policies will or should be made upon data-based research. One promising passage to change is to maintain national legislative programs but allow state and local educational agencies the flexibility to develop experimental programs for serving all students with learning problems without reducing the existing level of support for special education services. States could be encouraged to develop 3- to 5-year plans that would permit selected school districts to create innovative experimental programs. Local educational agencies whose proposals are selected would (1) receive a waiver from meeting the existing rules and regulations requirements, (2) receive an appropriate level of financial support for special education, and (3) in return, gather a data base on the efficacy of their programs.

A program waiver system would allow local educational agencies to use existing funds from categoric programs such as special education, vocational education, vocational rehabilitation, bilingual education, and Title I programs in more flexible ways to serve all students with learning problems.

All trial programs should be field tested. This would include systematic and rigorous monitoring and documentation and would permit carefully designed experimentation aimed at serving students in more comprehensive ways. Student data would be gathered to determine the effectiveness of these trial programs in improving student learning and behavior outcomes.

This experimental data-based approach could be supported by establishing Regional Institutes for Innovative Programs. These Institutes would have the responsibility for providing leadership and technical assistance to state and local educational agencies that are attempting to develop and evaluate innovative programs for assisting all students with learning and behavior problems. The Institute model would be very useful in creating a national data base upon which future program development and support could be based.

For this experimental plan to work, policymakers, professionals, parents, and advocates must make a broad commitment to monitor the experimental programs and to slowly revise policy guidelines in a responsible manner.

HOW WILL DECISIONS FOR CHANGE BE MADE?

Most professionals would agree that we should organize a more responsive, coordinated, and effective educational system for serving all students with learning and behavior problems (handicapped or not). Most people would agree that a regular education initiative, which brings regular educators more fully into the arena of individualizing instruction for students within the regular classroom, would be desirable.

Although these ideas are attractive, whether or not their implementation is in the best interests of learning-disabled students, depends upon how decisions for change will be made and the way in which these changes will be implemented. There are several concerns that can influence the future of services for the learning disabled.

First, many educators and persons in administrative and policy-making positions do not understand the difference between a learning problem and a LD. Failure to distinguish between learning LD and learning problems has three consequences. The nonhandicapped population are often not considered in program planning; planning for other mildly to moderately handicapped students is overlooked; and special services for the learning-disabled population often become a watered-down "opportunity room" kind of experience in a regular classroom setting.

Second, although there are few alternative programs for the non-handicapped, regular educators have not become heavily involved in the regular education initiative. This initiative seems to be led by special educators. Unless regular education leadership can be involved at the federal level as well as at the state and local levels, this initiative will be short-lived and have little impact.

Third, will the decision for change result from experimental data-based research, or will decisions be based on political action or public opinion or mandated through legislation and/or rules and regulations?

There is need for change, and such change is possible provided that school personnel, parents, and students work together on a national initiative to meet the needs of all students. To accomplish this task, we must remove the barriers and build a chain of three bridges: (1) reform at the building level, (2) the development of creative program alternatives in special education and regular education, and (3) mobilization of existing staff and resources more effectively. We must retain the positive aspects of our educational system, eliminate the rigidity that leads to inefficiency and ineffectiveness in our schools, and create a system that meets the individual needs of all students.

Harold J. McGrady

Public policy should be represented by appropriate statutes, regulations, and judicial decisions at the federal, state, and local levels. Educational practice should also reflect those laws, rules, and court conclusions.

How does society determine what is "right" for public education? Is educational practice driven by public opinion, accepted best practice, or research findings? How much effect is produced by legislation, litigation, or adjudication? Do these formal mechanisms reflect public opinion or standards established through professional societies and research?

One indication would be to reflect upon attempts over the past 10 years to implement the federal Education for All Handicapped Children Act (EHA), commonly known as Public Law 94-142. What most influenced its passage? Was it precedence-setting court decisions, such as the PARC and Mills cases? Was it public concern over undesirable practices with certain types of handicapped children? Or, was it the effects of significant research articles in the professional literature?

Each of these occurrences was a factor in the passage and eventual implementation of Public Law 94-142. It is clear, however, that none of these factors was solely responsible for instituting that law or for shaping current educational practice.

What is done in the schools today is the result of an interaction among all the aforementioned forces, plus a multitude of others. Data-based research, however, is probably the factor with the least direct influence on public policy decisions and current educational practice. Chalfant is clearly saying in his presentation that research should have a much more prominent role in the public policy and decision making that influences educational practice for the field of LD.

The field of LD is at a watershed. What will happen at this crucial dividing point in its history? Will school practices be allowed to meander, unchecked, in many directions until an acceptable water level of common practice is reached? Will there be a tide of public opinion that will drown professionals in a pool of watered-down rules, regulations, and practices? Will there be a flood of court cases that will create a reservoir of case law decisions from which to draw? Or, through research, can we engineer an organized system that would be the most appropriate, efficient and effective means to deliver services to learning-disabled youngsters in the mainstream?

There is considerable public and professional disagreement as to how best to serve learning-disabled children in our schools today. There is some agreement that learning-disabled children should spend more time in the mainstream classrooms. Special educators believe that regular educators need to be pulling more of the oars in the passage of learning-disabled students through that mainstream. However, regular educators sometimes believe that learning-disabled children are being dumped unfairly back into the mainstream without having been taught how to swim. Many questions are being posed: What is a *real* LD? What are the best ways to teach learning-disabled children? What is *special* about special education? Who should bear primary responsibility for education of learning-disabled children? What is the role of the regular teacher? What are the changing roles of the LD teachers?

These are important questions. Chalfant has done his usual insightful analysis of the major issues surrounding services to learning-disabled children and the implications for public policy and programs. He has correctly stated that the problem lies in the current two-systems approach. In presenting the current status of the problem, Chalfant identifies five areas of issues: specialized programs, regular teacher intervention, administrative problems, categoric funding, and personnel preparation. These are all valid areas for concern, and each offers opportunities for research.

This author is in agreement with Chalfant when he identified the following research needs:

1. A student data base from which researchers can test the effects of various interventions or delivery systems.
2. Analysis of the effects (regular classroom interventions on children with various I
3. Examination of the effects of certain rules, regulations, and administrative structures or procedures on the progress exhibited by learning-disabled students.
4. Study of how differing funding patterns or formulae influence the provision of services and the achievement of learning-disabled pupils.
5. Methods to increase the accountability of teacher training and other personnel preparation programs.

Chalfant states that "Future program policies will be made upon data-based research." That is a sound premise with which this author is in complete agreement. Past history, however, indicates a different scenario. Perhaps the professional community would agree that program policies *should* be driven by data-based research.

It is the challenge for that community to create the types and quality of research that will demand attention, produce results that will bring definition to the problems, and generate concrete answers to the questions that have been raised.

Chalfant has created a script for researchers to follow. He has posed a number of significant questions and issues. With appropriate study of these questions, perhaps the millenium will occur: Research results will drive public opinion, legislation, litigation, adjudication, and educational best practice. When that day arrives, the hopes and dreams of the participants in the DLD/Utah Research Symposium (the authors of this volume) will have been realized.

REFERENCES

Barriers to excellence: Our children at risk. (1985). Boston: National Coalition of Advocates for Students.

Bennett, W.J. (1985). Excellence for all: A statement from Secretary of Education William Bennett. *Exceptional Parent, 15,* 11–12.

Bogdan, R. (1983). A closer look at mainstreaming. *Educational Forum, 47,* 425–434.

Boyer, E. (1983). *High school: A report on secondary education in America.* New York: Harper & Row.

Chalfant, J.C. (1984). *Identifying learning disabled students: Guidelines for decision making.* Burlington, VT: Trinity College, Northeast Regional Resource Center.

National Center for Educational Statistics. (1983). *Bulletin.* Washington, DC: Department of Education.

National Commission on Excellence in Education. (1983). *A nation at risk: The imperative for educational reform.* Washington, DC: Department of Education.

National Education Association. (1983). *The teaching profession.*

Parks, J.R. (1985). *A national review of special education certification requirements.* Unpublished report, University of Arizona, College of Education.

Sarason, S. (1982). *The culture of the school and the problem of change.* Boston: Allyn & Bacon.

Task Force on Federal Elementary and Secondary Education Policy. (1983). *Report of the twentieth century.* Washington, DC: Department of Education.

Will, M.C. (1984). Let us pause and reflect—but not too long. *Exceptional Children, 51*(1), 11–16.

Will, M.C. (1986). *Education students with learning problems—shared responsibility.* Washington, DC: Office of Special Education and Rehabilitative Services.

PART VII

Conclusions

Moving from Consensus to Action: An Agenda for Future Research in Learning Disabilities

Sharon Vaughn
Candace S. Bos
Stevan J. Kukic

F rom its inception, the field of learning disabilities (LD) has been bombarded with problems and suggested solutions to these problems. From multiple task forces established to solve definitional issues to crackpots recommending the use of hair dryers to stimulate brain functioning, a wide range of solutions have been proposed to solve problems in LD. As a field, we have spent what seems to be an endless amount of time and energy battling many of the issues related to definition, identification, eligibility, and intervention. Seeking a solution to "the" LD definition is time that could be better spent assembling a taxonomy or classification system that tells us more about the characteristics of poor learners. According to authors in this book, we are taking the first steps toward assembling a body of knowledge that will allow us to have empirical support for solutions to such persistent problems as identifying the many subtypes of learning-disabled students and potent methods of intervening with their cognitive and academic difficulties.

In reading the chapters in this volume, it is clear that the authors have taken a critical view of research problems and issues in LD. What is striking is that they provide guidance for where future research should be aimed and what methodologic issues we can successfully handle. It is the intent of this chapter to identify the major issues and directions for research in LD and provide extensions of positions discussed.

ISSUE

There is a need to use theory and knowledge from related disciplines and to develop theories and taxonomies in LD.

The study of LD lacks a robust scientific perspective. Keogh (Chapter 1) describes it as "...fragmented and diverse, lacking in coherence and focus." The purpose of good theory is to organize our current knowledge and to assist in systematically acquiring more knowledge. Theory is noticeably missing from much of the research in LD.

Theory provides "Systematically organized knowledge applicable in a relatively wide variety of circumstances: especially, a system of assumptions, accepted principles, and rules of procedure devised to analyze, predict, or otherwise explain the nature or behavior of a specified set of phenomenon" (American Heritage Dictionary, 1970, p. 1335). The field of LD lacks systematically organized knowledge and often ignores knowledge and theory from other disciplines (Torgesen, this book). Consequently, many of the identification and treatment processes and practices are built on assumptions that are loosely structured and may be faulty.

After reading the chapters in this book that discuss the importance of theory in research, one is struck by the lack of theory-driven research in the field of LD. There are several possible explanations, including the age of the field, the number of diverse professionals interested in LD, the personal motivations for involvement in LD, the social and political influences on the field, insufficient understanding of normal learning and development, and the training of researchers in LD. Previous chapters may have reminded us of our negligence relative to theory building and utilization, but they also provided encouragement for future directions.

Future Directions

One direction is to develop research based on already existing theories and/or focused on the development of theories explaining LD. We need to be cautious about doing single unrelated studies that provide little information relating to previous studies or contributing to the understanding of LD.

Early in its history, psychology thought that small, more local theories would assemble into broad theories (Farnham-Diggory, 1986). What resulted was the investigation of very specific phenomena with little attention to the larger context. Researchers attempted to develop their own theories with little integration from the work of others or consideration of how they might generate a more broad-based theory that would envelop other work. Much of the work in LD has proceeded this same way. Although it is probably fruitless to attempt to develop a grand theory that explains all LD, it is useful to conduct research cognizant of the status of current theories and paradigms and of how the research under investigation can use these theories to extend knowledge in the area of study and/or contribute to the theory. The lack of attention to theory in LD can be partially explained by the diverse disciplines that study the condition, as well as by a lack of adequate models. In the last 10 years, we have made progress in the development of paradigms for studying learning and teaching (Shulman, 1986; Torgesen, this book), and these should be applicable in future research.

A second direction is to conduct broad-based interdisciplinary reviews of the literature related to the target research area. Often, literature reviews are limited to journals most closely related to the researcher's field. Reading specialists conducting research on LD review reading-related journals, speech and language specialists review journals related to their specialties, and professionals in special education review their field's journals. We need to cross boundaries in culling research to include all related fields, including psychology, neuropsychology, and sociology. Kavale surveyed journals in which articles related to LD had been published during a 2-year period and found that there were more than 25 different journals representing more than five disciplines. Torgesen (this book) urges us to stay abreast of the basic sciences and to use information from them to guide research in LD. We need to develop our research ideas and strategies from a larger interdisciplinary context.

A third direction is to provide training at the doctorate level in the basic sciences as well as research and design so researchers interested in LD are adequately equipped to investigate the condition (Keogh, 1986; Johnson, this book). In addition, teachers need to be educated in the critical skills necessary for reading and evaluating research.

Training in special education has necessarily emphasized assessment, program development and evaluation, and public policy, often resulting in minimal preparation in research methodology and theory. For this reason, doctoral students in special education are often less familiar with theory and research in related fields such as psychology, neuropsychology, and sociology. Many universities are responding to the need for broad-based training and research skills and are including more comprehensive training in basic sciences as well as research and design in their doctoral programs.

Stanovich (1985, 1986) reminds us of the principle of converging evidence when interpreting research in a particular area. Individual studies rarely produce resolutions to important educational issues. It is the compilation of a series of studies, each converging in a direction that provides insight into difficult problems. Teachers need to be informed as to how to read and interpret the range of studies conducted in a particular area and, rather than seeing them as a debate with the side producing the most persuasive argument winning, interpreting the research in terms of its findings converging on a particular conclusion that most educators can accept. Teachers need to understand that many scientific investigations across field produce contradictions and that these contradictions can result from methodologic error, chance, or other unknown factors (Stanovich, 1985, 1986).

A fourth direction is to be patient in our pursuit of theory and taxonomy development. While many investigators involved with the field of LD may want quick answers, it will take time to allow theory to develop so that we can provide tested solutions to important problems. The current funding structure for research and development is directed toward obtaining quick solutions to very complex problems. This approach provides only answers that have not been adequately investigated nor have withstood the test of time. Funding needs to be directed at developing long-term research programs that will allow time to adequately explore issues. Keogh (this book) reminds us that although practical application is of the utmost importance, we cannot be so impatient with our need for immediate application that we forgo the type of scientific investigation that would guide us toward theory development. The use of theory in guiding research is necessary if the field of LD is to develop empirically sound ways of identifying, classifying, and treating the learning disabled.

ISSUE

There is a need for well-designed and well-implemented programmatic intervention research.

Intervention research needs to look beyond the question "What instructional method is best?" We often approach intervention research in a naive way. For example, we first select a method that we believe holds instructional promise. To determine the efficacy of this particular instruction approach, a common design is to assign school-identified learning-disabled students to experimental and control groups. Students in the experimental group are given some special intervention, whereas those students in the control group are given the usual intervention. We test students prior to and following intervention to determine the efficacy of the special intervention. For a variety of often unexplained reasons, the experimental group does or does not perform better than the control group, and we conclude that one intervention is more effective than another with learning-disabled students. In addition to such factors as subject selection, characteristics, and teacher variables, there are other important questions that we need to have answered before we can satisfactorily address issues related to the efficacy of the special intervention and its application to various learning-disabled students.

Future Directions

One direction is to look beyond how the group as a whole performed after intervention. Researchers need to examine and report group variability and the characteristics of students who fail to profit adequately from the specialized intervention as well as those of students for whom intervention is successful. As Senf (1986) has explained elsewhere, significant group differences tell us how students compare on the average. Some of the students in the experimental group may score lower than some students in the control group despite the fact that the mean experimental group scores were higher. Conversely, some of the students in the control group may score higher than the average score in the experimental group despite lower scores on the average in the control group. Although we frequently conduct group intervention research to determine the efficacy of the intervention, we also need to know with whom the intervention is effective. Thus, overgeneralizing group results may be dangerous when applied to individual students.

We might address this issue by studying both the role of the trainee's deficient knowledge and how the learning-disabled student's processing problems interact with a given instruction (Wong, this book). This involves a more dynamic approach to assessment; in addition to assessing the child's level of competence, it also assesses his or her understanding of the process and potential for learning (e.g., Feuerstein, Rand, & Hoffman, 1979) as well as how he or she interacts with the teacher and curriculum demands (Deno, 1985; Gickling & Thompson, 1985; Mercer, this book). Applying dynamic assessment requires a detailed analysis of the learning processes (not just the tasks) in the major academic domains (Brown & Campione, 1986). We also need to examine questions that address how differing subtypes of students with serious learning problems perform on intervention strategies capitalizing on a different process and over time (Lyon, this book).

A second direction is to ensure that intervention research is well grounded in sound theory. Through carefully controlled studies, one can examine the assumptions of the theory to determine their efficacy with a specific student sample. For example, in intervention research, it is not uncommon for methods of instruction to be compared. However, it is less common that these intervention are tied to theory and that the assumptions underlying the theory of the method are tested. Simply determining which method works best is a dead end. It does not teach us how principles of teaching interact with individual differences, nor does it add to the growing body of research in education and psychology, developing and testing principles of teaching and learning (Bloom, 1976; Bruner, 1966; Gage, 1978; Gagne, 1977; Walberg, 1986).

A third direction is to select and describe the sample carefully. The most important part of determining the success of an intervention strategy is to know "with whom" it is successful. Sampling and describing the sample should allow us to answer "with whom." As mentioned by almost every author in this book, sampling is a serious problem in research with learning-disabled students. Like many of our difficulties in research with learning-disabled students, sampling problems stem from definition and identification difficulties. As discussed by several authors in this book (Chalfant, Johnson, Lyon, McGrady, McKinney, this book), the students who end up in classes for the learning disabled vary by school district and reflect a heterogenous sample that includes students with low verbal IQ's, low achievement, language problems, brain injury, and mental retardation and may include other students who may not be learning up to grade level for a host of other reasons. Selecting a sample from these students without imposing any other criteria affords the researcher and reader only a few clues regarding the "with whom" question, even when teaching one method is generally more instructive than another.

A fourth direction is to match research design to the questions being asked (Kirk, this book). This may require creativity in our approach to how to best answer the question. We may need to conduct observational studies to from the research hypotheses for more controlled studies. Ethnographic research may serve as the precursor to studies with more controlled experimental designs. Case studies and other types of naturalistic and observational inquiry (Evertson & Green, 1986; Guba & Lincoln, 1981) can provide data rich with descriptions of the interactions among learner, task, and context variables.

The fifth direction is to incorporate the research from regular education that has focused on the impact of teaching and teacher effectiveness on student performance (Brophy & Good, 1986; Rosenshine, 1983; Stallings, 1980). While instructional research in LD has been heavily influenced by cognitive and developmental psychology with focus on within-child variables, it has not been as concerned with "teaching" as has been characterized in the research on teaching literature (MacMillan, Keogh, & Jones, 1986). This educational reseach has investigated the role that teachers and their interactions with students play in learning. Syntheses of this research indicated that such teaching variables as the structure and clarity of presentation, the degree of redundancy, particularly in the form of repeating general rules and key concepts, the quantity and pacing of instruction, classroom management, and academic learning time are related to academic achievement (Brophy & Good, 1986; Doyle, 1986). Measuring teacher variables (Kukic, Ryberg, Link, & Freston, 1986) could assist us in ascertaining the interactions between student, teacher, and intervention characteristics and facilitate the study of contextual variables that function outside the child.

The previously stated directions address the need to conduct systematic, programmatic research. Programmatic research goes beyond one-shot studies that compare methods to determine their efficacy. It requires the examination of the intervention components to determine which components of the method are necessary and the power of selected components under differing conditions (Wong, this book). Programmatic research requires careful selection and description of the sample, specifying characteristics of students who do not profit from the intervention as well those who do.

ISSUE

We need to provide appropriate services for students who have serious learning problems while responding to the sociopolitical and economic factors that influence the field of LD.

Given the current public policy governing identification, assessment, and intervention for learning-disabled students, what do we do today while we are waiting for research to provide the insight we need?

At this time, sociopolitical and economic forces do and will continue to influence the field of LD. It is important to be aware of these forces and their influence on research (Chalfant, Martin, Senf, this book).

The authors in this volume have alerted us to our need for a classification system as well as empirically useful and clinically relevant definitions of LD. We have been warned that our present system for identifying learning-disabled students, which yields a widely varying percentage of the population depending upon the school district and the state, will not continue to be supported and tolerated. Despite our recognition of the problem, its resolution does not come quickly (Keogh, this book). The challenge to practitioners is to do the best possible, given the state of the art available. We may create even greater problems by making unfounded changes in our haste for quick solutions. Change is not necessarily progress, and we may need to continue with our best efforts until research is able to provide solutions to these complex problems. Despite the sociopolitical and economic pressures that govern the field of LD and our difficulties with definition and classification, we have taken steps forward that hold promise.

Future Directions

One direction is to preserve the fundamental rights provided learning-disabled students in Public Law 94-142 and Section 504 of the Rehabilitation Act. Martin (this book) describes the process for the inclusion of learning-disabled students within Public Law 94-142 and Section 504 of the Rehabilitation Act. To preserve Public Law 94-142—a significant human rights document—researchers need to be involved in answering fundamental questions about the impact of public policy. Martin (this book) identifies the more important of these questions: Who qualifies as handicapped?, Is overplacement in special education occurring and why? Are special education programs helping? For whom, and under what conditions? An important perspective that researchers need to keep in mind is that their work is capable of influencing public policy if presented so that the results are understandable, applicable, and persuasively presented (Martin, McKinney, this book).

A second direction is to attempt to understand and account for the sociopolitical forces that affect the identification and treatment of learning-disabled students. As Senf (this book) describes it, the sociologic function of LD has been to resolve the educational problems facing regular education. LD has become a label and a means for providing services for students who are failing to meet educational expectations for a range of reasons. The range of reasons for identification results in a heterogeneous sample, which, without further identification criteria, forms an unsound group for research. There are other social and political forces that influence LD, including parents and professionals who have vested interests in LD (Lyon, this book), which influences the objectivity with which they approach its investigation.

Although it may seem obvious to conclude that the definitional issue is the corrupting force behind the identification and eligibility problems that have created such a heterogeneous group of students, the answer is unlikely to be found in additional task forces or committees that attempt to provide "the definition" of LD. In addition, definitions in LD need to consider LD across the life span (Vogel, this book; Weller, this book).

Furthermore, because of the social and political forces that influence LD, solving the problem of identification and classification of learning-disabled students will not solve who is eligible to receive services through the various agencies organized to serve the learning disabled, including the public schools. Even if we knew tomorrow how reliably and validly to determine the learning disabled from other low achieving students, we would still continue to have an enormous problem in the public schools—how to deal with students who are not achieving up to the expectations of the teacher or educational system. The reason that there are so many students identified as learning disabled is not merely because we are not adequately able to identify them, but, even more importantly, because the system wants them identified as learning disabled (Chalfant, McKinney, this book). Special education is a great consolation as well as a headache to regular education.

Addressing the directions for future research outlined in this chapter provides a hefty agenda for researchers, practitioners, administrators, and public policy officials. The success of this agenda depends upon the resources available, the patience of policymakers and school administrators, and the persistence and focus of researchers.

REFERENCES

Bloom, B.S. (1976). *Human characterics and school learning*. New York: McGraw-Hill.

Brophy, J.E., & Good, T.L. (1986). Teacher behavior and student achievement. In M.C. Wittrock (Ed.), *Handbook of research on teaching* (3rd ed., pp. 328–375). New York: Macmillan.

Brown, A.L., & Campione, J.C. (1986). Psychological theory and the study of learning disabilities. *American Psychologist, 14*(10), 1059–1068.

Bruner, J.S. (1966). *Toward a theory of instruction*. New York: W.W. Norton.

Deno, S.L. (1985). Curriculum-based measurement: The emerging alternative. *Exceptional Children, 52*(3), 219–232.

Doyle, W. (1986). Classroom organization and management. In M.C. Wittrock (Ed.), *Handbook of research on teaching* (3rd ed., pp. 392–431). New York: Macmillan.

Evertson, C.M., & Green, J.L. (1986). Observation as inquiry and method. In M.C. Wittrock (Ed.), *Handbook of research on teaching* (3rd ed., pp. 162–213). New York: Macmillan.

Feuerstein, R., Rand, Y., & Hoffman, M. (1979). The dynamic assessment of retarded performers: The learning potential assessment device, theory, instruments, and techniques. Baltimore, MD: University Park Press.

Farnham-Diggory, S. (1986). Time, now, for a little serious complexity. In S.J. Ceci (Ed.), *Handbook of cognitive, social, and neuropsychological aspects of learning disabilities* (Vol. 1, pp. 123–158). Hillsdale, NJ: Erlbaum.

Gage, N.L. (1978). *The scientific basis of the art of teaching.* New York: Columbia University, Teachers College Press.

Gagne, R.M. (1977). *The conditions of learning.* Chicago: Holt, Rinehart & Winston.

Gickling, E.E., & Thompson, V.P. (1985). A personal view of curriculum-based assessment. *Exceptional Children, 52*(3), 205–218.

Guba, E.G., & Lincoln, Y.S. (1981). *Effective evaluation.* San Francisco: Jossey-Bass.

Keogh, B.K. (1986). Future of the LD field: Research and practice. *Journal of Learning Disabilities, 19,* (8), 455–460.

Kukic, S.J., Ryberg, S.L., Link, D., & Freston, J. (1986). *The scales of effective teaching.* Salt Lake City: The Change Agency.

MacMillan, D.L., Keogh, B.K., Jones, R.L. (1986). Special educational research on mildly handicapped learners. In M.C. Wittrock (Ed.), *Handbook of research on teaching* (3rd ed., pp. 686–724). New York: Macmillan.

Rosenshine, B. (1983). Teaching functions in instructional programs. *Elementary School Journal, 83,* 335–351.

Senf, G.M. (1986). LD research in sociological and scientific perspective. In J.K. Torgeson & B.Y.L. Wong (Eds.), *Psychological and educational perspectives on learning disabilities* (pp. 27–53). Orlando: Academic Press.

Shulman, L.S. (1986). Paradigms and research programs in the study of teaching: A contemporary perspective. In M.C. Wittrock (Ed.), *Handbook of research on teaching* (3rd ed.). New York: Macmillan.

Stallings, J. (1980). Allocated academic learning time revisited, or beyond time on task. *Educational Researcher, 8*(11), 11–16.

Stanovich, K.E. (1985). Explaining the variance in reading ability in terms of psychological processes: What have we learned? *Annals of Dyslexia, 35,* 67–96.

Stanovich, K.E. (1986). New beginnings, old problems. In S.J. Ceci (Ed.), *Handbook of cognitive, social, and neuropsychological aspects of learning disabilities* (Vol. 1, pp. 229–238). Hillsdale, NJ: Erlbaum.

Walberg, H.J. (1986). Syntheses of research on teaching. In M.C. Wittrock (Ed.), *Handbook of research on teaching* (3rd ed., pp. 214–229). New York: Macmillan.

Author Index

Aaron, P.G., 124
Abrams, H., 122
Abrams, R., 122
Achenbach, T.M., 74
Ackerman, P., 145
Adams, K.M., 76
Adelman, H.S., 178
Alberg, J.Y., 223, 225, 226, 227, 231
Algozzine, B., 3, 11, 70, 71, 72, 78, 90,
    111, 113, 123, 155, 217
Alley, G.R., 147, 177, 197, 217
American Heritage Dictionary, 258
Anderberg, M.R., 94
Anderson, C.S., 111, 112
Andreski, S., 19
Antonoff, S., 129
Applebaum, M.I., 7, 39, 228, 230
Astin, A., 132

Bailey, K.D., 10
Baird, N., 125
Baker, C, 124
Baker, R., 130
Ball, D.W., 166
Baratta, A., 147
Bauer, J.N., 88
Beauchamp, G.R., 5
Belmont, I., 70
Belmont, L., 70
Bennett, W.J., 241
Berk, R.A., 6, 11, 154
Berliner, D.C., 177
Best, L., 13, 123, 130
Bickel, D.D., 156
Bickel, W.E., 156
Billingsley, F.F., 94
Blaha, J., 40
Blalock, H.M., 20, 24
Blalock, J., 124, 125, 145
Blankenship, C., 160
Bloom, B.S., 189, 262
Boalt, G., 20, 28
Boder, E., 39
Bogdan, R., 240
Bonstrom, O., 156, 157
Boodoo, G.M., 6, 11
Boring, E.G., 36
Borkowski, J.G., 189
Boyer, E., 240

Bradley, L., 57
Brophy, J.E., 263
Brown, A.L., 261
Brown, B.S., 41
Bruner, J.S., 262
Bryan, J.H., 117
Bryan, T., 45, 189, 190
Bryan, T.H., 117
Bryans, B.N., 7
Bryant, P.E., 57
Buchanan, M., 39, 117

Cable, B., 148
Calfee, R., 148
Campbell, D.T., 36, 37, 42
Campione, J.C., 261
Carlberg, C., 159
Casey, A., 156, 157
Chalfont, J., 126, 142
Chalfont, J.C., 111, 114, 155, 157, 158,
    173, 174, 240
Chi, M.T.H., 187, 191
Churchman, C.W., 26
Clements, S., 142
Clements, S.D., 4
Cohen, C., 145
Cohen, J., 132
Colarusso, R., 211
Coles, G.S., 154
Cone, T.E., 11, 154, 218, 219
Connor, F.P., 177
Cook, L.K., 191
Cordoni, B., 125, 132
Cosden, M., 190
Cox, J., 6, 11
Cronbach, E.J., 22
Cronbach, L.F., 37
Crowder, L., 61
Crowdes, M.S., 9
Cruickshank, W.M., 4

Daddi, B., 129
Danielson, L.C., 88
de Hirsch, K., 142
DeLoach, T.F., 41
Denckla, M.B., 39
Denhoff, E., 142
Deno, S.L., 111, 113, 160, 261
Deshler, D.D., 45, 58, 118, 147, 177, 197, 217

Dice, C., 57, 61, 70
Dinklage, K., 128
Doehring, D.G., 7
Donahue, M., 45, 189
Doyle, W., 263
Drake, C., 129
Dunn, L., 92
Dykman, R., 145

Earl, J.M., 41
Education of the Handicapped staff, 205
Eighth Annual Report to Congress on the Implement of the Education of the Handicapped, 173
Ellis, E.S., 45, 58, 177
Epps, S., 71
Estes, W.K., 46
Everitt, B., 76
Evertson, C.M., 262

Farnham-Diggory, S., 198
Feagans, L., 72, 189, 220, 228, 229, 230
Federal Register, 4, 116, 117, 121, 142, 156
Feige, H., 24, 28
Ferrell, W.R., 40
Feuerstein, R., 44, 261
Fimian, M.J., 156
Fisk, D.W., 36, 37
Fletcher, J.M., 7, 70, 72, 75, 76
Forgnone, C., 4
Forness, S.R., 11, 19, 21, 22, 24, 27, 69, 70, 72, 81, 82, 155, 212, 216, 218, 219
Foth, D., 197
Fowler, C.A., 61
Freedman, D., 77
Freston, J., 263
Friel, J., 72
Frith, U., 145
Furlong, M.J., 154–155, 159

Gaffney, J.S., 198
Gage, N.L., 262
Gagne, R.M., 262
Gajar, A., 125
Galagan, J.E., 160
Gallagher, J.J., 44
Gelzheimer, L.M., 60
Gerber, M., 157
Germann, G., 160
Gickling, E.E., 261
Glass, G.V., 159
Goetz, E.T., 189
Good, T.L., 263
Goodman, L., 211
Goodman, N., 23
Gottlieb, J., 207

Graden, J., 3, 111, 113, 123
Graden, J.L., 156, 157, 262
Greenspan, S., 44
Guba, E.G., 262
Guilford, J.P., 44
Guthrie, D., 11, 154
Gutkin, T.B., 6, 17

Hagin, R.A., 121
Hainsworth, M., 142
Hainsworth, P., 142
Hallahan, D.P., 4, 116, 117
Hammill, D.D., 4
Harris, A., 218
Harris, S.P., 46
Hartman L., 121, 125
HEATH, 115
Heaven, R.K., 7
Hedley, C., 147
Heller, K.A., 155
Hemond, M., 132
Hempel, C.G., 23
Hendrickson, J.M., 163
Herkweck, A., 9
Hoffman, M., 261
Holcomb, P., 145
Holtzman, W.H., 155
Horvath, M.J., 40
Hoshko, I.M., 7
Houck, D.G., 9
Houck, G., 57, 188
Howard, R., 13, 123, 132
Hughes, C., 116, 154
Hunt, F., 125
Hunter, M., 177
Hutchinson, N., 195

James, K., 147
Jansky, J., 142
Jenkins, J.J., 45
Johnson, D.W., 125, 143, 147, 190
Johnson, R.T., 190
Johnston, M.B., 189
Jones, R.L., 263

Kanter, M., 13, 123
Kass, C.E., 40, 89
Kauffman, J.M., 4
Kavale, K.A., 19, 20, 21, 22, 24, 27, 69, 70, 72, 81, 82, 159, 212, 216
Keller, C.E., 116
Keogh, B.K., 4, 7, 8, 9, 15, 45, 57, 65, 66, 72, 73, 95, 97, 98, 142, 217, 259, 263
Kiesler, C.A., 210, 212, 213
Killburg, R.R., 211, 212
Kirk, J., 179
Kirk, S.A., 40, 44, 70, 88, 158, 173, 174, 178

Kirk, W.D., 40, 70
Kirstner, 189
Korinek, L., 217
Kuhn, T.S., 28, 36, 70
Kukic, S.J., 263
Kurtz, J., 125, 132

Lahey, B.B., 40
Lakatos, I., 23, 25
Langford, W., 142
Larsen, R.P., 88, 94
Larsen, S.C., 4
Lauden, L., 24
Leigh, J.E., 4
Lerner, J., 70
Lewin, J., 198
Licht, B.G., 45, 58, 189
Lieber, J., 181
Lilly, M.S., 160
Lincoln, Y.S., 262
Link, D., 263
Lloyd, J.W., 7
Long, J.S., 37
Lovitt, T., 117
Luick, A.H., 94
Lyon, G.R., 7, 70, 73, 75, 76, 77, 79, 94

MacCorquodale, K., 22
MacMillan, D.L., 9, 263
Magee, B., 76, 79
Magnusson, D., 160
Major-Kingsley, S., 7, 8, 45, 57, 72, 95, 142
Mangrum, C., 122
Mann, L., 6, 17
Mann, V.A., 58
Marks, P., 206
Marston, D., 160
Mastropieri, M., 198
Mattson, D.P., 212
Mayer, R.E., 191
McConaughty, S.H., 39
McGrady, H.J., 107, 108, 110, 111, 112
McGue, M., 217
McKinney, J.D., 7, 39, 63, 65, 66, 69, 72, 75, 94, 95, 98, 114, 142, 189, 216, 220, 228, 229, 230
McLeod, J., 70
McLoone, B., 198
McNutt, G., 4
McREL staff, 158, 159
Meehl, P.E., 22, 93
Mehan, H., 9
Meihls, J.L., 9
Mellard, D., 13, 123
Mercer, A.R., 116, 154

Mercer, C.D., 69, 116, 154
Mercer, L.D., 4
Merton, R.K., 23, 26, 29
Messick, S., 155
Meyers, C.E., 9, 44
Miller, M.L., 179
Mitroff, I., 21, 25
Miyake, N., 188
Moran, M., 124, 132
Morris, R., 7, 72, 75, 76, 77, 142
Morrison, G.M., 9
Moultrie, R., 157, 158
Murphy, J., 125
Musgrave, A., 22, 25
Myklebust, H.R., 89, 142, 143

Nagel, E., 23
National Advisory Committee on Handicapped Children, 4
National Center for Educational Statistics, 240
National Coalition of Advocates for Students, 240
National Commission on Excellence in Education, 244
National Education Association, 244
National Joint Committee on LD, 124
Nihira, K., 44
Nolte, R.Y., 194
Norman, D.A., 188
Northropp, F.S.C., 22
Nye, C., 20, 81

O'Connell, J., 125, 132
Olivier, C., 129
Omori-Gordon, H., 7, 8, 45, 57, 72, 73, 95, 142
Ostertag, B., 130
Ozols, E.J., 40

Page, E.B., 6, 11, 17
Palincsar, 193
Pallack, M.S., 211, 212
Palmer, D.J., 189
Parks, A., 129
Parks, J.R., 246
Patton, J.R., 132
Pearl, R., 44, 189, 190
Pearson, M., 13, 123
Peck, C.A., 181
Pelco, L., 125
Phillips, L., 93, 94
Piontkowski, D., 148
Platt, J., 28
Polansky, N.A., 26
Polloway, E.A., 132
Poplin, M.S., 41
Popper, K.R., 27, 29, 76, 80

Porch, B., 77
Prater, M.A., 198

Ramaniah, N., 125, 132
Rand, Y., 261
Ravetz, J.R., 25, 26
Rawson, M., 121
Raymond, M., 125
Reid, H., 72, 73
Reid, H.P., 7, 45, 57, 94, 142
Reid, M.K., 189
Rescher, N., 21, 24
Reynolds, C.R., 6, 11, 118, 153, 154, 165
Rhodes, J., 77
Rietta, S., 77
Richardson, G., 132
Richey, L., 3, 123
Riscucci, D.A., 76, 77
Ritter, D.R., 39
Robinson, E.J., 40
Robinson, S., 117
Rogan, L., 121, 125
Rosenshein, K., 125, 132
Rosenshine, B., 263
Rourke, B.P., 40, 73, 94, 145
Ryan, E.G., 43
Ryberg, S.L., 263
Ryckman, D.B., 40

Salvia, J., 155
Sarason, S., 244
Satz, P., 7, 70, 72, 75, 76, 77, 142
Scheiber, B., 122, 128
Scheffelin, M., 142
Schumaker, J.B., 45, 58, 177, 197
Scruggs, T., 198
Sedito, J., 136
Semel, E.M., 46
Semmel, M.I., 181
Senf, G.M., 6, 7, 8, 38, 40, 45, 58, 59,
   60, 70, 71, 72, 88, 90, 91, 93, 94, 95,
   97, 211, 261
Shepard, L., 114, 123, 219
Shepard, L.A., 152, 154, 174, 217
Shepard, L.A., 3, 11
Shepherd, M.J., 60
Shinn, M.R., 217
Short, E.J., 43, 228, 230
Showers, B., 159
Shulman, L.S., 259
Shumaker, J.B., 217
Siegel, L.S., 7
Silver, A., 121
Simpson, E., 121
Sinclair, E., 11, 154, 218, 219
Singer, H., 194
Sixth Annual Report to Congress on the
   Implementation of Public Law
   94–142: The Education for All
   Handicapped Children Act, 3
Skinner, H.A., 76, 77
Smith, D.D., 117
Smith, J.D., 132
Smith, M.L., 3, 11, 114, 123, 153, 154,
   174, 217
Sneath, D.H.A., 94
Snow, R.E., 36, 46
Sokal, R.P., 94
Solar, R.A., 60
Speece, D.L., 7, 39, 230
Stallings, J., 263
Stanovick, K., 58, 61, 260
Stark, J.H., 217
Stempniak, M., 40
Sternberg, R., 43, 44
Stevens, L.J., 70, 78, 89
Stewart, N., 77
Strang, J.D., 40
Strausser, S., 38, 39, 40, 41, 44, 45, 117
Strichart, S., 122
Summers, E.G., 22

Talpers, J., 122, 128
Task Force on Federal Elementary and
   Secondary Education Policy, 239
Taylor, H.G., 72
Taylor, L., 178
Thompson, V.P., 261
Thurlow, M., 111, 113
Thurlow, M.L., 155
Tindal, G., 160
Torgesen, J.K., 7, 9, 31, 35, 38, 45, 57,
   58, 61, 62, 63, 64, 65, 66, 70, 72, 188,
   189
Tucker, J., 70, 78, 89
Turner, M.B., 25, 36
Tyroler, M.J., 40

Underwood, B.J., 36
U.S. Office of Education, 69, 88

Vance, 40
VanDusen Pysh, M., 157, 158
Vaughn, S., 79
Vellutino, F., 58, 62
Vogel, S.A., 13, 122, 123, 124, 125, 126,
   129, 130, 131, 132
Voress, J., 117
Voss, J.F., 188, 191

Walberg, H.J., 262
Walbrown, F.H., 40
Warner, M.M., 41, 177, 197, 217
Watson, B.L., 73, 77, 94
Wechsler Adult Intelligence Scale—
   Revised, 125, 131

Weed, K.A., 43
Weener, P., 23, 93
Weiss, I., 129
Weisz, J.R., 74
Weller, C., 38, 39, 40, 41, 42, 44, 45, 117
Wesson, C., 111, 113
Wiederholt, J.L., 211
Wiener, J.R., 39, 40
Wiig, E.H., 46
Will, M.C., 240, 241
Wilson, B.C., 76, 77
Wilson, L.L., 218, 219
Wilson, L.R., 9, 116, 154
Wilson, V.C., 6, 11
Winch, P., 21

Wolf, J.S., 39
Wolford, G., 61
Wolking, W.D., 4
Wong, B.Y.L., 7, 9, 23, 38, 62, 117, 193, 195, 196, 197
Wong, R., 197

Yanagida, E.H., 154–155, 159
Ysseldyke, J.E., 3, 11, 58, 70, 71, 72, 78, 89, 90, 111, 113, 117, 123, 155, 217

Zetlin, A., 44
Zigler, E., 93, 94
Ziman, J., 24, 28
Zojonc, 189

SUBJECT INDEX

Academic outcomes of LD children, relationship of IQ/achievement discrepancies to, 228–230
Achievement, definition of, 142–143, 149
Acquisitional-developmental frame in intervention research, need for, 186–187
Administrative issues in providing services to all students
policy implications, 247
research implications, 247
Adults, definition of LD in, 124–128. See also Postsecondary education, eligibility and identification considerations in
Assessment in LD
challenge of, 153–155
conclusions on, 166–167
and consultation, 155–164
district level multidisciplinary team, 159
regional diagnostic teaching center, 159–164
school-based support team, 157–159
purpose of, 155
response to, 166–167
Assessment issues in LD research
environmental attributes, 146
experimental procedures, 146–148
intervention methods, 148–149

media attributes of, 146–148
population attributes of, 142–145
purpose of, 141–142
response to, 149–150
terminology, 146
tests, attributes of, 146–148
Assessment of LD, 131–132

Bureau of education for the Handicapped (BEH), 204

California Achievement Test (CAT), 223
California Community College System, 130
Carolina Longitudinal Learning Disabilities Project, 228
Case studies, use of in intervention procedures, 179
Center for Advanced Studies in Learning Disabilities, 29
Children, LD identified, characteristics of, 227–228
Children, research on identification of LD in. See Identification of LD children, research on
Classification of LD, description of, 106–109
Classification system for LD, need for, 6–7, 9, 10–11, 12
Clinical diagnostic batteries, 144
Coaching, 158–159

Component analysis in intervention
   methodology, 195
   counter argument to, 195
Conceptual issues in interventions with
   LD. See Interventions with LD,
   conceptual issues in
Consultation and assessment
   district-level multidisciplinary team, 159
   MDTP center
      consultation model evaluation, 161–164
      description of, 160–161
      rationale, 159–160
   review of literature, 156
   school-based support team, 157–158
      coaching, 158–159
      teacher-assistance teams model, 158
Consultation model of intervention
   research, 176
Control procedures, weak, 56–57
"Control" variables, problems with,
   60–61
Curriculum-based assessment (CBA),
   160

Definition problems in LD, 4–5
   empirical approaches to, 7–8
   problems in understanding, 9
Developmental longitudinal research
   programs in LD, need for
   impediments, 73–74
   programmatic research, lack of, 73
   sample selection, present, 72–73
   studies needed, 74–75
   traditional practices, 74
Disabled Student Services Office, 130
Disciplinary matrix, 70
District-level multidisciplinary team of
   assessment, 159
Division of Rehabilitation Services
   (DORS), 122
DLD/Utah Symposium, 29, 35, 72, 105
Domain-specific strategies, inducing,
   191

Ecologic validity, issue of, 192–193
Education Daily, 205
Education for All Handicapped
   Children Act of 1975 (EHA),
   a.k.a. Public Law 94-142, 121, 207,
   252. See also Public Law 94-142
Education of the Handicapped Act, 204
   amendments to, 204–205
Eligibility concepts in LD
   classification, 106–107
      category abuse, 108
      clarification need, 107
      labels, 107–108
      misclassification in schools, 107

research task, 108–109
   conclusions on, 115
   decision-making process, 109
      concepts underlying, 110
      exclusionary factors, 109, 110
   definition of, 106
   identification, 106
   research related to, 110–115
      University of Arizona studies,
         111–112
      University of Minnesota studies,
         113–114
      U.S. Office of Special Education,
         programs sponsored
         research, 114–115
   response to
      definition versus eligibility and
         identification, 116–117
      heterogeneity, 117
      perspective, 117–118
Eligibility and identification
   considerations in postsecondary
      education. See Postsecondary
      education
Environmental attributes in research,
   146
Exclusion, diagnosis of LD by, 109, 110
   decisions made in University of
      Arizona study, 111
Experimental procedures, attributes of,
   146–148
Experimental programs in providing
   services to all students, 250. See
   also Services for students,
   providing
   alternatives, 243
External validity, 77

Frank Porter Graham Child
   Development Center, 215
   review of study findings. See
      Identification of LD children
Funding issues, categoric, in providing
   services to all students, 247–248
   policy implications, 248
   research implications, 248
Future program policies in providing
   services to all students, 250
Future research in LD
   programmatic intervention issue,
      260–261
      future directions, 261–262
   services for students issues, 263–264
      future directions, 264–265
   theory development issue, 258
      future directions, 258–260
Future research problems in LD. See
   Research problems in LD

George Washington University course in oral interviewing techniques, 128

Heterogeneity groups, misleading sample averages of, 60
Heterogeneity of groups
lack of appreciation for, 60
solutions to sample, 63
Heterogeneity, problems of, 90–91
and subject sample selection, 92–93
Heterogenous symptoms of LD, 143–144

Identification and eligibility considerations in postsecondary education. See Postsecondary education, eligibility and identification considerations in
Identification of LD children, research on
academic outcomes, relationship of IQ/achievement discrepancies to, 228–230
background of, 216
conclusions on, 232–233
North Carolina evaluation of changes, 223–228
policy implications, 230–233
policy issues, 216–217
prevalence of LD among 1st and 2nd grader students, 220–223
quantifying IQ-achievement discrepancies, methods for, 217–220
deviation from grade level, 218
expectancy formulas, use of, 218
regression equation, use of, 219
response to, 233–235
Identification process, research implications of, 243
Instruction, individual versus small-group, 189–190
Instructional strategies in intervention research, 177–178
Internal validity, 76–77
Intervention research in LD
definition of, 185–186
methods of research, 178–180
models of
ecologic intervention research, 175–177
instructional strategies, 177–178
response to, 180–182
underachievement, reasons for, 173–175
Intervention studies on LD, 148–149
Interventions with LD, conceptual issues in
affective variable neglect and, 189
description of, 186

individual versus small-group instruction, 189–190
need for, 186–187
process problems, 188–189
response to, 197–199
trainee's knowledge base, 187
IQ/achievement discrepancies
relationship of to academic outcomes, 228–230
research on use of, 217–220. See also Identification of LD children, research on

Language tests, inspection of, 147
LD. See Learning disabilities
Learning disabilities (LD)
classification and identification issues of, 10–11
definition of, 30, 91–92, 142
definition problems of, 4–5
description of, 3, 4–5
prevalance of, 89–90
problems in understanding, 9
statistics on, 3–4
Learning Disabilities Act, 1969, 88
Learning disabilities among 1st and 2nd grade students, prevalence of, 220–223
Legislation and LD, 203–204, 207–208. See also Public policy and LD
Longitudinal research programs in LD, developmental, 72–75

Maintenance tests, use of in intervention research, 193
Marker variables, routine use of, 7–8
detailed markers, 8
UCLA, 7, 8(t)
Marker variables, strict use of, in subject selection, 73
Math disability, 128
Mayor Koch's Commission on special education, 206–207
McBurney Learning Center of the University of Wisconsin-Madison, questionnaire on LD, 128
MDTP. See Multidisciplinary and Training Programs
Media, attributes of, 146–148
Methodological issues in interventions with LD
description of, 190
developmental nature of intervention, 91
domain-specific strategies, development of, 191
ecologic validity, issue of, 192–193

Methodologic issues in interventions
  with LD (continued)
  interpretations of interventions effects,
    195
  issues of importance
    processing time allowed subjects,
      195
    skill and strategy mastery, 196
  maintenance and transfer, 193–195
  response to, 197–199
  sustained and programmatic
    interventions, 191–192
Methods in multifaceted hierarchical
  theory of LD
  layer I, 43–44
  layer II, 44–45
Models. See specific models
Monothetic classification scheme, 6–7,
  14
Multidisciplinary and training
  programs (MDTP) model, 159–161
  description of, 160–161
  evaluation of consultation model, 161,
    162(t), 163–164
Multifaceted hierarchical theory of LD
  conclusions on, 46
  description of, 36, 37
  layer I methods
    adaptability, 44
    cognitive competence, 43
    experimental competence, 43–44
  layer I traits
    severity, 40–41
    subgroups, 38–40
  layer II methods
    adaptability, 44–45
    examples of, 45
    experiential competence, 45
  layer II traits, 41–42
  rationale for, 36–37
  response to, 47–48
Multiple function tests, 144, 145
Multitrait-multimethod matrix, 37
National Advisory Committee on
  Handicapped Children, 204
National Joint Committee on Learning
  Disabilities (NJCLD), 124–125
North Carolina Annual Testing
  Program, 223, 224
North Carolina Department of Public
  Instruction evaluation of LD
  children
  characteristics of children identified,
    227–228
  comparison of prevalance estimated,
    223–226
  impact on school-identified LD
    students, 226–227

Office of Handicapped Student
  Services, 122
Office of Special Education Programs in
  the Department of Education, 242

Paradigm selection, theoretical,
  problems of, 62–63
Parent-school relationships, research
  implications of, 244
Personnel preparation issues in
  providing services to all students,
  248–250
  policy implications, 249
  research implications, 249–250
Policy implications in identification of
  LD children, 230–233
Polythetic classification scheme, 7, 14
Postsecondary education, eligibility and
  identification considerations in
  categories of, 122–123
  definition of LD in adults, 124–128
    failure to achieve, 127–128
    intellectual functioning, 126–126
    potential-achievement discrepancy,
      126–127
  future research, 132
  identification procedures, 129–131
    diagnostic testing, 131
    intake interview, 130–131
    referral process, 130
  response to
    admission and support issue, 134–135
    receptivity issue, 133
    success capability issue, 134
Prescriptive direct teaching, 149
Problems in research in LD. See
  Research problems in LD
Process problems, role of in
  intervention research, 188–189
Program issues in providing services to
  students, specialized
  research implications of, 242–244
  experimental alternatives, 243
  identification process, 243
  impact on students, 244
  parent-school relationships, 244
Programmatic intervention research,
  well-designed and implemented,
  future need for, 260–263
Programmatic and sustained
  interventions, 191–192
Public Law 94-142, 88, 114, 204–205,
  207, 210, 217, 241, 248, 252. See
  also Education of the
  Handicapped Act of 1975
Public Policy and LD
  issues facing practitioners and
    researchers, 205–208

legislation, 203–205
research specialist roles for, 208–210
response to, 210–214
    relevant issues today, 213

Qualitative research in intervention
    procedures, 179
Quantifying discrepancies, methods for,
    217–220. See also Identification of
    LD children, research on
Quantitative research on intervention
    procedures, 179

Reading comprehension tests, 144–145
Reading, research in, 187
Regional diagnostic teaching center
    description of, 160–161
    evaluation of, 161–164
    rationale for, 159–106
"Regression-to-the-mean," 225
Rehabilitation Act of 1973, Section 504,
    121–122, 123, 129, 205
Research in LD, shortcomings of
classification needs
    description of, 75
    developmental classification of LD
        subtypes, 77–78
    external validation, 77
    internal validation, 76–77
    misuse, 75
    theoretical considerations, 76–77
conclusions on, 79–80
developmental longitudinal research
    studies, need for, 72–75
enduring, 69–70
future directions, 69, 71–72
response to, 80–82
Research problems in LD
conclusions on, 64
response to, 64–66
solvable, 56–61
    "control" variables, 60–61
    failure to embed in theoretical
        framework, 57–58
    failure to report characteristics of
        samples, 57
    heterogeneity groups, misleading
        sample averages, 60
    unknown bias samples, use of,
        58–60
unsolvable at present
    heterogeneity samples solutions, 63
    operationally defined samples,
        61–62
    theoretical paradigms selection,
        62–63
Resource rooms, use of in intervention
    research, 175–176

Sample characteristics
    biased in unknown ways, 58–60
    failure to report, 57
    heterogeneity, 63
    operationally defined, 61–62
        problems with, 61–62
School-based support teams, 157–158
    coaching, 158–159
    teacher-assistance teams, 158
School-identified LD students, impact
    on, 226–227
Schools, eligibility misclassification in,
    107
Schools, LD identification and
    placement process within, 9–10,
    15
Self-contained classes, use of in
    intervention research, 175, 176
Services for students, future research
    directions in, 263–265
Services for students, providing
    administrative issues and, 245–247
    change decisions, 251
    funding issues, 247–248
    future program policies, 250
    personnel preparation issues, 248–250
    problems, extent of, 240
    problems of system, 240–242
    response to, 252–254
    specialized program issues, 242–244
    teacher intervention issues, 244–245
"Severe discrepancy," North Carolina
    criteria for defining, 225
Shared attribute model of LD, 3, 5–6
    classification and identification in,
        10–11
    conclusions on, 11–12
    definition problems of, 4–5
    empirical approaches to, 7–8
    future directions, 11–12
    purposes of classification, 9–10
    response to, 13–15
    taxonomy, need for, 6–7
Shortcomings of research. See
    Research, shortcomings of
Single-subject research in intervention
    procedures, 179
Small-group instruction versus
    individual, 189–190
Sociologic sponge, LD as
    absorbing problems, 88–91
    response to, 97–99
    subjects, obtaining, 92–96
    summary of, 96
Special education and vocational
    rehabilitation, 205
Specialized program issues. See
    Program issues, specialized

Student services programs, research
implications of, 244
Students, providing services to all. *See*
Services for students, providing
Subject samples, selection for LD,
obtaining, 92–96
achieving stable clusters, 94
heterogeneity, 92–93
single-subject designs, 93–94
smaller samples, 95–96
Subtypes of LD, 7–8
developmental classification of, 77–78
Sustained and programmatic
interventions, 191–192

Taxonomies in LD, future development
in, 258–260
Taxonomy of LD, need for, 6–7, 12
Taxonomy, theoretically based, need to
develop
classification description, 75
classification misuse, 75–76
developmental classification of LD,
subtypes, 77–78
external validation, 77
internal validation, 76–77
theory formulation, 76
Teacher-assistance team model, 158
Teacher intervention issues in providing
services to all students, 244–245
policy implications, 245
research implications, 245
Test of Cognitive Skills (TCS), IQ data
from, 223
Tests, attributes of, 146–148
Theoretical framework, failure to embed
research in, 57–58
Theoretical paradigm in future
research, 63
Theory development in LD
conclusions on, 28–29
data and theory in, 22–23
function of, 26,
future directions of, 28–29
modifications for, 27–28
problems of, 20–21

reasons for, 25–27
response to, 30–31
status and function of, 23–25
basic aim of theory, 24
types of, 24–25
study of, 21–22
Theory on LD, future development in,
258–260. *See also* Specific
theories
Trainee's knowledge base in
intervention research, 187–188
Training in special education, research
implications of, 249–250
Traits in multifaceted hierarchical
theory of LD
layer I, 38–41
layer II, 41–42
Transfer tests, use of in intervention
research, 193–195

UCLA marker variables, 7, 8(t)
Underachievement, factors influencing,
173, 174(f), 175
Univeristy of Arizona studies on LD
eligibility
conclusions on, 112
exclusion decisions, 111
inclusion decisions, 112
University of Florida Multidisciplinary
and Training Program. *See*
Multidisciplinary and Training
Program (MDTP)
University of Minnesota studies of LD
eligibility, 113–114
U.S. Office of Special Education
Programs sponsored research,
114–115

Variables, control problems of, 60–61
Variables in intervention research,
affective, 189
Vocational Rehabilitation
Administration, 205

WISC-R test, 222
Woodcock-Johnson Achievement test, 222